MANAGING
THE
STRUCTURED
TECHNIQUES

MANAGING THE STRUCTURED TECHNIQUES

Fourth Edition

EDWARD YOURDON

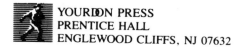
YOURDON PRESS
PRENTICE HALL
ENGLEWOOD CLIFFS, NJ 07632

Library of Congress Cataloging-in-Publication Data

Yourdon, Edward.
    Managing the structured techniques / Edward Yourdon. -- 4th ed.
        p.   cm.
    Bibliography: p.
    Includes index.
    ISBN 0-13-551680-3
    1. Electronic data processing--Structured techniques. 2. Computer
software--Development--Management.   I. Title.
QA76.9.S84Y68 1988
005.1'13--dc19   88-31643
                                                                       CIP

Editorial/production supervision: Jacqueline A. Jeglinski
Cover design: Bruce Kenselaar
Manufacturing buyer: Mary Ann Gloriande

The publisher offers discounts on this book when ordered
in bulk quantities. For more information, write:
         Special Sales/College Marketing
         Prentice-Hall, Inc.
         College Technical and Reference Division
         Englewood Cliffs, NJ 07632

Printed in the United States of America
10   9   8   7   6   5   4   3   2

ISBN 0-13-551680-3

Prentice-Hall International (UK) Limited, *London*
Prentice-Hall of Australia Pty. Limited, *Sydney*
Prentice-Hall Canada Inc., *Toronto*
Prentice-Hall Hispanoamericana, S.A., *Mexico*
Prentice-Hall of India Private Limited, *New Delhi*
Prentice-Hall of Japan, Inc., *Toyko*
Simon & Schuster Asia Pte. Ltd., *Singapore*
Editora Prentice-Hall do Brasil, Ltda., *Rio de Janeiro*

To my son,
David Nash Yourdon,
who is already a better writer than his father.

Contents

             Techniques   **223**

             19.1   Automated tools 223
             19.2   Reusable code 227
             19.3   Complexity models 229
             19.4   Proofs of correctness 230
             19.5   Project management 231
             19.6   Visual programming 233
             19.7   Artificial intelligence 235

Appendix A   Suggested COBOL Coding
             Standards   **238**

Appendix B   Suggested PL/I Coding Standards   **247**

             Bibliography   **254**

             Index   **263**

Preface

Structured analysis is obsolete. Structured design is irrelevant. And structured programming is passé.

If you believe these gloomy pronouncements, here are a few more: Capitalism is doomed; greed is out. Organized religion is on the wane; soon, there will be no more churches. And Congress is going to vote next year to abolish alcohol and tobacco. They're even going to balance the budget.

No, the structured techniques are not dead. They are very much alive, and they continue to evolve to adapt to new technologies and to new *paradigms*. One important paradigm that emerged in the 1980s and that has become widely accepted is prototyping. Its proponents argue that there is no point trying to "pre-specify" the requirements for a system because users don't really know what they want, don't really know what possibilities and alternatives are open to them, and simply cannot understand abstract models such as data flow diagrams.

Thomas Kuhn discusses the concept of "paradigm shifts" eloquently in his book, *The Structure of Scientific Revolutions* ([Kuhn, 1962]); serious students of the software engineering revolution must read this book to put current (and future) developments in perspective. But the systems development field differs from some other scientific disciplines in at least one important way: New paradigms do not necessarily replace old paradigms, but rather enlarge and refine the older ones. When Copernicus proposed a rather radical paradigm shift in the field of astronomy, he presented his audience with a binary choice: People either had to believe that the earth revolved around the sun, or that the sun revolved around the earth. You couldn't have it both ways.

But in the systems development field, you *can* have it both ways. There is no need to make a binary choice between the prespecified (structured analysis) paradigm and the prototyping paradigm. They both work. Sometimes it makes more sense to build a formal, abstract system model on paper and explore its characteristics; sometimes it makes more sense to build a prototype and let the user kick the tires and drive the system around the block to get a feeling for it.

The *really* significant change in the past ten years is the recognition, in the "savvy" MIS organizations, that there is an enormous spectrum of information systems; different paradigms (and methodologies, guidelines, techniques, programming languages, etc.) are required, depending on the kind of system being built, the users who want the system, the environment in which the system will operate, etc.

From this perspective, I now view *structured systems development* as a "metaparadigm": an attempt to bring together several independent paradigms that have heretofore been advertised as competitive and mutually exclusive. I use the word "advertise" deliberately. It is unfortunate that both the academicians and the consultants in this industry have been driven by greed and ego to promote their ideas in "brand name" form. But this has happened throughout history. As Kuhn points out, the fiery, young revolutionary eventually becomes a conservative, old fussbudget, desperately trying to defend his old paradigm against the onslaught of new ideas.

In the systems development field, practical programmers and analysts won't tolerate this any longer. Any single-minded paradigm becomes quickly tarnished and discredited if it is applied in a maniacal fashion to *all* systems and *all* projects. Thus, there is more and more of a movement underway to take the best concepts and ideas from each competing brand-name methodology—the best ideas of the Gane-Sarson approach, the Warnier-Orr-Jackson approach, the Yourdon-DeMarco-Constantine approach, the Martin approach, and the concepts of Dijkstra, Wirth, Parnas, Brooks, and dozens of others—into a metaparadigm that "works" within the framework of a specific MIS organization. As this happens, brand names will disappear.

This process has just begun, and it has a long way to go; along the way, there will still be onslaughts from new paradigms that seek to obliterate existing paradigms by forcing yet another binary choice. As this edition was being written, *object-oriented design* was playing that aggressive role in MIS organizations around the country. So we will have several years of "two steps forward and one step back" before we have a seamless integration of paradigms in even the best of MIS organizations.

Indeed, it is more likely to be an ongoing, never-ending process, because as long as we continue to have quantum-leap improvements in hardware technology, we will continue to change the way we think about computers and systems. I think we will be well into the next century before advances in hardware technology begin to level off— and that's a conservative view at best.

The primary purpose of this book is not to show how the technical aspects of various paradigms mesh together; that would require *several* books. However, I have incorporated some of the changes that have taken place in the well-defined field of structured analysis and structured design; specifically, this book eliminates the classical concept of building a "current physical" and "current logical" model in structured analysis. Instead, it presents the "event partitioning" approach discussed in such books as [McMenamin and Palmer, 1984], [Ward and Mellor, 1985], and [Yourdon, 1989]. And the discussion of CASE tools has been updated to reflect current developments; however, I have omitted references to specific vendors and products in this area, because they would surely be obsolete by the time this book is published.

Most of the book, though, is not concerned with the technical issues per se, but rather with the *management* and *cultural* issues surrounding structured techniques. Anticipating and preventing paradigm wars is probably the most important thing you an MIS manager can do as we end this turbulent decade of the 1980s; helping your staff grow and accommodate new paradigms, thus enlarging their ability to build systems, is the most important long-term investment you can make.

A few other changes in this edition require brief comment. The chapter on program librarians in the previous edition has been dropped. CASE tools and other productivity aids have rendered the notion of a human assistant obsolete in most MIS organizations. The chapter on chief programmer teams still takes a gloomy view of its practicality in large MIS organizations, but acknowledges its stunning success in many of the smaller PC-based software development organzations. And, of course, the bibliography has been enlarged and brought up-to-date; it is by no means an exhaustive list of everything that has been written on software engineering and structured techniques, but it certainly represents a basic library for the professional systems developer.

It is a pleasure to acknowledge the assistance of many people who helped me produce this new edition of *Managing the Structured Techniques*. Bob Spurgeon and Adrian Bowles read the manuscript and made many helpful suggestions. Ed Moura, the managing editor of Yourdon Press, encouraged the project from the beginning and never complained as deadline after deadline was missed. And last (though probably first given my verbosity), my editor, Jackie Jeglinski, for her invaluable help and patience throughout the project.

Edward Yourdon
New York City
January, 1989

Chapter 1
INTRODUCTION

1.1 THE STRUCTURED REVOLUTION

The issue here is not technology, but the *management* of technology. I don't care whether you've ever heard of structured analysis, or whether you know what a leveled data flow diagram is. It's not important whether you are familiar with the structured design concepts of coupling and cohesion, or whether you believe that structured programming is more practical in Pascal than in COBOL.

What *does* matter is the way you introduce these and other new software development technologies into your organization, and how you manage their use. With no management involvement, structured techniques and software engineering will attract some followers at the grass-roots level, but will not have any significant impact. *Programmer* productivity might be increased for the few individuals who decided to follow an organized, disciplined approach to the development of systems, but *project* productivity would not necessarily increase.

And *project* productivity is not even enough. As we enter the 1990s, it is vitally important that we begin focusing on *enterprise* productivity—because other enterprises around the world are focusing on this level of productivity, and it promises to have an ever-increasing impact on the profitability and very survival of many organizations.

Indeed, we must eventually focus on *national* productivity, for information systems are becoming a larger and larger part of our overall economy. In 1985, the information processing industry represented approximately 8 percent of the Gross National Product in the United States; in 1990, it will be 15 percent. Thus, the *quality* of our information systems and the *productivity* of the people building those systems are now every bit as important as quality and productivity were in the steel industry in the 1960s and in the automobile industry in the 1970s. Just as American dominance in many of the traditional "smokestack" industries came under heavy attack from Europe, Japan, Asia, and various Third World countries, so the American computer industry, both hardware and software, is coming under attack from these same countries today.

At the enterprise level, I think it's safe to assume that if you were a totally successful Director of MIS (or whatever title is used for the top-level manager in charge of information systems development), you wouldn't be reading this book. If your customers smiled and applauded when you delivered a new system, if your programmers wrote code that worked correctly the first time, if your systems ran year after year with no bugs or failures, if your maintenance programmers complained only that their job was boring because it was so easy— if all of these things were true, you would probably be spending your days sipping piñā coladas at your villa in the Caribbean. Or, maybe you would be spending your time trying to determine how your computers could *really* do something effective for your users.

But you are reading this book. Conclusion: Your customers grumble and complain when you deliver new systems to them. They grumble and complain more loudly about the systems that you *don't* deliver to them; your organization, like so many other major enterprises in the United States, has a backlog of four to seven years of application development projects. Your programmers spend inordinate amounts of time writing relatively small pieces of code; your systems crash, abort, and produce garbage output with disconcerting regularity; and maintenance is such a dirty word in your organization that you assign the task to trainees and misfits.

This description could continue. Your programmers quit after two years in your organization and go to work for a consulting firm or a PC-based software development organi- zation, where they have *fun* and also double their salary . . . and they always wait until the final stages of a critical project to resign from your organization. The documentation that you forced them to write at gunpoint turns out to be unreadable, obsolete, and completely inaccurate— so you're told by the new programmer, who promptly throws the old coding and documentation into the wastebasket and begins anew. And on and on . . . .

Sound familiar? It should. Indeed, these problems are almost universal. As a consultant and educator, I have visited hundreds of organizations around the world during the past 25 years, and everyone seems to be having the same problems. It doesn't matter whether you are using IBM or Burroughs computers, whether your programmers code in COBOL, FORTRAN, or Ada, or whether your documentation is written in

English, French, Japanese, or Norwegian. Things just aren't what they ought to be.

Because these problems are so prevalent, there has been a strong interest in the past decade in *structured techniques*, that is, a collection of technical procedures and concepts that is capable of doubling the productivity of a data processing organization, and increasing the quality of information systems (as measured by the number of defects in the system delivered to the customer) by a factor of ten, and sometimes as much as a factor of 100. The components that make up this "structured revolution" include the following:

- *Structured analysis.* A collection of graphical modeling tools that allows the systems analyst to replace the classical functional specification with a model that the users can actually understand. Structured analysis is the linchpin of the structured techniques, for if the system developers don't know the requirements of the system they are building, the best design and coding techniques will be of no avail.

- *Top-down design and implementation.* The strategy of designing a system by breaking it into major functions, and then breaking those into smaller sub-functions, and so on, until the eventual implementation can be expressed in terms of program statements.

- *Structured design.* A set of guidelines and techniques to help the designer distinguish between "good" and "bad" designs. Proper use of structured design will lead to a system composed of small, highly independent modules, each of which is responsible for carrying out one small single-purpose function.

- *Structured programming.* An approach to programming that constructs all program logic from combinations of three basic forms. As a result, reasonable programs can be written in a straight-forward manner, with little or no use of potentially dangerous constructs such as the GOTO statement.

Associated with these techniques are the following aids to implementations:

- *Chief programmer teams.* The concept of building a team of EDP specialists around a "super-programmer," who can develop programs 10 to 20 times faster than the average programmer. The team includes a "program librarian"—a programming secretary who relieves the programmer of the clerical aspects of programming and who also controls access to source programs, listings, and other documents.

- *Structured walkthroughs.* The use of peer group reviews in which an entire project team walks through the specification, design, code, and/or test data produced by one of its members.

Much discussion and controversy have arisen about each of these techniques, as we will see later in this book. Some of the methods are more controversial than others; some are more effective than others in certain situations. Indeed, some of the techniques may not work at all in your organization!

In general, though, the structured techniques *do* work. They double the productivity of the average programmer/analyst, increase the reliability of the developed system by an order of magnitude, and decrease the cost and effort of maintenance by a factor of two to ten. Finally, they substantially improve the chances that you will deliver a system that your customers will accept—and maybe, just maybe, on time and within budget!

No one can promise that structured techniques will improve your programmers' sex lives or decrease the number of cavities found in their annual dental checkups, but what the techniques can do is impressive. Chances are that if you can successfully implement structured techniques within your organization in the next couple of years, you'll be sipping your piña colada in your Caribbean villa before long. And if you don't implement structured techniques, well, chances are you'll eventually be replaced by someone who does.

1.2   MANAGEMENT IMPLICATIONS

At this point, a bit of cynicism may be expected. "Hrumph! My systems analysts and programmers have been doing these things for years. I don't see what the big fuss is all about."

Obviously, the world has not been entirely ignorant of the structured techniques for the past decade. Some managers have been implementing the techniques for years in their departments, and some programmers have been writing structured programs since the 1960s. However, most data processing professionals have not been using the techniques, *even if they thought they were.*

If the structured techniques are so wonderful, why weren't they universally adopted years ago? Why are they just now gaining strong support in some organizations? These questions are particularly relevant because the various components of the structured techniques have been discussed in the literature and among academic computer scientists for more than two decades, but have only been introduced into commercial organizations since the early 1980s.

During the 1960s and 1970s, limitations in computer hardware technology and systems software made adopting the structured techniques difficult. Expensive, inefficient hardware, restrictive programming languages, and inadequate compiler implementations were common excuses for the resistance offered by programmers and systems analysts. In the early 1980s, a new technological constraint appeared: Many programmers and systems analysts lacked the automated tools (such as "programmer's workbench" or "analyst's workbench") that would make it possible to develop and maintain the graphical models of structured analysis and structured design efficiently and conveniently. This problem has disappeared in the late 1980s with the advent of powerful, PC-based or workstation-based CASE (**C**omputer-**A**ided **S**oftware **E**ngineering) tools— so that just as no one complains about inefficient computer hardware or unsophisticated programming languages any more (except people burdened with maintaining old systems!), eventually no programmer or systems analyst should have to be without the automated tools needed to implement the structured techniques effectively.

While these technology problems have been important, an even more fundamental reason exists for the long delay in implementing structured techniques on an enterprise-wide basis: *management.* Perhaps it would be kinder to say that it has been a *cultural* problem, rather than blaming the delay on the incompetence of one or two individual managers in an organization. As Capers Jones points out, it took the military 75 years to evolve from the technology of muskets to the technology of rifles; perhaps we should not be surprised that the data processing community, with its 30-year traditions and culture, should be slow to move to new technologies. This is less of a problem in small EDP organizations with only a dozen analyst/programmers and one level of management; it is an *immense* problem in large organizations with several thousand system developers, and three or four levels of management.

It would be hard to introduce new technologies and change the culture of the organization, even if everyone agreed, a priori, that the new technologies would bring about substantial improvement. Matters are made worse by the fact that not everyone *does* agree that structured techniques *or any other new paradigm* will dramatically improve productivity and quality of information systems. Thus, one often finds resistance— usually at the second or third levels of management— articulated in the question, "How do we know that this stuff is going to produce any real results?"

But there is an even more pervasive and fundamental problem than this. The *real* problem, in my opinion, is that most American organizations have not yet made a fundamental commitment to quality and productivity *over the entire life cycle of the system.* Largely influenced by America's short-term objectives of producing ever-better quarterly results for the shareholders, there is a constant pressure on the systems development organization to deliver *any* system, of *any* level of quality, to the users— as long as the system can be put into operation within the stated deadline.[1]

The fact that the delivered system is riddled with bugs is not yet perceived as a major problem; the fact that the delivered system costs an extravagant amount of money to maintain is of little concern to the development team, since (a) they won't have to do the maintenance, (b) the manager is not being evaluated on maintainability, and (c) maintenance will be paid for out of someone else's budget.

Thus, the most important management implication of the structured techniques is that they force management— not just senior MIS management, but management all the way up to the board of directors— to squarely face the issue of enterprise productivity and enterprise quality. Without a board-level commitment to productivity and quality, success with the

---

[1] It turns out that we're not even very good at doing this: A study of 200 large U.S. organizations by Capers Jones concluded that 25 percent of large software development projects *never* finish, and that the average project is one year late and 100 percent over budget. This situation gets worse when you consider the large number of systems which get into operation but which never really satisfy the users for whom they were developed.

structured techniques— or any other productivity techniques— on individual projects will be haphazard. *With* a board-level commitment, there is still the difficult, time-consuming job of changing the 30-year-old culture of the systems development organization. I will deal with the issue of "culture change" in later chapters.

1.3   CHANGING RELIGIONS

Unfortunately, many MIS organizations treat the structured techniques as a highly political, almost religious, issue. Hence, the question of whether the organization should endorse the structured techniques becomes almost as sensitive as the issue of whether one should endorse the Catholic religion or the Republican party.

The controversy has become more intense throughout the 1980s with the emergence of several new trends and methodologies, including:

- the widespread use of personal computers.

- the emergence of powerful, user-friendly, fourth-generation programming languages.

- the emergence of application prototyping packages that allow systems analysts and programmers (and end-users, too!) to implement quickly a rough approximation of the user's requirements and operate it on a computer so the user can observe it.

- the growing recognition of data modeling and information modeling as an important discipline.

- the development of new design "paradigms" such as object-oriented design.

- the growing emphasis on strategic planning, and attempts at combining systems development methodologies with enterprise modeling methodologies.

Advocates of these new trends often remark, rather loudly in many cases, that the structured techniques are "the techniques of the 1970s" and that they should be replaced in favor of personal computers or prototyping or some other new trend. Indeed, some are even beginning to suggest the "new" techniques listed above are obsolete, and that they will soon be replaced by *fifth*-generation computer systems containing artificial intelligence-based "expert systems."

My position on this "religious" argument is rather simple. There are some techniques that certainly will be replaced by new methods and technologies (e.g., as the practice of coding systems in assembly language was largely replaced by COBOL and FORTRAN, so there will eventually be a trend toward building a wide class of systems in higher-level fourth-generation languages). *But the major philosophical concepts used to build reliable, maintainable information systems, which is what the structured techniques are all about, can continue to embrace new technologies and paradigms without destroying the concepts themselves.*

Thus, fourth-generation programming languages are often a better alternative for coding than current third-generation languages like COBOL or PL/I, but the major philosophical concerns for developing well-organized, well-documented, maintainable code don't change. Application prototyping packages may provide an alternative to the top-down implementation approach discussed in Chapter 4, but prototyping doesn't replace the paradigm of providing the user with a visible, tangible model of a working system as early as possible.

As we will see throughout this book, most of the "new" techniques of the mid-1980s, as well as those to be introduced in the 1990s, are consistent with the structured techniques that began to emerge in the mid-1970s, and which continue to evolve. Fourth-generation languages, prototyping packages, and personal computers are not competitors of the structured techniques; they are complementary techniques that help implement the structured techniques more and more effectively.

1.4   OBJECTIVES OF THIS BOOK

The primary objective of this book is to make it possible for you, as an MIS manager, to implement the structured techniques in your organization with a minimum of problems.

I will begin by discussing how to *sell* the techniques to and within your organization. Usually, there will be some resistance, either from the senior managers above you, the more junior managers below you, or from the systems analysts, designers, and programmers themselves. The nature of this resistance is predictable, and Chapter 2 presents some techniques for dealing with it.

Chapters 3 through 9 deal individually with the components of the structured revolution described in Section 1.1. The intent is to provide a sufficient technical overview of each of these techniques, with a suggested bibliography for further reading, so that you won't be bamboozled by your staff or a vendor trying to sell you a new hardware or software package or methodological religion. More important, though, specific management problems associated with each structured technique are addressed and, wherever possible, specific solutions are recommended.

The next five chapters of the book discuss other practical management issues involved in implementing the structured techniques. Chapter 10 discusses the problem of deciding which specific technique should be introduced first in your organization. Chapter 11 presents the concept of a pilot project as a formal experiment in structured analysis, structured design, and structured programming. Chapter 12 deals with the problem of revising your systems development standards in light of the structured techniques. Chapter 13 explores the impact of the classical budgeting/scheduling/controlling activities of project management. Chapter 14 examines the most practical subject of all: What can you expect to go wrong when you implement some or all of the structured techniques?

The last five chapters discuss the "competing religions" that were introduced in the mid-1980s as possible replacements for the structured techniques, but which this book regards as complementary enhancements to the structured techniques. Chapter 15 addresses the phenomenon of personal computers in major organizations, particularly PCs in the user organization and under the user's direct control. In many such situations, the user is developing systems himself without guidance from the MIS organization or other programmers or systems analysts; how does this affect the use of structured techniques? Chapter 16 discusses the use of fourth-generation programming languages, such as FOCUS, RAMIS, and ADR/IDEAL. Chapter 17 discusses the use of application prototyping packages and their impact on the structured techniques. Chapter 18 discusses the role of information modeling object-oriented design, concepts that in the 1970s and early 1980s were often regarded as separate from and perhaps even opposed to the structured techniques. Finally, Chapter 19 addresses the future of structured techniques, that is, the developments that we can expect in this area in the early 1990s.

Chapter 2
HOW TO SELL THE STRUCTURED TECHNIQUES

2.1 INTRODUCTION

It is convenient for me to assume that you are already convinced of the virtues of structured analysis, top-down implementation, structured design, and structured programming, and that your only problem is to convince the rest of your organization that the structured techniques are something more than plots by the computer vendor to sell more hardware and by consulting firms to sell new "methodology" packages.

These assumptions may be unnecessarily pessimistic. Both you and the other members of your organization may already have been sold on the new techniques. If so, skip the rest of this chapter and begin reading Chapter 3 about the specific management problems associated with structured analysis.

On the other hand, these assumptions may be slightly optimistic. Perhaps you are unconvinced, and the rest of your staff has not even heard of the structured techniques. (What cave have they been living in? This is the 20th century!) If so, the balance of this chapter serves a double purpose: While giving you suggestions about how to sell your organization on the advantages of the structured methods, it should also be possible for *me* to sell *you*.

The remainder of this chapter addresses the various concerns of this selling stage. I must first ask whether your organization, as well as the kind of projects it undertakes, is the right environment for the structured techniques. Then we can ask whether it is necessary to sell structured development techniques through the art of gentle persuasion. Are there other approaches that would work as well? If we assume that friendly persuasion is the best approach, we must then ascertain who in your organization needs to be told: senior management, middle management, first-level project leaders, or the people who actually develop the systems. Finally, let's examine the selling approach itself. How do we convince someone that the structured techniques— or any other productivity technique that purports to do what structured techniques do— are desperately needed in today's data processing environment? The following pages provide some answers.

2.2   THE ENVIRONMENT FOR STRUCTURED TECHNIQUES

No company is entirely like another, nor are any two MIS organizations exactly alike. Nor are the end-users in one company the same as the end-users in another, nor are the MIS systems they want built the same as the MIS systems that are necessary in other organizations. While the structured techniques discussed in this book can be used in almost any company, they make far more sense in some companies than in others.

In general, the structured techniques will be most successful in the following kind of environment:

- *An MIS organization that does a significant amount of new applications development work.* Some organizations spend 97 percent of their MIS budget maintaining systems that were developed ten, fifteen, or even twenty years ago. While some of the documentation techniques in Chapter 7 and the walkthrough technique in Chapter 9 may be useful, such topics as structured analysis and structured design will not evoke much enthusiasm in such an MIS organization. Indeed, it is hard to imagine *anything* evoking much enthusiasm in a shop that spends 97 percent of its resources maintaining old code, because the old code is likely to be undocumented and well-nigh unmaintainable. My advice in this situation is to invest heavily in research in the area of restructuring programs and reverse engineering processes that can help determine the original user requirements represented by the existing code (for more on this, see [Bush, 1985]).

    Also, if the MIS organization spends most of its time installing vendor-supplied packaged software— which makes sense in many organizations where user policies can be developed from the beginning to be compatible with the quirks of a particular commercial application package—then one could argue strongly that many of the topics in this book may not seem crucial. However, I would argue strongly that structured analysis is appropriate to carefully define requirements *before* deciding which commercial package should be obtained; similarly, the data modeling concepts discussed in Chapter 18 are important.

- *Systems being developed are large, complex, and vital to the success of the organization.* If the MIS organization is in the fortunate position of writing tiny systems for the most part, then many of the topics in this book may not seem very important. For example, an organization may have developed a comprehensive data model for the enterprise and installed a fourth-generation language for fast implementation of user-requested reports and ad hoc inquiries into the corporate database. This scenario means that (a) the data modeling techniques discussed in Chapter 18 (which are also a part of the structured analysis techniques discussed in Chapter 3) must have been employed; and (b) the organization must have already successfully implemented the standard "operational" systems, such as, payroll, inventory, general ledger, order entry, etc., that will continue to feed the organization's database and keep it up to date.

- *An organization that is accustomed to organizing its large, complex projects with a "life cycle" that breaks the project into recognizable phases or activities.* In a few organizations, projects still are carried out on an ad hoc basis, with communications between users, MIS project managers, programmers, and systems analysts occurring on an informal, verbal basis. For example, this informality may exist in some research organizations and in some personal computer software companies where the software is developed by "wunderkind" programmers. In such organizations, anarchy prevails; the structured techniques are the antithesis of anarchy and thus would not be welcomed. The easiest way for an outsider like me (or perhaps for a senior manager like you) to determine whether or not the organization is ready for structured techniques is simply to ask first whether there is an official project life cycle, and then see whether anyone is actually following it on systems development projects.[1]

- *Management, end-users, and the MIS organization are all vitally and passionately concerned about issues of the productivity of the MIS function throughout the entire enterprise, as well as the quality of the systems they produce.* If nobody cares, then the structured techniques will almost certainly not be implemented successfully. The same is true if only the bottom-level technicians are concerned. If the MIS organization is concerned, but end-users and senior management don't care, then it will be difficult to achieve the requisite commitment and support to implement the structured techniques successfully. The rest of this chapter is concerned with the ways to obtain that support.

2.3   INTRODUCING THE STRUCTURED TECHNIQUES WITHIN YOUR ORGANIZATION

Not too long ago, a major insurance company in New York City (the Center of the Universe to those lucky enough to live there!) was introduced to structured analysis and related techniques by one of its vendors. Assorted levels of MIS managers were assembled for a one-hour sales pitch, to which they all listened quietly and politely. At the end of the presentations, after the vendor's representative had been thanked for his efforts and excused from the meeting, the managers talked things over. After a lively exchange of opinions, one manager summarized the feelings of a majority of people in the room: "It seems to me that the problem is to find out how we can *avoid* using these new techniques. If we can manage to stall for a year or two, all of this will surely disappear—just like decision tables a few years ago."

This reaction is one way of dealing with the structured revolution and other productivity techniques: pretending that they don't exist. I can sympathize with the management of this organization. They were worried about the new standards manuals that they would have to write, the training of over a thousand people that would be necessary, and all of the other

---

[1] For different views of project life cycles, see Philip Metzger's *Managing a Programming Project* [Metzger, 1983], Edward Yourdon's *Managing the System Life Cycle,* 2nd edition [Yourdon, 1988], or Brian Dickinson's *Developing Structured Systems* [Dickinson, 1981].

organizational changes that certainly would accompany the introduction of such new techniques.

While you and your organization probably won't adopt this head-in-the-sand attitude, you might adopt other equally extreme approaches. Some of the more common approaches include an edict from the boss, the "sheep-dip" approach, and sending out a scout.

The first of these approaches is typically the least successful. An edict is often passed down from the top MIS manager (who usually is totally unfamiliar with data flow diagrams, nested IF statements in COBOL, functionally cohesive modules, and the other technical issues of structured systems development), and it frequently is expressed in such hard-line terms as, "Troops! Thou shalt not GOTO! Thy modules shall be functionally cohesive! Thou shalt draw many bubbles, but never more than seven on one page!" One such edict in a large military organization caused a great deal of scurrying around in the lower levels of the organization, for no one had any idea what the new techniques were all about.

Of course, some degree of management persuasion, perhaps in the form of an edict, may be necessary to shake the troops out of their lethargy. But if the programmers' first introduction to structured programming is a dictatorial memo from a high-level manager whom they have never seen and whom they suspect has never written a line of code on anything more modern that an IBM 1401, their reaction will be predictable: resistant and subversive in one form or another.

Next, there is the manager who believes in the "enlightened" approach to the new techniques, which usually takes the form of mass training, or what Gerald Weinberg likes to call the sheep-dip approach.[2]

The consulting and training firm that I formerly ran, YOURDON inc., frequently received phone calls from MIS managers who would say, for example, "I would like to put every one of my 300 programmers, designers, and systems analysts in a class for a day or two, and have you teach them everything there is to know about structured programming, structured design, top-down implementation, structured analysis, and all

---

2 Weinberg, whose work you should know, is author of *The Psychology of Computer Programming* [Weinberg, 1971], which laid the groundwork for the structured walkthrough concept discussed in Chapter 9. He is also the author of *Rethinking Systems Analysis* [Weinberg, 1976] and several other interesting, provocative books.

that other structured stuff. Then, as soon as they get back from class, we can cut their schedules in half—after all, they'll be twice as productive as they were!" We usually found that some progress was made by this approach, but not much. The confusion and misunderstandings caused by superficial exposure to new concepts, and the unrealistic management expectations, can easily exceed the positive benefits of using the new techniques.

Then there is the approach of sending a scout to evaluate the structured techniques. Whether or not management formally recognizes the phenomenon, there is usually one person or group that is the first to become aware of interesting new hardware/software technologies; it may be a research group, or the training group, or simply an aggressive, curious young technician. The scout in your organization probably began reading about structured programming in college in the early 1970s. He or she probably first heard about structured design in the mid or late 1970s, and probably explored some of the early ideas on structured analysis in the late 1970s or early 1980s. The scout tried the concepts on one or two small projects of his own with impressive results, and now is trying to introduce the techniques to members of your staff who never read any literature, never attend any conferences, and never are exposed to any new ideas.[3]

The trouble is, as in many other fields, that nobody wants to listen to the scout. Everyone else is too busy. As one manager put it, "We're too involved in patching the old programs to listen to any ideas about how to develop the new programs." In addition, nobody really trusts the scout: In the past, he's brought back a few ideas that didn't work. Personality problems may further complicate matters. The scout may be too inarticulate or too arrogant to communicate his ideas effectively.

You may argue that these examples are exaggerated and that they wouldn't occur in *real* organizations. Or, you may argue that the problems outlined above are the result of incompetent management and that you never would make such silly mistakes. Perhaps so, but we should remember that what begins as a good, common-sense idea in the mind of a manager sometimes is translated into something quite ridiculous when it is communicated to the rest of the staff. The examples discussed earlier *did* occur in organizations that generally conducted their

---

[3] This is not just a snide remark; the Luddite mentality of large MIS organizations is a major cultural problem. I will dwell on the problem in more detail in Chapter 14.

data processing in a levelheaded way, but that began doing rather silly things with the new techniques.

In summary, it is important to recognize that first, the brute force approach is risky; second, there is some resistance to new techniques in any MIS organization, so it will probably be necessary to sell the new techniques to a rather dubious audience; and third, the new techniques will be most effective if they are introduced slowly, gently, and with a healthy dose of diplomacy.

2.4   WHO NEEDS TO BE SOLD?

Before we can address effective methods of selling the structured development techniques, we have to identify our target audience.   Whom are we trying to convince that structured analysis is the greatest invention since peanut butter? Although every organization is different, we can usually identify several categories of people, each of which must be sold in a slightly different manner:

1.   Senior management
    a.   Corporate management not involved in MIS
    b.   Senior MIS management, usually without a programming background, such as from the accounting department

2.   Middle management
    a.   First-level managers, or team leaders
    b.   Second-level managers, third-level managers, and so forth

3.   Technicians
    a.   Veterans, with six or more years' experience
    b.   Junior programmers, with one to five years' experience
    c.   Trainees, just out of school
    d.   Maintenance programmers

2.4.1   Selling senior management

My experience is that senior management is relatively easy to sell. Two points should be considered:

1.   Senior MIS managers often know nothing about the technical details of programming, systems design, and systems analysis. They couldn't tell you, for

example, whether or not the GOTO statement should be removed from COBOL. Consequently, they are not likely to argue with any technical suggestions.

2.   Senior MIS managers are usually interested in the overall economics of data processing in their organization, as well as the economic impact of data processing on the enterprise as a whole. If they are told that structured analysis will double the productivity of their people, they will be sold.

However, an interesting point illustrates how senior management is likely to perceive the value of *everything* that the MIS group does. Commonly accepted accounting standards in the United States do not allow a corporation to show its corporate data (e.g., a customer data base) as an asset on the balance sheet. A senior manager who is only concerned with the bottom line, net worth of the organization could conclude that the organization's data has no value— and thus, MIS systems that produce data have no value.

Fortunately, the economic importance of high-quality information systems and highly productive MIS personnel is attracting the attention of senior managers in at least some organizations. However, senior management in most organizations will not commit the entire data processing staff to a new technique without the concurrence of their middle-level managers.

More importantly, senior management has not communicated to middle-level managers, or to the technicians who build the MIS systems, that they are willing to make a long-term investment (i.e., a capital expenditure of the same financial magnitude as automating a factory, or rebuilding an assembly line) in order to create high-quality information systems. Perhaps part of the reason is that senior management has been "burned" once or twice before by the MIS organization— "management information systems" in the 1960s and 1970s that failed to provide any useful information, and large systems development projects in the 1970s and 1980s that suffered massive cost overruns and schedule delays.

But the most likely cause for lack of support from top management is that nobody has presented them with a cogent, articulate proposal for a massive capital investment program to dramatically improve *enterprise* productivity and quality. Such a proposal would have to be couched in the same financial terms as any other capital investment proposal: It would have to show the cash flow impact on the organization, the extent of savings or improved profitability caused by improved MIS productivity and quality, and the return on investment (ROI) or internal rate of return (IRR) associated with the investment of monies. Good sources of information about the economics of software productivity may be found in [Boehm, 1981], [DeMarco, 1982], [Jones, 1986], and [Grady, 1987].

2.4.2   Selling middle management

Surprisingly, middle management has frequently resisted the structured techniques. When the Chief Information Officer asks the Manager of Systems Development for his opinion of, say, structured design, he is likely to get one or any combination of the following reactions:

- "We've been doing that for years. All of these new structured techniques are really just the same as modular programming, which we started doing in 1968 (when dinosaurs roamed the earth)."

- "It'll never work. We tried these ideas a couple of years ago, and they didn't work then, so they won't work now."

- "Are you suggesting that my staff and I have been doing our jobs wrong for the past ten years? I resent that. Our current methods work just fine."

These objections are similar to those made by the veterans who design, code, and test programs. There's a reason for the similarity: Many middle-level MIS managers rose from the ranks of programming and systems analysis and thus react to new technological concepts as if they were still technicians.

This reaction is particularly true of the "We've been doing it for years" reaction from the middle-level manager. Indeed, maybe he and his staff *have* been using structured analysis, structured design, structured programming, and related techniques for the past ten years without telling anyone, but it's unlikely from what I have seen in the average American and European data processing organization. It's possible that the manager sincerely thinks his staff is using structured techniques.[4] The organization's standards manuals may even dictate something resembling structured programming and structured design, but that doesn't mean that anyone is actually doing it.

Let's imagine a somewhat more optimistic scenario. Once upon a time, when the manager was a technician, he designed and coded good programs. Now that he's a manager, he has tried to pass on his experiences and ideas to his staff, a staff composed of intelligent programmers, designers, and systems analysts who are trying to do a good job. Everyone thinks that he is designing good, modular programs that will be easy to debug, maintain, expand, and modify. Everyone is trying to do good work.

Unfortunately, each programmer/analyst has a slightly different interpretation of the design/coding philosophies espoused by the manager; after all, phrases in the standards manual such as "All programs should be designed in terms of functionally independent modules with a single entry and a single exit" leave a lot to the programmer's imagination. The result has been a nonuniform, informal, sloppy implementation of the basic philosophies that the manager had practiced diligently ten years earlier, particularly if the organization is not using the walkthrough techniques discussed in Chapter 9. Consequently, the programs written by today's staff are not so easy to maintain and not so easy to expand and modify as those the manager developed.

This consideration brings us to the middle-manager reaction, the one characterized by "Whaddya mean with this structured stuff? Our old way of doing things is just fine!" Generally, it would be more accurate for the manager to say that he hasn't had any obvious disasters in his department, that things appear to be relatively stable, and, therefore, the old way of doing things must be satisfactory. Later in this chapter, I will discuss statistics taken from the data processing industry that will indicate the old way is *not* satisfactory.

I don't mean to suggest that middle-level managers are ignorant or that they should be ignored when they react

---

[4] The Peter Principle may also be involved. Years ago, when the manager was programming, he may have been a *super* technician and used structured programming. Because he was a good technician, he was promoted until he reached his level of incompetence. The mediocre programmers who had reached their levels of incompetence *as programmers* were left to design and code unstructured, unreliable, unmaintainable programs. The manager often makes the mistake of assuming that because *he* was competent as a technician, his current staff must be, too.

negatively to the introduction of structured techniques. They
have survived vendor hardware that was too small and inefficient
to permit many of the structured techniques to be implemented
practically; they have survived several generations of vendor
software (operating systems, compilers, database management
systems, telecommunication monitors, etc.) that didn't meet
expectations or that didn't work at all, and they have survived a
couple of decades in which the major problem was not the
complexity of the application but the reliability of the vendor-
supplied hardware and vendor-supplied software.

However, today things are different. Technology is
radically different from that of even ten years ago, so we can
afford to do things in a radically different way. It's also true that
most organizations are operating in a radically different
marketplace and economic situation than they were ten years
ago, so they *must* adopt radically different methods and
approaches to remain competitive, and even to survive. The
end-users' applications are more complex, so it's no longer
sufficient to lock one brilliant programmer in a room for six
months and expect him to develop a perfect system.[5]

Also, our problems today are different. Software reliability
is more important, maintenance costs are a greater
consideration, hardware costs generally are lower, and
programmers and systems analysts are more expensive than they
were ten years ago.

2.4.3   Selling the technicians

Finally, there is the question of selling the people who
actually develop the systems: senior programmers, designers,
and systems analysts; junior programmers; trainees; and
maintenance programmers. A few brief comments are in order.

1.   The senior programmers, designers, and systems
      analysts often display much the same reaction to the
      structured techniques as do the middle-level
      managers. Although many of their specific
      objections and complaints are discussed in later
      chapters, they seem to fall into the same general
      categories: "It'll never work," or "My old way of
      doing this is just fine," or "I've been writing

---

[5] It may be possible if the programmer has a fourth-generation language; but then there is
a different set of problems. See Chapter 16 for more details.

structured programs for years and years— I just use a
different way of describing it."

2.   Junior technicians tend to be less negative.
      Although converting them from their initial training
      may not be easy, they usually do not have strong
      opinions about the technical aspects of the new
      techniques, and they usually have fewer bad habits to
      break.

3.   Trainees don't have to be sold. By definition, they
      know nothing about programming and systems
      analysis, and they are perfectly happy to learn good
      techniques or bad techniques.   Indeed, leading
      American, Canadian, and European universities now
      introduce structured programming and structured
      design in first-year programming courses, and the
      students have no difficulty dealing with the
      concepts.[6]

4.   Maintenance programmers do not need to be
      convinced that the current method of designing and
      writing programs is unsatisfactory.   They are the
      ones who have had to patch and debug sloppy
      software for the past thirty years.

Occasionally, subtle political problems make the selling job
more difficult. For example, trainee programmers can be taught
how to design and code programs using all the new techniques;
but what do they do if their first project requires them to work
with or under senior programmers who persist in using the old
unstructured techniques?

What about the maintenance programmer who agrees that
current programming and design approaches are unsatisfactory,
and who would like to use as an example the program he is
maintaining, except that the program was designed and coded
years ago by a person who is now his manager? Obviously, it's
impolitic to suggest that a system that is the full-time occupation
of a whole department, a system that built the manager's career
and reputation, is a bad system!

---

[6] On the other hand, we now have to deal with the problem of poor training at the
elementary and high-school levels. It has been estimated that a child born in 1980 will
graduate from high school near the end of this century having written 10,000 lines of
code—most of it in BASIC, and most of it without any disciplined training on proper
program design and construction.

Or, a maintenance programmer agrees that classical programming techniques are terrible, but his first structured program turns out to be even more difficult to maintain than the old programs. I will discuss this problem further in Chapter 6 when we look at structured programming. A program that *appears* to be structured may not actually *be* structured, and, in fact, may be worse than a classical program.

2.4.4   Some final comments on selling the organization

Throughout this section, I have suggested that senior management may have a different reaction to the new techniques than middle management, and that programmers and systems analysts may respond differently depending on whether they are trainees or veterans or somewhere in between.

Accordingly, I recommend that your organization be sold on the structured techniques from the top down. I have seen organizations in which structured design or structured analysis was introduced at the grass-roots level, only to be stymied by suspicious middle-level managers and ignored by senior management. Management commitment is essential *before* any significant effort should be made to sell the approach to the technicians themselves.

There are exceptions— for example, when senior management immediately turns to middle managers for a technical opinion. In this case, initial selling of the structured techniques may have to begin with the middle-level managers themselves. They can convince senior management of the favorable economic aspects, and can persuade the programmers of the strong technical arguments in favor of the techniques.

2.5   HOW TO PROMOTE THE STRUCTURED TECHNIQUES

Having discussed other aspects of the selling of structured systems development techniques, we are still left with one fundamental question: How do we convince a dubious audience (whether programmers, designers, systems analysts, or managers) that the structured techniques are worth exploring?

I have found that the most effective approach is a double-whammy. First convince the audience that the current approach used by the organization leaves much to be desired. Second, convince them that the structured techniques are demonstrably better than any of the methods currently used by the organization.

To do this properly, you need ammunition: some statistics, case studies, and documented evidence that the current organizational approach is unsatisfactory, and that the structured techniques are good. The remainder of this chapter discusses some useful statistics, beginning with figures describing the current state of the systems development profession.

2.5.1 The average application programmer is not very productive

On average, an application programmer can produce 10 to 15 debugged program statements per day; for systems programmers, particularly those working on large operating systems, the number drops to as few as two or three debugged statements per day. Given the salary of system developers in the late 1980s— typically $30,000 to $60,000, plus another 50 to 100 percent overhead for insurance, benefits, office space, computer support, clerical support, etc.— this means that each program statement in a new application system costs somewhere between $10 and $50. *And this does not include the cost of maintenance, which will increase the cost of each program statement by at least a factor of two!*

The figure of average programmer productivity has been documented in many places, including the delightful classic by Fred Brooks, *The Mythical Man-Month* [Brooks, 1975]. What makes the figure so interesting— and discouraging!— is that it seems to be invariant over a long period. IBM first observed the productivity statistics on projects in the late 1950s. They were confirmed over and over again in major projects throughout the 1960s, 1970s, and 1980s, and it appears that they will be valid as we enter the 1990s.

The productivity figures seem to be both machine independent and language independent. That is, the available statistics strongly suggest that the average application programmer can generate 10 to 15 debugged statements per day regardless of whether he programs on an IBM, Honeywell, or Burroughs computer. Similarly, it appears that he will write 10 to 15 statements per day regardless of whether he programs in COBOL, FORTRAN, Ada, assembler, or any other major programming language.[7]

---

[7] Since one can accomplish much more with ten COBOL statements than with ten assembler statements, or with ten FOCUS statements compared to ten COBOL

Controversy arises with the definition of programmer productivity, particularly when it is expressed in terms of debugged statements per day. Some of the commotion is made by programmers themselves, who always remember that wonderful day when they wrote six hundred lines of code. What they usually forget, and what the figure of 10 to 15 statements is drawn from, is the tremendous amount of time required to design, debug, and document the code.

There are other reasons for the controversy surrounding the measurement of productivity:

- The Hawthorne Effect may become significant when measuring the productivity of an individual programmer over a short period of time. If a programmer knows that he will be judged by the number of lines of code he writes, then he will automatically write more lines of code—but they may be trivial lines of code. In the extreme case, a simple in-line loop that iterates a thousand times could be rewritten as a thousand in-line instructions. However, my experience has been that programmers do not react in this fashion because (aside from their sense of professionalism and their desire to write good programs) they know, deep in their hearts, that their salary will not increase proportionately to the number of lines of code they write.

- There can be extreme variations in productivity, from project to project, from programmer to programmer, and from day to day. The Hawthorne Effect ceases to be a problem even when measuring an individual programmer, if the time scale is increased from a day to a more reasonable period— say, six months to a year (people can sprint at amazing speeds for a short period of time, but nobody can sprint for the duration of a marathon). And it ceases to be a factor at all if one measures productivity at the *project* level or the *enterprise* level over any reasonable period of time.

---

statements, it is fair to say that a programmer is producing much more "functionality" when he programs in a higher-level language than in a lower-level language. However, writing ten assembly language statements represents approximately the same level of intellectual effort as writing ten COBOL statements. This argument is used in the late 1980s to promote the use of fourth-generation languages. This is discussed in more detail in Chapter 16.

- People measure productivity differently. When we measure productivity, should we include only the coding activity itself, or should we include testing? What about documentation, design, and systems analysis? Do we include only the people who write the programs, or do we include the clerical support people (e.g., the program librarian discussed in Chapter 8), and the managers? And if we are concerned about productivity at the *enterprise* level, should we include the cost of canceled projects? Should we include the cost of maintenance? If one is measuring the dollar-cost of each developed statement, should we include the cost of travel time to visit user sites? Should we include the cost of hiring, relocation, and turnover of employees?[8] As Capers Jones points out in [Jones, 1986], productivity figures can vary by a factor of 100 to 1, depending on what activities are included, and what people in the organization are included.

The rest of this book could be devoted to a discussion of productivity metrics, but there are already several excellent books on the subject. For more information, consult [DeMarco, 1982], [Boehm, 1981], [Jones, 1986], or [Grady, 1987]. However, it is sufficient to conclude this section by stating that productivity, if measured consistently, is not very high— and that it can be *substantially* improved, often by as much as a factor of two, by using structured systems development techniques.

2.5.2   There is a substantial variation in programmer abilities

Things would be bad enough if all programmers wrote ten debugged COBOL statements every day; at least it would give us a uniform measure with which to plan and budget our projects. What is more disturbing is that ten statements is an average, or mean— and the variation between high productivity and low productivity is staggering.

This point was first made in a classic paper in 1968 [Sackman et al., 1968]: Professor Harold Sackman reported that in an experiment with a group of experienced programmers, the

---

[8] Paul Strassmann points out in *Information Payoff* [Strassmann,1985] that the easiest way of increasing productivity is to shift costs to someone else's budget. Thus, a manager can dramatically improve the apparent productivity of the *development* team by doing a "quick and dirty" job, which causes an even more dramatic decline in the productivity of maintenance.

best was able to design, code, and test a program 25 times faster than the worst. Similarly, he found that one programmer could produce a program that was ten times faster, and required ten times less memory, than the program produced by the worst in the group.

What makes Sackman's experiment so interesting is his observation that there was no significant correlation between programming performance and years of experience, and no correlation between programming performance and scores on programming aptitude tests.[9]   This is no surprise to many programming managers, who know that a programmer with ten years of experience may have had one year of real experience, repeated nine times.

As with the statistics concerning programmer productivity in the preceding section, there is much dispute about the Sackman statistics.   It may be argued, for example, that Sackman studied only a small sample of programmers (approximately one dozen people), and that universal conclusions about the entire programming industry cannot be drawn from the sample.   One might also argue that the programmer who takes a long time to design and code a program may require substantially less time to test it; similarly, one could expect that a programmer whose program occupies a large chunk of memory would have written it in such a way as to require less CPU time, and vice versa.

Although these comments may be valid, there is still the strong impression that some programmers are substantially better—typically an order of magnitude better—than their colleagues.   I have confirmed this several dozen times in informal experiments in programming seminars I have taught throughout the United States and Europe.   An equally distinct impression is that a high IQ and ten years of experience may not be sufficient qualifications to make a really good programmer.

If this is the case, what should we do?   Should we identify those programmers who are an order of magnitude better than their colleagues, and then shoot everyone else?   The Sackman statistics provide a slightly more civilized solution: the chief programmer team concept discussed in Chapter 8.

---

[9] Actually, this is true only of the *experienced* programmers. Sackman found that, for trainee programmers, there *was* a correlation between programming performance and scores on aptitude tests.

Others propose that we examine what makes the "good" programmer so good, and then teach those skills to the average programmer.   Indeed, this approach provides much of the motivation for structured programming and structured design. Some programmers are successful largely because of their *instinctive* ability to break a large system into small, independent modules, and then code those modules with well-organized (i.e., well-structured) statements.[10]   The technologies of structured programming and structured design might be regarded as an attempt to capture in words what a few of these programmers have been doing by instinct for years.

In the meantime, you as a manager should recognize that you have a potential problem. If you have a staff of ten or twenty programmers, and if there is an order-of-magnitude difference in their abilities, then *your* ability to schedule, manage, and budget projects is seriously impaired.   The difficulty is compounded by the probability that you don't know precisely how good or bad your programmers are in the area of designing, coding, testing, and writing efficient programs.

Sackman was able to do something that most programming organizations *never* do: He had a dozen programmers working on the same programming problem at the same time, under the same conditions.   In the real world, Charlie works on program A, while Susan works on program B. Since program A and program B are intrinsically different, it is difficult to determine whether Charlie codes faster than Susan, and whether Charlie's code is more efficient or more maintainable than Susan's code.

Sackman's experiments thus confirm what we could only guess at before: There are substantial variations in programmer abilities. This knowledge should give us motivation to try some of the structured system development technologies that are discussed in subsequent chapters.

---

[10] This has also been observed with young children who, in many schools, are now learning to program in a language like LOGO. Some children instinctively follow a top-down problem-solving approach, while others develop monolithic programs. It should be noted that children of seven and eight can easily be taught the concept of top-down design, and that with a language like LOGO, they easily learn the concept of procedures (subroutines), the notion of passing arguments (parameters) to procedures, and even the concept of recursion.

2.5.3   The average programmer spends very little time programming

One reason for the low productivity of programmers is that we don't give them enough opportunity to program. In a typical organization, a programmer spends a significant portion of his time attending meetings, filling out reports, walking downstairs to the computer room to pick up his output listings, walking across the hall to discuss some esoteric programming issue with another programmer, and so on.

An early study published by George Weinwurm [Weinwurm, 1970] indicated that the average programmer spends only 27 percent of his day doing something that could be interpreted as programming—writing program statements, looking at a listing, debugging, etc. The remainder of the programmer's working day is spent performing basically clerical activities or duties that have nothing to do with programming.

To see whether this statistic is relevant in your organization, you might spend a few hours watching your programmers and systems analysts as they carry out their normal duties. Then ask yourself: How many of their activities really require an M.B.A., or a B.S. in Computer Science, six months of on-the-job training, and a $40,000 annual salary? How much of the work could be done by an intelligent clerk?

As you might have anticipated, Weinwurm's study provides some motivation to apply the program librarian concept, discussed in Chapter 8, and for automating much of the clerical work done by programmers and systems analysts, which is discussed in Chapter 19.

2.5.4   Testing typically occupies 50 percent of a programming project

One-third of the time, energy, and money expended in a programming project is for analysis and design; roughly one-sixth is spent on coding; and the remaining half is spent trying to make the thing work![11]   Indeed, it has been known for so long that testing consumes half the time allocated to a project that everyone seems to accept it as a law of nature. That it is *not* a law of nature has become painfully apparent in some of the

---

[11] For a discussion of these statistics, see [Metzger, 1983] and [DeMarco, 1982].

recent programming projects in which the code virtually worked correctly the first time it was run.[12]

In other words, we spend so much time on testing primarily because the programmers, designers, and systems analysts make so many unnecessary mistakes. With the use of structured analysis, structured design, structured programming, and structured walkthroughs, we can cut the number of unnecessary bugs almost to zero. Thus, if you're spending 50 percent of your resources in a systems development project on testing, you're probably wasting a substantial amount of time and money.

In addition, the way we conduct testing on most projects causes trouble. The current approach in most organizations is roughly as follows: First, test all the modules in a stand-alone fashion; then, combine modules into whole programs, and carry out program testing; next, combine several of the programs into subsystems, and conduct subsystem testing; finally, combine the subsystems into a system and do system testing. Largely as a result of this approach to testing, many projects encounter the following problems:

- There is little tangible evidence of progress during the testing phase. It is largely during this time that programmers remark that they are 98 percent finished or that there is only one more bug to find.

- The worst bugs—interface bugs—are most often found at the end of the testing phase, while trivial bugs—for example, local logic errors within a module—are found at the beginning. If they had their choice, most programmers (not to mention managers and users!) would like to reverse the sequence, finding the major bugs first and cleaning up the trivial bugs last.

- Deadlines frequently are missed, and since the classical approach to testing usually means that nothing works until it *all* works, the project can become politically vulnerable. When the deadline arrives, the user is not impressed with 50,000 lines of code that have passed a module test phase, but that don't do anything as a system.

---

[12] For an interesting discussion of this phenomenon, see the discussion of "cleanroom programming" by Harlan Mills in [Mills, 1986].

- The user discovers that he doesn't like the system, which I regard as a fault of the testing approach, since the user doesn't see anything tangible until he sees the entire system in operation.

Each of these problems will be examined in Chapter 4 in the discussion of top-down implementation. At this point, it is sufficient to recognize that the current method of doing things is fraught with problems.

2.5.5   Bugs last forever in large systems

One of the most interesting statistics in the software profession came from an employee of IBM, who remarked at a landmark software engineering conference that every release of IBM's OS/360 operating system had at least a thousand bugs.[13]

Obviously, IBM is not unique in this area, nor is this a phenomenon restricted to operating systems. Large programs or systems have a number of residual bugs that will never be completely eliminated. Indeed, there is increasing evidence to suggest that large programs—whether payroll programs, order-entry programs, compilers, operating systems, or air defense systems—behave in the manner shown in Figure 2.1.

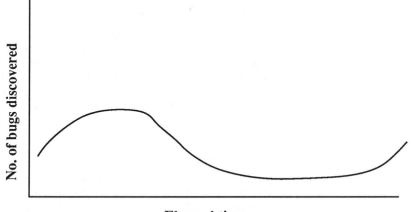

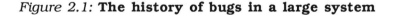

Figure 2.1: **The history of bugs in a large system**

---

[13] See the republished proceedings of the NATO Software Engineering Conference in [Buxton, 1976].

During the first few months of a system's use, more and more bugs will be discovered. There are various reasons for this. The users become increasingly experienced with the system and thus push it harder. The volume of processing builds up, exposing bugs that were in the code all the time, but which did not come to light during the early use of the system.

At some point, the bug-discovery curve turns downward (otherwise, the system will be discarded by the users). Each month, the users find fewer and fewer bugs. Eventually, though, the curve levels off and then remains relatively constant over a long period. In the case of IBM's operating system, the curve apparently leveled off at a thousand bugs per release. For a medium-sized payroll system, we might measure this as one bug every third payroll period, while the measure for an on-line airline reservation system might be one system failure every week. However we measure it, one fact remains clear: *The system will probably never be bug-free.*

In fact, if we wait long enough, the curve will inevitably turn up again; that is, there will gradually be more and more bugs discovered per unit time. This usually occurs with old systems, which have been so heavily patched and modified that nobody understands them. In such a situation, every time the programmer fixes one old bug he unwittingly introduces two new ones into the system.

Another way to assess the reliability of a system is by considering the total number of bugs discovered during its lifetime. Currently, classical methods of developing computer programs turn up an average of three to five bugs per hundred statements, bugs that appear *after* the program has been tested and put into production. Thus, if we develop a payroll system with 10,000 COBOL statements, we should expect to find between 300 and 500 bugs in productions during the eight to ten year expected lifetime of the system. Obviously, the majority of those bugs will be found during the first few months of production, but they will continue to appear even after five, six, or seven years of use.

The point of this is quite simple: The unreliability of our current systems is a problem, and the "state of the practice" in most organizations is *far* below the "state of the art" in the systems development industry. This is particularly true when typical American application systems are compared with, say, typical Japanese systems, where there are typically three to five bugs per *10,000* lines of code—in other words, only one percent as many bugs. In later chapters, we will see how we can improve the reliability of our systems dramatically.

2.5.6   Bugs are more critical in today's systems

As pointed out in the preceding section, most current information systems have a substantial number of bugs, a phenomenon that has been with us ever since the first programmer wrote the first program. The problem is not that programmers today are less knowledgeable or conscientious than that first programmer, but that the methods now used are outdated.

In addition, the bugs matter much more today than they did in the early days of programming. We are beginning to appreciate that it is expensive to put bugs into a program and then go through the laborious, time-consuming process of finding them and removing them. It is considerably cheaper to avoid bugs in the first place.

A more serious reason for being concerned about bugs is that our customers, our companies, and our entire society are becoming less tolerant of buggy programs. Twenty years ago, a computer bug often was the source of an amusing newspaper article— for example, when a billing program produced a customer invoice for $0.00, or even worse, *minus* $0.00, and sent nasty dunning letters to the customer who refused to pay. True, such events were considered an irritation and a public relations problem, but a small price to pay for the marvels of the electronic computer.

Today, however, we are faced with a very different situation. Consider the consequences of a bug in a payroll system for 100,000 people. I once saw a nationwide wildcat strike in Canada triggered by a payroll system's failure to pay correct overtime wages. Or, imagine the effects of a bug that shuts down a nationwide on-line order entry system, or an airline's reservation system, or a bank's on-line ATM system.

At an even more serious level are the potential repercussions of a bug in any of the computerized telephone switching systems that are now installed in most of the developed countries around the world. A software bug could leave an entire city without telephone service until a programmer could figure out how to eliminate the problem. Or consider a failure in a computerized air traffic control system, or, worse still, a malfunction in an air defense system or in any of the sophisticated military command-and-control systems under development today. The ultimate example, as this book was being written, is the American "Star Wars" system, which some experts estimate will require as much as *100 million* lines of code. I leave it as a simple arithmetic exercise to calculate how many errors such a system would have at an average of one to five bugs per hundred lines of code.[14]

The moral is simple and clear and increasingly urgent with each passing day: We cannot afford bugs— *any* bugs— in the large, complex, "mission-critical" systems being designed today.   Nor can we afford to continue introducing bugs into our current systems.

2.5.7   Programmers are not very good at fixing bugs

To complicate matters further, once bugs are discovered, programmers are not very good at fixing them.   A classic study by Barry Boehm ([Boehm, 1973]) indicated that, at best, a programmer has approximately a 50 percent chance of successfully eliminating a bug on his first attempt, if he modifies only five to ten lines of code.   If he changes more lines of code, his chances of success drop.   If, for example, the bug requires 50 lines of code to be changed, the programmer's chance of success drops to approximately 20 percent on the first try.

Interestingly, if the programmer modifies fewer than five to ten lines of code in his attempt to correct the bug, his chances of success also drop, though only slightly.   Although this might seem surprising at first, it can be explained by the normal human psychology associated with making "trivial" changes to a program.   Programmers are overconfident when making such changes; on the other hand, if the bug is serious enough to require several lines of code to be changed, the maintenance programmer will usually be much more careful.

Obviously, some of the problems associated with correcting bugs are human problems: typographical errors when program statements are entered, coding mistakes, psychological errors, and so forth.   However, many problems are of a different sort: We may successfully fix a bug in subroutine x, only to find later that the supposed fix has introduced a new bug in subroutine y.   This phenomenon, often called the "ripple effect," is becoming more troublesome, particularly in regard to larger systems having many modules with which the programmer is unfamiliar.   It is even more impossible for him to be aware of the subtle interactions between the modules.

---

[14] For a rather alarming list of errors in such critical systems, see [Neumann, 1985] and [Bellin, 1987].

Largely because of this problem, interest has grown in the techniques of structured design, which attempt to minimize the interdependencies between modules. This is discussed at length in Chapter 5.

2.5.8 Maintenance is becoming too expensive

A survey in the October 1972 issue of *EDP Analyzer* [Canning, 1972] indicated perhaps for the first time that many MIS organizations were spending about 50 percent of their budgets on maintenance. More recently, Professors B. P. Lientz and E. B. Swanson confirmed these figures in a detailed study of nearly 500 United States MIS installations [Lientz, 1980]. Indeed, many large organizations spend as much as 75 percent or more of their data processing budgets maintaining existing systems.

Nobody is suggesting that maintenance could be eliminated altogether, and it is not even clear, a priori, that there is anything wrong with 75 percent of the MIS budget being devoted to maintenance; it could just mean that the organization has finished developing all of its "core" information systems. However, an expenditure that consumes such a large part of the MIS budget deserves to be examined more closely to see if it is being well spent. Consider how we currently spend our maintenance money:

- Ongoing debugging

- Changes required by new hardware, new versions of vendor operating systems, new compilers, and so on

- Changes to improve the efficiency of the program, or to improve its internal documentation, etc.

- Changes, expansions, and new features requested by the users

The first two categories should be possible to control and minimize. As I suggested earlier, *any* money spent on testing and debugging after the system is put into operation is too much. Lientz and Swanson reported in their study that approximately 12 percent of the MIS maintenance budget is spent on "emergency" debugging, and another 9 percent is spent on "routine" debugging. Thus, some 21 percent of the maintenance budget— or 10 to 15 percent of the overall MIS budget— is spent repairing errors in information systems after delivery to the end-user. The dollar cost of this activity in MIS organizations around the world is staggering, and one estimate is that it represents approximately $75 per year for every man, woman, and child in the United States (see Chapter 20 of [Yourdon, 1986] for more details).

The last category in the maintenance list above—new features for the end-user—never can be eliminated. Lientz and Swanson report that most organizations spend about 41 percent of their maintenance budget in this category. However, some portion of this expenditure may be the result of poor systems analysis: What is reported as a "new feature" may be something that the users wanted all along, but which the systems analysts never understood. In any case, the cost for these changes could be minimized if our information systems were easier to change. A rule of thumb to follow is that if a modification or a new feature to a system can be easily explained by the user, then it *should* be easy to introduce into the system. If it is not easy, then the system was probably poorly designed. The impact of such poor designs is rather remarkable: A well-designed system can be maintained as one-tenth that of a poorly designed system.

2.6   STATISTICS SUPPORTING USE OF STRUCTURED TECHNIQUES

Thus far we have understood that the current approach to systems analysis and design is not as successful as we would like. It is fair to offer criticism only if we can come up with something better. This raises the obvious question: Why should we believe that things will improve with the use of structured programming, structured design, structured analysis, and the other techniques?

Some people argue that using the new techniques is simply a matter of common sense—for example: "It makes *sense* to use structured programming because of increased pro- ductivity, fewer bugs, and easier maintenance, among other reasons." Indeed, I have already used such arguments in this chapter, and I will repeat them in subsequent chapters.

Unfortunately, common sense and rational arguments are not always sufficient to convince data processing managers. Perhaps that's because these battle-scarred veterans have already been promised too many miracles in the form of relational database systems, virtual memory, fourth-generation languages, and goodness knows what else. Or, perhaps it's because the common-sense sales pitch makes structured analysis sound like just another brand of toothpaste or dog food, and we all have grown a little cynical and skeptical about *that* kind of selling.

From my experience, the most convincing arguments have been based on real experiences, or case studies, in which people have actually used structured programming, chief programmer teams, walkthroughs, or some other aspect of the structured techniques, with documented results. Fortunately, the number of case studies is growing. At least one such case study is described at each computer conference, and almost every issue of *Datamation, Infosystems, Software, IEEE Transactions on Software Engineering,* or *Computerworld* contains some kind of we-tried-it-and-here's-what-happened report. In addition, there have been major studies published in journals such as the *IBM Systems Journal* (see [Walston-Felix, 1977]) and such books as *Programming Productivity* [Jones, 1986] and *Software Engineering Economics* [Boehm, 1981], which show the impact of structured techniques on both development and maintenance. These and other journals, books, and references are a good source from which to build your own file of testimonials to convince skeptical members of your data processing department.

The only problem with using case studies is that they all measure their results differently, thus making comparisons and generalizations difficult. As I pointed out earlier, some organizations include system testing and documentation in their productivity measures, while others do not; some organizations include systems analysts, managers, and clerical staff in their measurements, while others count only the programmers. Current work by Capers Jones [Jones, 1986], Basili [Basili, 1984], and Weiss [Weiss, 1985] is concentrating on finding standardized ways of measuring productivity and quality data for software engineering.

In the meantime, the studies published in the various references cited above indicate that diligent use of structured techniques can improve productivity during the development phase of a project by 50 to 100 percent; can reduce maintenance costs by as much as 90 percent; and can reduce errors in operational systems by as much as 99 percent. The figures may be slightly higher or lower for your organization, but they should still be enough to impress the skeptics in your organization. You can be sure that they have impressed your competitors; aggressive MIS organizations around the world have begun to practice the use of structured techniques with a fervor that approaches religious fanaticism.

Chapter 3
STRUCTURED ANALYSIS

3.1   INTRODUCTION

Perhaps the most important of the structured disciplines discussed in this book is structured analysis. As the term implies, structured analysis is the first phase of an MIS systems development project, when the user's requirements are defined and documented.

To understand why structured analysis is so important, let's examine the steps that usually occur in classical systems analysis. The analyst prepares a document describing the proposed system. The document, which may contain hundreds and even thousands of pages of technical jargon and terms, is submitted to the user for review. In most cases, it might as well be written in a foreign language because most users have neither the time nor the technical knowledge to wade through and understand the implications of the proposed system. In contrast, structured analysis recognizes that the user does not have a good understanding of what the data processing people are going to develop for him, unless it is an utterly trivial MIS project.

The user's inability to interpret classical analysis documents comes as a rude shock to many systems analysts, who complain, "But we gave the user a detailed functional specification, and he signed off on it!" Many systems analysts sincerely believe that "signing off" on a thousand-page functional specification guarantees that the user knows what kind of MIS system he is getting. Unfortunately, this assumption isn't valid. Most users acknowledge that they never read the specification in detail because it's too long and too technical. Moreover, I am convinced that if they did read the specification, they probably would not understand it.

The reasons for the user's difficulty with classical functional specifications can be summarized as follows:

- They're *monolithic* and must be read from beginning to end. A user cannot easily find information about a particular part of the proposed system without searching the entire document.

- They're *redundant*, giving the same information (or worse, conflicting information) in numerous locations throughout the document, but without benefit of cross-reference.

- They're *difficult to modify* and *difficult to maintain.* A simple change in the user's requirements may necessitate changes to several different parts of the functional specification— and, because the document is monolithic and redundant, it's exceedingly painful to change. Consequently, the specification is usually not kept current during subsequent maintenance activities, and is often obsolete even by the end of the analysis phase of the project!

- They're often *physical* instead of *logical*, in that they describe the user's requirements in terms of either the physical hardware or the kind of physical file structure or programming language that will be used to implement the system. Such information often muddles the discussion about *what* the user wants his system to do by giving details about *how* the system will do things.

- They are *not a useful target* for ongoing development of the system; indeed, as one of my clients said, the classical functional specification is "of historical significance only." As a result, the system that is designed may differ considerably from the system that was specified.

Three other drawbacks should be stressed about functional specifications. Because they are usually long narratives, they tend to be boring. It's extremely difficult to read through a thousand pages of narrative text without feeling the urge to assume the fetal position and fall fast asleep! Since our society is increasingly video-oriented, there's less and less of a chance that users actually will spend time poring over hundreds of pages of turgid prose.

There is an additional problem connected with the length of the functional specification. Because it is so long and monolithic, feedback between user and systems analyst typically takes weeks or even months. Thus, if the user *does* read the specification, and if he does find something that he wants changed, so much time elapses before he sees the modified specification that he will have forgotten what he wanted changed in the first place.

The last problem is perhaps the most important: *Things change.* While the specification is being developed, the user's external environment is constantly changing: The economy is changing, the competition is changing, the government regulations are changing, the social climate is changing. Indeed, even the user himself is changing. It's not unusual to deliver a finished MIS system to an end-user who inherited his position from an earlier user who first asked for the project to be done. The problem with all of this is that if things change, then the user's system requirements change; if the requirements change, then the functional specification needs to be changed. But, as we have seen above, this is problematical.

As systems analysis continues, all of these problems become compounded, causing the classical analysis phase of most large projects to be painful and time-consuming. Typically, everyone involved feels desperate to end the analysis phase as soon as possible, and few people ever go back to reexamine or revise the functional specifications. Once classical analysis is done, it's done forever— much to the relief of both the users *and* the analysts. And the document that is produced is a dead document, stillborn after months of painful labor. It might as well be written in Latin.

3.2   THE TOOLS OF STRUCTURED ANALYSIS

What, then, is *structured* analysis? Basically, structured analysis is the use of graphical documentation tools to produce a new kind of functional specification— a structured specification. The primary documentation tools of structured analysis include the following items:

- Data flow diagrams

- Data dictionary

- Process specifications

- Entity-relationship diagrams

- State transition diagrams

Data flow diagrams, or DFDs, provide an easy, graphic means of modeling the flow of data through a system—any system, whether manual, automated, or a mixture of both. Figure 3.1 shows the basic elements of a data flow diagram: data flows, processes, data stores, and terminators. The data flows can be thought of as pipelines that carry elements of data from one place to another; the processes (often known as "bubbles") carry out the computations and processing work of the system; the stores represent data "at rest" (once the system is implemented, these will probably be traditional *files* or *databases*); and the terminators are people, organizations, or other systems external to the system being developed.

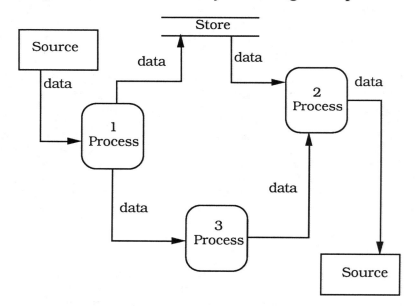

Figure 3.1: **The elements of a data flow diagram**

A typical system requires several *levels* of data flow diagram, though even the largest system will usually not have more than six or seven levels. For example, an overview of the system might be provided in a DFD such as the one shown in Figure 3.2. Each of the processes shown in Figure 3.2 can be "exploded"—that is, it can be defined in terms of a lower-level DFD. For example, bubble #3 in the "parent" diagram can be exploded, or decomposed, into a "child" diagram shown as Figure 3.3. Note that the detailed DFD is a replacement for its parent bubble, having the same net inputs and outputs.

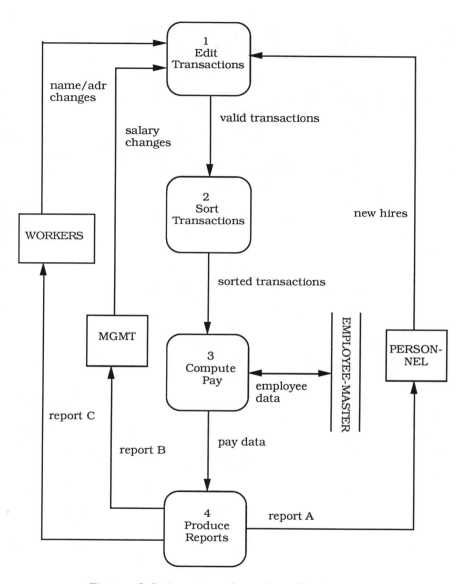

Figure 3.2: **An overview data flow diagram**

The second major tool of structured analysis is the *data dictionary.* A data dictionary is an organized collection of logical definitions of all data elements that occur in the system. In a typical systems development project, there are likely to be several thousand such data definitions. For example, one of the

data elements shown on the DFD in Figure 3.1 might be called
CUSTOMER-ORDER, and it might be defined in the data
dictionary as follows:

CUSTOMER-ORDER =   ***description of a customer
                          order***
                          CUSTOMER-NAME +
                          ACCOUNT-NUMBER +
                          [SHIPPING-ADDRESS|"TAKE-AWAY"] +
                          (SALESPERSON) +
                          {ITEM-ORDER}

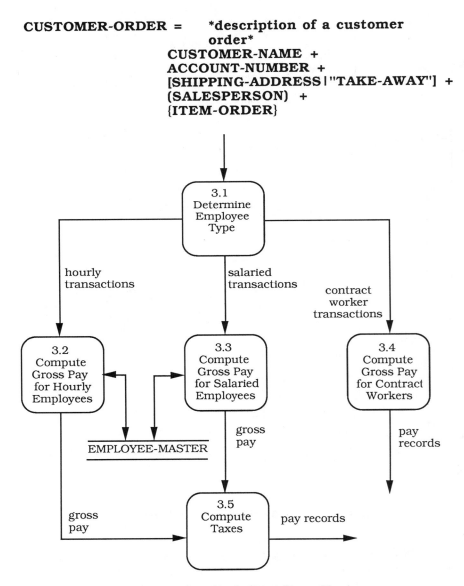

Figure 3.3: **A detailed data flow diagram**

For the most part, this data definition can be read by the end-user without any explanation once the mathematical operators, or notations, are understood. These are defined as follows:

NOTATION	MEANING
* *	encloses a descriptive comment
x = a+b	x consists of data elements a and b
x = [a|b]	x consists of either a or b, but not both
x = a + (b)	x consists of a and the optional occurrence of b
x = {a}	x consists of zero or more occurrences of a
x = y{a}	x consists of y or more occurrences of a
x = {a}z	x consists of z or fewer (possibly zero) occurrences of a
x = y{a}z	x consists of between y and z occurrences of a

Thus, the data element description at the top of the page tells us that a **CUSTOMER-ORDER** consists of a **CUSTOMER-NAME**, together with an **ACCOUNT-NUMBER**, together with either a **SHIPPING-ADDRESS** or the literal text string "TAKE-AWAY," together with an optional **SALESPERSON** description, together with zero or more **ITEM-ORDER**s.

Just as with a data flow diagram, the data dictionary can present a top-down definition of a complex data element. For example, having defined **CUSTOMER-ORDER**, it behooves us to provide an appropriate description of some of its component data elements. Thus, the data dictionary would probably also contain a definition for **ITEM-ORDER**s:

ITEM-ORDER =   ***an individual item being ordered***
                         PART-NUMBER+(PART-NAME)+
                         QUANTITY+UNIT-PRICE+(DISCOUNT)

Indeed, a proper job of systems analysis requires that every data element eventually be defined, down to the lowest level of detail. Elementary items (those that need no further decomposition) should also indicate the relevant *units* and *values* or *range*; for some applications, it may also be important to specify the *precision* with which the item is measured. For the example above, we might expect to see the following definition of **QUANTITY**:

QUANTITY =   ***quantity of an individual item ordered***
                        units: integers; range: 1-999

The term data *dictionary* is an apt one. Just as nobody
expects to read Webster's dictionary from cover to cover, nobody
seriously expects an end-user to read the data dictionary from
cover to cover. Its primary purpose is to serve as a *reference*
document, to clarify any confusion over a term. (However, the
systems analysts who build the data dictionary must review each
individual entry, preferably using a walkthrough approach
described in Chapter 9, to ensure its accuracy.)

To those who are concerned about the user's ability to read
and understand the notation shown above, I point out that there
are many other examples of formal notations that are
understandable by "ordinary" people. One such notation is
shown below in Figure 3.4; another is shown in Figure 3.5.

Figure 3.4: **Musical notation**

The third major tool of structured analysis is the *process
specification.* The purpose of the process specification is to
allow the analyst to describe, rigorously and precisely, the
business policy (but *not* the implementation tactics) represented
by each of the bottom-level bubbles in the bottom-level DFDs. At
the same time, the description is intended to be
comprehensible to the end-user. These bottom-level process
descriptions are often referred to as "mini-specs," since each
one is a miniature functional specification. The process
specification can be written in a variety of forms: formulas,
graphs, decision tables, or—as I prefer—in a form known as
"structured English," consisting of a limited set of verbs and
nouns organized to represent a compromise between readability
and rigor.

For example, a bottom-level bubble entitled **CARRY-OUT-
BACK-BILLING** might have associated with it the structured
English shown on the next page.

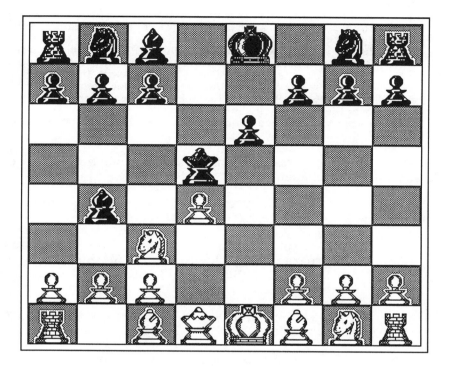

Figure 3.5: **Chess notation**

STRUCTURED ENGLISH FOR CARRY-OUT-BACK-BILLING

1. IF the dollar amount of the invoice times the number of weeks overdue is greater than $10,000 THEN:
   a. Give a photocopy of the invoice to the salesperson who is to call the customer.
   b. Log on the back of the invoice that a copy has been given to the salesperson, with the date on which it was done.
   c. Refile the invoice in the file for examination two weeks from today.

2. OTHERWISE IF more than four overdue notices have been sent THEN:
   a. Give a photocopy of the invoice to the salesperson to call the customer.
   b. Log on the back of the invoice that a copy has been given to the salesperson, with the date on which it was done.
   c. Refile the invoice in the file to be examined again one week from today.

3.   **OTHERWISE (the situation has not yet reached serious proportions)**
   a.   **Add 1 to the overdue notice count on the back of the invoice (if no such count has been recorded, write "overdue notice count = 1")**
   b.   **IF the invoice in the file is illegible THEN type a new one.**
   c.   **Send the customer a photocopy of the invoice, stamped "Nth notice: invoice overdue. Please remit immediately," where N is the value of the overdue notice count.**
   d.   **Log on the back of the invoice the date on which the Nth overdue notice was sent.**
   e.   **Refile the invoice in the file for examination two weeks from today.**

In its most extreme form, structured English consists of only the following elements:

-    A limited set of action-oriented verbs, such as "Compute," "Get," "Put," etc.

-    Control constructs borrowed from structured programming (see Chapter 6)—for example, IF-THEN-ELSE, DO-WHILE, CASE, and so forth.

-    Data elements as defined in the data dictionary.

The example above was chosen deliberately to show the difference between *essential* business policy and *implementation* tactics. For example, the systems analyst might ask the following questions about the back-billing policy:

-    "Is it necessary to make photocopies of invoices, or is that just the way things happen to be done today? Is it OK if we think of other ways of providing the appropriate information to the salesperson or customer?"

-    "Why does the date have to be logged on the back of the invoice? As long as we somehow keep track of the data on which an overdue date was sent, is that OK?"

-    "Similarly, why do we have to log on the back of the invoice the name of the salesperson to whom it was given?"

-    "Why are you sending these notices every two weeks or every four weeks? Is that just because of the limitations of the staff you presently have? If you had perfect technology and could, in theory, send out additional overdue notices automatically every microsecond, how often would you want to do it?"

While some of these issues may seem trivial, there may be a number of subtle policy issues dictating the way things must be done, regardless of whatever perfect technology the analyst can imagine (e.g., government regulations, union agreements, contractual obligations, etc.).

As noted earlier, other methods can be used to document the business policy for the bottom-level processes in the data flow diagrams. Depending on the application, decision tables, mathematical formulas, graphs, or even narrative English might be appropriate. The key point is that each mini-spec describes only one small piece of the system. Also, a mini-spec, if properly written, tells *what* the process has to accomplish without saying or even implying *how* the process eventually will be built.

The next major tool of structured analysis is the *entity relationship diagram*, or ERD. An example of an ERD is shown in Figure 3.6.

The purpose of an ERD is to highlight the major objects or entities of stored data that the system must deal with, as well as to highlight the relationships[1] among those objects. Many of the early books and articles on structured analysis, written in the 1970s, did not not include ERDs as a modeling tool, but it has become evident that in most information processing systems, the information modeled by the ERD is just as important as the *functions* that are modeled with the data flow diagrams.

It is also important to note that the DFD and the ERD highlight two different aspects of the same system; consequently, there are one-to-one correspondences that the systems analyst can check to ensure that he has a consistent set of models. Specifically, each data store shown on the DFD should correspond to an object or a relationship on the ERD.

---

[1] Specifically, these are relationships that must be *remembered* by the system; if a relationship can be calculated or computed automatically, it need not be shown on the ERD. In Figure 3.6, for example, the "receives" relationship exists because the system has to remember which customer(s) are associated with which invoice(s). If there was an algorithm for associating invoice numbers with customers (e.g., based on their Social Security number), then the "receives" relationship would not be shown on the ERD.

There is one last modeling tool that is important for the class of systems characterized as real-time systems; examples of such systems are process control systems, telephone switching systems, command and control systems for many defense applications, and embedded systems that control such devices as intelligent photocopiers. In these systems, the *time-dependent behavior* of the system is important: The end-user has business policy requirements concerning the sequence of activities, the response time required to respond to various external signals, and so on. To help highlight these aspects of the system, we use a *state transition diagram*, or STD; a typical STD is shown in Figure 3.7. In this diagram, each of the rectangular boxes represents a "state" in which the system may reside from time to time; the arrows indicate the allowable changes of state.

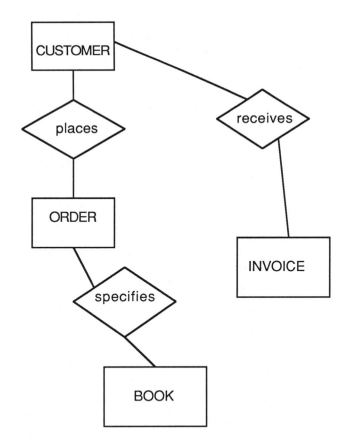

Figure 3.6: **An entity relationship diagram**

STDs are usually associated with a modified form of the standard data flow diagram, a modification that allows the systems analyst to show control signals (or "control flows" or "event flows") and "control processes," whose purpose is to coordinate and synchronize the activities of other bubbles. A typical real-time DFD is shown in Figure 3.8. The STD diagram represents a process specification for the "inside" of the control process.

Once again, there is a way of checking the consistency of these diagrams. Each of the inputs to the control process should correspond to the condition that causes the state change in the STD, and each of the outputs from the control process should correspond to the actions that take place during the state change in the STD.

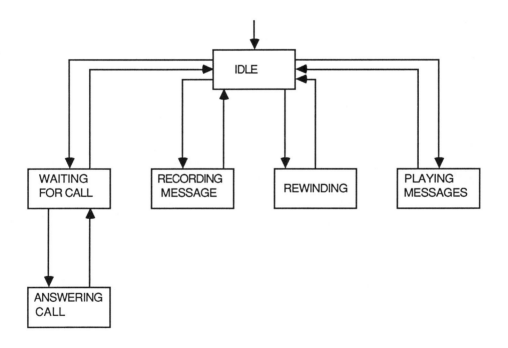

Figure 3.7: **A state transition diagram**

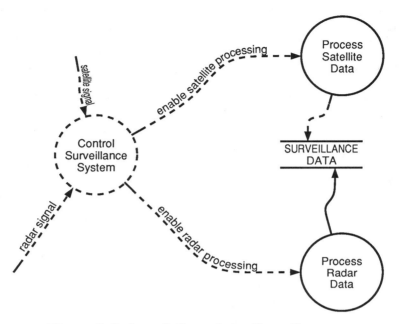

Figure 3.8: **A real-time data flow diagram**

Even though this discussion of the major tools of structured analysis has been brief, you should see that a structured specification resulting from these graphic tools has a number of desirable characteristics, summarized as follows:

- It is partitioned, rather than monolithic.

- It is graphic, consisting largely of pictures rather than words.

- It is top-down, presenting a description of the system at progressively detailed levels.

- It is logical, depicting an implementation-inde-pendent model of the system that will be developed for the user.

3.3   APPLYING THE TOOLS OF STRUCTURED ANALYSIS

The previous section presented an overview of the graphic tools that can be used to develop a top-down partitioned model of a data processing system. This section shows how the tools of structured analysis can be applied to the typical project's systems development life cycle today.

In most MIS projects, the systems analysis phase is preceded by a brief feasibility study, or project survey. The major purpose of the survey is to determine whether a proposed MIS project warrants the investment of significant amounts of time and money. The output of the survey may be called the project charter and usually consists of three parts:

- *a project abstract,* listing the name of the project and the responsible user, the starting date of the project and the target delivery date, the original budget allocation, and any other suitable information

- *a statement of goals and objectives,* listing functions to be implemented, deficiencies to be remedied, and features to be added to or modified in the present system

- *schedule constraints,* including key dates and deadlines and usually presented in PERT format

When structured analysis was first introduced in the 1970s, it was commonly argued that the systems analyst should develop four distinct models. These are shown in Figure 3.9.

The *current physical* model is a model of the "actual" system that the user is presently using. It may be a manual system, or an automated system, or a mixture of the two. Typically, the processes (bubbles) in the data flow diagram for the current physical system represent the names of people, or their titles, or organizational units, or computer systems which do the work of transforming inputs into outputs. An example is shown in Figure 3.10. Note also that the data flows typically show physical forms of data being transported from bubble to bubble; also, the data stores may be represented by file folders, magnetic tape files, or some other form of implementation technology.

The *current logical* model is a model of the "pure" or "essential" requirements being carried out by the user's current system. Thus, arbitrary implementation details are removed, and the resulting model shows what the system would do if "perfect" technology were available. An example of a current logical model is shown in Figure 3.11.

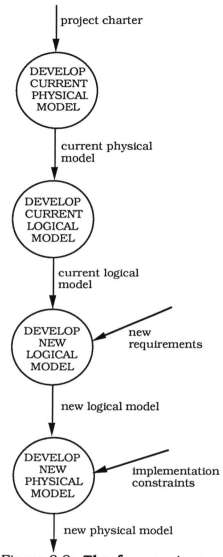

Figure 3.9: **The four system models**

The *new logical* model is a model of the "pure" or "essential" requirements of the *new* system that the user wants. In the ideal case (from the systems analyst's point of view), it is the same as the *current logical* model (i.e., it contains the same functions and the same data). This situation could occur if the user was completely satisfied with the functionality of his current system, but was dissatisfied with its implementation.

In most cases, though, the user will ask for additional functions—"While you're at it, could you add another transaction to take care of the following situation . . . ." Or the user may ask that the system keep track of a new form of data. Thus, while 80 to 90 percent of the new logical model may be identical to the current logical model, there are likely to be at least a few changes and additions.

The *new physical* model is a model showing the implementation *constraints* imposed by the user. One of the most important such constraints is the determination of the *man-machine boundary*—the determination of which functions in the new system will be automated, and which will be performed manually. The new physical model corresponds to what we now call the *user implementation* model, which is discussed in more detail in Chapter 5.

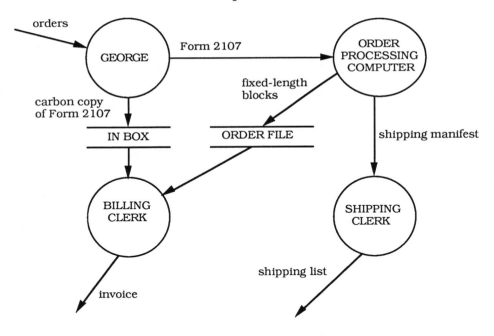

Figure 3.10 : **A current physical model**

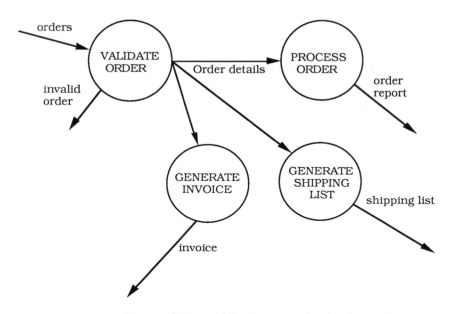

Figure 3.11: **The current logical model**

The classical approach described above was based on three major assumptions:

- The systems analyst may not be very familiar with the application or business area. He may be an expert in computer technology, but only superficially knowledgeable about banking, insurance, inventory control, or whatever area the user is working in. Because of this, it is important for the systems analyst to begin with a current physical model as a way of educating himself. The model he draws will be relatively easy to verify, because it will contain a number of physical "landmarks" that can be observed in the user's current physical environment. Once having gathered this "background" information, the systems analyst can continue by transforming the physical model into a logical model.

- The user may be unwilling or unable to work with a new logical model at the beginning of a project. The most common reason for this is suspicion of the systems analyst's ability to develop a logical model of the new system. Even if the systems analyst thinks that he is an expert in the user's business area, the user himself may not agree. "Why should I trust you to design a new system for me," he will ask, "when you don't even understand how my business works now?" Also, some users find it difficult to look at an abstract system model with no recognizable landmarks; they may need a model of the current physical system as a way of familiarizing themselves with the process of structured analysis, and assuring themselves that the analyst hasn't overlooked anything. (An alternative is the prototyping approach discussed in Chapter 17.)

- The transformation of a current logical model into a new logical model does not require much work, and, in particular, does not require much *wasted* work. As indicated above, the user will typically add some new functions, or new data, to the system he already has—but most (if not all) of the existing *logical* (or "essential") system remains in the replacement.

These assumptions have indeed turned out to be correct in many projects. However, they ignore a much larger danger: *The process of developing a model of the current system may require so much time and effort that the user will become frustrated and impatient, and ultimately cancel the project.* To appreciate this, you must keep in mind that:

- Some users (and some managers, and some programmer-analysts) regard *any* form of systems analysis as a waste of time—as a way of "resting up" until the *real* work of the project (i.e., coding) begins.

- Many users are understandably dubious about the merits of carefully modeling a system *that, by definition, will be superseded and replaced as a result of the development of the new system.*

The problem occurs most often because the systems analyst gets carried away with the task of modeling the current system, and begins to think of it as an end unto itself. Thus, instead of drawing just the data flow diagram(s) and documenting a few key process specifications, we often find the systems analyst drawing *every* data flow diagram, documenting *every* process specification, and developing a *complete* data dictionary.

Unfortunately, this approach almost always involves a great deal of wasted time. Indeed, you can normally expect that as much as 75 percent of the physical model will be thrown away in the transition from current physical to current logical; or to put it another way, the current physical model is typically three to four times as large as the current logical model. This is because of redundancy (the same function being carried out in several different parts of the current system, and several data elements being duplicated or triplicated), and because of verification, validation and error-checking that is appropriate in the current physical system but not appropriate in the current logical system.[2]

All of this may seem rather obvious to the casual reader. However, in project after project, systems analysts have been observed getting so involved in the *process* of modeling that they have forgotten the user's ultimate objective: to produce a working system. As Steve McMenamin (coauthor of *Essential Systems Analysis* [McMenamin, 1984]) points out, "Bubbles don't compile."[3]

Consequently, this book recommends that the systems analyst should *avoid* modeling the user's current system if at all possible. The modeling tools discussed earlier in this chapter should be used to begin, *as quickly as possible*, to develop a model of the *new* system that the user wants. This new system—referred to in classical structured analysis textbooks as the "new logical" system— is referred to here as the *essential model* of the system.

There will occasionally be a situation where the systems analyst *must* build a model of the user's current system; this is true, for example, if the systems analyst needs to model the

---

[2] Regardless of whether we are building a logical (essential) or physical (implementation) model, it is usually appropriate to perform extensive error-checking of data *that comes into the system from the external world*. However, as data is transmitted from place to place *within* the system, the logical (essential) model does *no* error-checking, because it assumes that the system will be implemented with perfect technology. In the physical (implementation) model—*especially* a model of the *current* physical system—the error-checking is vital because (a) some of the processing is error-prone, especially if carried out by humans, and (b) the transportation of data from one process to another may be error-prone, depending on the communications medium used, and (c) the storage and retrieval of data from physical data stores may be an error-prone activity.

[3] Eventually, bubbles *will* compile. That is, the combination of data flow diagrams, data dictionary, and rigorous process specifications can become input to a code generator that will produce executable programs. However, even in this case, the effort to produce a complete, detailed *physical* model is a waste of time. Nobody wants a computerized replica of the current system.

current physical system in order to discover what the essential processes really are, or if documentation of the current system is important in its own right.

3.4   MANAGEMENT PROBLEMS WITH STRUCTURED ANALYSIS

In the systems development field, like all other activities in life, we are beginning to learn that there is no such thing as a "free lunch"; or, as Fred Brooks pointed out in a delightful article [Brooks, 1987], there is no "silver bullet" that will magically solve all of our development problems. Structured analysis of the nature described in this chapter is being used in approximately 60 percent of the MIS organizations in the United States, according to a survey conducted by *Software News* in the fall of 1986, and it is considered to be quite successful in many of those organizations. *But*, there have been some problems, and there will probably be programs for your MIS organization when it first begins to use structured analysis. The problems most likely to arise are as follows.

3.4.1   Fears that structured analysis may not work

Structured analysis did not begin to attract serious attention until the late 1970s, and was not widely used until the mid-1980s. Hence, you may still encounter a reaction similar to the one that accompanied the introduction of structured programming and structured design in the 1970s: "How do we know this stuff is going to work? It sounds like black magic!"

There are various ways of responding to such comments, but your answer should depend on whether the comments come from your boss, the end-user, or the systems analyst on your project. Depending on your situation, your response might be:

- *Direct confrontation.* To the person who asks, "How do you know that structured analysis will work?" you might respond, "How do you know it won't? Could it be any worse than what you have now?" Often, your boss and your systems analysts will agree that the problems listed at the beginning of Section 3.1 are true. You'll agree that the end-user rarely reads the voluminous specifications currently being produced and that such documents generally are obsolete and unmaintainable by the time programming begins. If everyone agrees that the current technology for producing functional specifications is a disaster and that there is no alternative approach, then all parties may be willing to accept structured analysis— at least on a trial basis.

- *Common sense.* To the person who expresses further doubts about structured analysis, you might respond, "But structured analysis is just common sense!" This kind of comment is best made if you can say it while looking utterly innocent, as if to say, "But, gee, isn't this the way we've been doing it all along?"

- *Testimonials.* Perhaps the most convincing way of dealing with these fears is to find a similar project in a similar organization, or perhaps another division of your own company that has tried the structured analysis techniques discussed in this chapter. You should be able to find case studies in recent issues of such journals as *Software News*, *Datamation*, *IEEE Software*, or in books (see, e.g., Audrey Weaver's *Using the Structured Techniques: A Case Study* [Weaver, 1987]).

These suggested ways for presenting the concepts of structured analysis work well in most organizations. However, if yours is particularly conservative, you may need to employ more political methods.

Indeed, it's extremely important for you to realize that the introduction of structured analysis necessitates a much more political approach than do the concepts of structured design and structured programming discussed later in this book. After all, nobody, except perhaps the programmer responsible for a piece of code, knows how the code is written, or whether it is good or bad, so you won't run into many arguments with managers or end-users when you begin to introduce new ways of design. But analysis clearly involves the end-user, who may have extremely strong views on the subject and who undoubtedly will ask for an explanation. In addition, the format and organization of the analysis product may be subject to various external constraints. For example, an aerospace vendor may find that the "statement of requirements" for a system built for the U.S. Department of Defense has to obey strict rules for format, substance, and organization (e.g., the standards known as DOD-Std-2167). Fortunately, it dictates a structured life cycle approach.

Further, the output of systems analysis may be visible to levels of management outside (and above) the MIS area itself.

So, it is important to be prepared to explain the merits of structured analysis to nontechnical people— clearly a political situation. If you're faced with this kind of situation, it could be better for you to begin with structured programming or structured design; when you've demonstrated that these newfangled techniques actually work, then you might try to sneak structured analysis into the organization. This last idea is discussed in more detail in Chapter 10.

3.4.2   Fears relating to the amount of time spent on analysis

Managers and users sometimes act as if *any* time spent on analysis (or design, for that matter) is just a way for the technical staff to rest up before they get to the real work of the project— programming.   This attitude has been around for a long time, perhaps because coding has long been viewed as the only tangible activity of systems development. As my colleague Scott Guthery says, "Coding is where the tire meets the road." Structured analysis seems to intensify this suspicion, particularly because roughly 30 percent of the total project manpower should be allocated for systems analysis, and another 20 percent for design.

There are rational arguments for devoting a substantial effort to properly defining the user's requirements.   Indeed, there have been studies [Boehm, 1976] that have documented that a systems analysis error is often two orders of magnitude— a factor of 100— more expensive to correct if it is not discovered until acceptance testing.   More recently James Martin has pointed out in [Martin, 1984] that approximately 50 percent of the errors, and 75 percent of the cost of error correction in operational systems, are attributable to errors of systems analysis.

But you probably know all of these arguments.   The problem is getting doubting users and skeptical non-MIS managers to believe them.   There is no definite way to convince the skeptics other than with testimonials and showing them that the methods work.   A small pilot project that demonstrates the virtues of structured analysis, as well as all the other structured techniques, is worth a try at this point. (Pilot projects are discussed in detail in Chapter 11.)

You may get some rational arguments from people who say that the users in your organization are simply not capable of articulating their requirements— and that any time spent developing formal models of their requirements will thus be wasted. This is usually the beginning of an argument in favor of *prototyping,* which is discussed in detail in Chapter 17.   An alternative method of "discovering" the user's requirements is top-down implementation, which is discussed in Chapter 4.

3.4.3   Justification of the time spent analyzing the current system

Managers and users frequently ask, "Why should we spend so much time studying the current system if we're about to throw it away?" They're right!   Studying the current system and environment can take a considerable amount of time; *indeed, it takes as much time as you're willing to allow the systems analysts to spend!* The time consumed by this activity adds to the frustration and impatience felt by the non-MIS personnel.

As we saw in Section 3.3 above, there are rational arguments in favor of modeling the user's current system. Nevertheless, the "bottom line" experience of many MIS organizations during the late 1970s and early 1980s was that modeling of the user's current system simply took *too long.* Horror stories circulated through the industry of projects that spent *three years* developing a model of the user's current physical system; projects were sometimes canceled before the analysts could even begin to specify the user's new system.

Modern structured analysis, as espoused by [Ward and Mellor, 1985] and [Yourdon, 1989], recognizes that a small amount of current system modeling may be necessary for the reasons discussed above, but the emphasis today is on beginning the modeling of the new system as soon as possible— preferably on the first day of the project!   How can this be accomplished, given the concerns discussed above? Here are some ideas:

- Find systems analysts who *do* know the user's business. If your MIS organization has been building systems for the past twenty years, surely there must be a systems analyst somewhere who has absorbed something about the user's application.

- Put several users on the project team, and make one of the users the project manager; put the whole project team *in* the user organization. This puts the systems analyst into a subordinate role, providing technical expertise when needed. The point here is that the users generally *do* know a lot about the requirements of their new system, and can be quite articulate about expressing them.

- Model the current system and the new system at the same time. This takes more effort and more people, and it requires coordination to ensure that the essential functions (and data) of the current system are carried into the new system, but it does contract the elapsed time schedule

3.4.4 Reluctance to recognize the techniques as anything different

Resistance to structured analysis may take the form, "Isn't this just the same old stuff that we've been doing for years?" This is a question you will hear repeatedly, and it will be asked equally frequently about structured design, structured programming, and every one of the other topics in this book. The simplest reply to such a question is, "Well, perhaps you have been doing it all along. Let's take a look at one of your functional specifications . . . ."

At this juncture, the we've-been-doing-it-all-along person will probably say something like, "Ahhhh, actually, well, errr . . . ummm, we really don't have any functional specifications lying around that I can show you. They are all marked **Top Secret**." Or, if this person does produce a sample specification for you to look at, he might say, "Actually, this one was produced in an awful hurry, so it's kind of sloppy. We didn't get around to doing the data dictionary, but that seemed like a lot of low-level work, and we figured that we would get the programmers to do it at some later point. And I have to admit that most of it *is* a monolithic narrative document, but— see, right here on page 509, there's a flowchart, and that's not too much different from a data flow diagram anyway. I mean, we've got the *idea* of structured analysis; it's just that we don't use all the fancy words, and we're not quite so formal about it."

Of course, that's just the point! The *idea* of structured analysis has probably been in a lot of people's heads for a very long time, but organizing, formalizing, and giving names to the ideas is what distinguishes a formal discipline from an apple-pie-and-motherhood set of fuzzy attitudes.

3.4.5 The urge to freeze the specifications

One of the advantages of the graphic, partitioned specification produced by structured analysis is that it can be modified very easily if the user's needs change during the analysis phase, or even during the design and programming phases of the project. Indeed, it is my strong feeling that the specification *must* be maintained and modified, along with the source code, for the entire 10- to 15-year life cycle of the system.

Unfortunately, many MIS organizations are convinced that the specification has to be frozen at a relatively early stage in the development phase, with no more consideration given to user changes until after the code has been completed. Perhaps this was appropriate for conventional specifications, in which a minor change to the requirements often created enormous amounts of clerical work, but it is a dangerous practice. If anyone is going to freeze the specifications, it should be the user. In particular, the user who bears the cost of the changes (cost, in this context, may mean money, manpower, and delays to the schedule) has the right to *insist* on change, making it unrealistic and unwise to freeze the schedule. Rather than abolishing change, we must learn to *control* change. Structured analysis facilitates such control.

3.4.6   The difficulty of maintaining graphical models

As we have seen, structured analysis depends heavily on pictures: data flow diagrams, entity relationship diagrams, and state transition diagrams. Despite the comments above about allowing changes from the user, many systems analysts complain that it is tedious and time-consuming to continue redrawing a diagram that may have required an hour or more of manual labor; this problem is compounded in a large system that has a hundred or more DFDs, as well as dozens of ERDs and STDs.

Until the mid-1980s, the only solution to this problem was the program librarian concept discussed in Chapter 8; after all, systems analysts should not be hired for their talents as artists. If that kind of talent is required, the MIS organization should hire specialists to do the work. More recently, though, a more attractive solution has appeared: PC-based CASE tools that allow the systems analyst to compose and revise DFDs, ERDs, and STDs, as well as the associated textual material in data dictionaries and process descriptions.

The future developments of CASE tools are discussed in Chapter 19, but the technology is, in my opinion, the least of our problems. Systems analysts have good reason to worry about the difficulty of manually maintaining DFDs and other graphical models, because it will take several years for large MIS organizations to provide an adequate number of CASE tools for their staff. As this book is being written, approximately 2 percent of the systems analysts have such tools available to them;

it is estimated that 10 percent will have them by 1990, but it will be the middle of the 1990s before even 50 percent of the community of system developers have such tools.

3.4.7 Fear that users won't look at structured analysis models

As suggested earlier, it's best to meet this fear head-on: You won't know whether users will look at the graphical models of structured analysis until you try.

Sometimes, though, the fear is well-founded. Occasionally users will not look at data flow diagrams. If this happens, check carefully to see how the models have been presented to the user. If your systems analyst says, "This is a top-down, third normal form, balanced data flow diagram, which I learned about last month while studying for my Master's Degree in Computer Science, and it represents the very latest software engineering approach to defining the logical essence of your system, after which we'll talk about various incarnations that we propose to implement," then you shouldn't be surprised if the user faints or throws the systems analyst out of his office. If, on the other hand, the systems analyst says, "This is a picture that I drew to show you my understanding of what you want your system to do," then it would be more surprising (and more serious) if the user objects.

Indeed, this latter situation is a good argument for prototyping, which also involves developing a model of user requirements. But the model appears to be more "real" because it actually runs on a computer, with "live" inputs and "real" outputs. Prototyping is discussed in more detail in Chapter 17.

3.4.8 Concern that the modeling techniques may not apply to real-time systems.

Many of the early books and articles on structured analysis concentrated on "business" systems, such as payroll, inventory, and general ledger. In such systems, any attempt to show interrupts or signals in the statement of requirements was usually a terrible mistake; at best, it represented an intrusion of implementation details in the statement of what the system had to do. Hence, these books abolished all efforts to show signals, interrupts, timing sequences, and so forth—much to the consternation of people building real-time systems, for whom such issues are of paramount importance from the earliest points in the project.

We saw in Section 3.1 that the structured analysis model now includes the state transition diagram as a vital component; it also has a provision for showing control flows and control processes in the data flow diagram. Since the mid-1980s, this approach has been well-documented (see, e.g., [Ward and Mellor, 1985]).

3.4.9   What about users with personal computers? They don't want to do ANY analysis!

This, of course, has become a concern since the mid-1980s, as powerful personal computers have begun springing up like mushrooms in many organizations. I will deal with this question in more detail in Chapter 15. The short answer is that *all* complex systems need to be modeled, regardless of who implements the system and regardless of whether it operates on a central mainframe or on a remote stand-alone personal computer. Remember the assumption at the beginning of Chapter 2: If your organization does nothing but build trivial systems (each of which, in the extreme case, executes once and is then thrown away), then you don't need any structured techniques. But if you're reading this book, it's presumably because you or your users are building more complex systems.

3.4.10   The myth of the perfect specification.

To conclude this discussion of typical problems, I must introduce a slightly pessimistic but realistic note: The structured analysis approach is not perfect, nor can it produce a perfect specification—mainly because people are not perfect.

Communication between two human beings always involves some risk of a misunderstanding of one sort or another. This potential is important to recognize because management in some MIS organizations believes that if one spends enough time, and enough money, and if one plays enough games, then one can eventually do a *perfect* job of systems analysis.

Playing the game right politically can provide the attempt to introduce structured analysis with a significant edge. Effective ways to play the game have already been mentioned above, and can be repeated here:

- Put a user on the project team. No, put *lots* of users on the project team. Not only will this help keep both parties honest, but it will also swing the balance of power toward the user organization, where it ought to be.

- Transfer the development team into the user's department. Team members are likely to be more responsive to user requirements if they know that those same users are paying their salaries.

- Write a formal contract between the user and the development team. If each page of the specification must be signed in blood by both parties, you can be somewhat more confident that the misunderstandings will be reduced.

Under the right circumstances, each of these games has some value— but even these ploys won't guarantee that you will do a perfect job of capturing the user's requirements. Indeed, even if you do, these requirements probably will change before the coding is completed; as noted earlier, technology, business conditions, government regulations, and even the identity of the user can change during the project.

Perhaps the most dangerous assumption is that the user knows what he wants his system to do. Chances are that he has a pretty good idea, but there are lots and lots and *lots* of details that he hasn't thought out carefully. Or that he's not sure about. Or that he thinks are unimportant, but later decides are *very* important. Hence, no matter how hard the systems analyst and user try to develop the perfect functional specification, they are doomed to failure.

One solution to this dilemma, as we will see in Chapter 4, is top-down implementation.

Chapter 4
TOP-DOWN DESIGN AND TESTING

This chapter deals specifically with two related techniques: top-down design and top-down testing. The format of the chapter is simple: first, a brief overview of the technical concepts behind the top-down approach; second, a review of the management-oriented benefits of the approach; and third, a discussion of the problems and difficulties that you as a manager are likely to encounter when implementing the top-down approach in your organization.

4.1   AN OVERVIEW OF THE TOP-DOWN APPROACH

Top-down design and top-down testing have been practiced instinctively by many programmers and system developers for years.   In academic circles, the top-down approach has been referred to as "systematic programming," "stepwise refinement," "levels of abstraction," and a variety of of other names. The phrase "top-down," however, today seems to dominate the other buzzwords.

The purpose of this section is to provide you with enough of an understanding of these important concepts of design and implementation to enable you to discuss them intelligently with your technical staff and with other MIS managers. This chapter is not intended to make you an expert on top-down design, and certainly doesn't cover everything about the subject. Consult the references in the bibliography for further reading, if you and/or your programmers require a more detailed discussion.

Many MIS people use the phrase "top-down" loosely. For reasons that are largely historical, top-down design and structured programming have long been discussed together. Indeed, you'll notice that many of the references in the bibliography emphasize structured programming, but that few include "top-down" in the title.   There is nothing wrong with the association, but you should make sure that when you are discussing top-down design with one of your colleagues, he or she is not thinking about structured programming. The two are not synonymous, as you will see in the discussion of structured programming in Chapter 6.

Also, when you are discussing the top-down approach with a colleague, make sure that you're both discussing the same aspect of the top-down approach. There are three related, but distinct, aspects of the top-down approach:

- *Top-down design:* a design strategy that breaks large, complex problems into smaller, less complex problems and then decomposes each of those smaller problems into even smaller problems, until the original problem has been expressed as some combination of many small, solvable problems.

- *Top-down coding:* a strategy of coding high-level, executive modules as soon as they have been designed and generally before the low-level, detail modules have been designed.

- *Top-down testing* or *top-down implementation*: a strategy of testing the high-level modules of a system before the low-level modules have been coded, and possibly before they have been designed; in the extreme case, the user requirements for the low-level modules may not have been specified at the time the high-level modules are tested.

What a perfectly simple idea! Indeed, what more does one need to say to introduce the top-down approach? Perhaps a simple example would be useful to illustrate the top-down aspects of design, coding, and testing. The example that I will use is that most universal of all business-oriented data processing systems, the payroll system.

A few years ago, I participated in the development of a payroll system for a government agency in Australia. We began the project by breaking the entire system into an edit, an update, a sort, and several print modules. ("What's so special about that?" you ask. "We've been doing that sort of thing for years!" That's just the point. Many organizations have followed some form of top-down design all along.) Having identified the edit, update, and print levels as top-level modules and having determined the next few levels of modules beneath them, we immediately wrote code for the top-level modules, in many cases writing code to call lower-level modules that we had not yet designed.

Our primary reason for writing this code was to make it possible to test— or *exercise*, as we preferred to call it, since the testing was not exhaustive— a preliminary version of the payroll system, but one that was, in a sense, a *complete* payroll system. Approximately six weeks after the beginning of the project, we produced what we referred to as "Version 1": a payroll system that accepted input transactions and a master employee file, and that produced paychecks.

Of course, our Version 1 payroll system had a few minor limitations. The user was required to provide error-free transactions, for our payroll system made no attempt to validate them. In addition, the user was required to provide transactions that already had been sorted, as our system was too lazy to do the sorting. Furthermore, our system was unwilling to allow the user to hire new employees, fire existing employees, give any employees a salary increase, or, for that matter, make *any* change to an employee's current status.

Worse, our payroll system uniformly paid everyone a salary of $100 per week, and withheld a uniform $15 in taxes from everyone's paycheck. The system insisted that all employees be paid by check, instead of allowing the convenience of being paid by cash or having one's paycheck deposited directly into a bank account. The final indignity: It printed all of the paychecks in octal.

Not a very exciting payroll system. On the other hand, it did involve all of the top-level modules. What made the system so primitive was the fact that all of the lower-level modules existed as "stubs," or "dummy routines." For example, the top-level module in the update portion of the system called a lower-level module to compute an employee's gross salary. For the Version 1 system, that module simply returned an output of $100— in all cases. Similarly, the top-level module in the edit part of the system called a module to determine the validity of a specific transaction. For Version 1, that module simply returned with an indication that the transaction was valid, without going to any effort to actually validate the transaction.

Subsequent versions of the payroll system merely involved adding lower-level modules to the existing skeleton of top-level modules. A second version of the system, for example, allowed the user to hire and fire employees (which exercised the system's ability to add and delete records from the master file). It also sorted the transactions, and in a few very simple cases, it actually computed an employee's gross pay. However, Version 2 still made no attempt to validate the input transactions. In most cases, it still paid employees $100 per week. In all cases, it withheld $15 in taxes and printed paychecks in octal. Subsequent versions rectified these limitations, until a final version produced output that was satisfactory to the user.

That process in a nutshell is the top-down approach. The concept of top-down design is simple and has been around for a long time. Indeed, one could argue that it is just a variation of Julius Caesar's "divide and conquer" strategy. Many programmers and systems designers would argue that they've been doing top-down design all along, and most MIS managers would insist that they have always enforced top-down design in their organization.

However, my visits to several hundred organizations around the world during the 1970s and 1980s suggest otherwise. Many managers promote good design strategies in their standards manuals, but fail to enforce them. Many programmers follow such a sloppy, informal version of top-down design that they are unable to take advantage of its benefits. Some programmers attempt to practice bottom-up design; that is, they first try to identify all of the bottom-level modules that will be required, and then try to figure out how to put them together. Alternatively, they might try to figure out how to use existing system modules (e.g., the library routines in a UNIX® environment) to build their system from the bottom up. Finally, there is still a Luddite minority of system developers who do *no* design, but rather begin coding as soon as they have been given specifications.

Still, it is probably fair to say that many MIS organization attempt to practice top-down design. In contrast, very few organizations make any conscious attempt at top-down testing. Those organizations that have a formal test plan unfortunately tend to advocate a bottom-up strategy, as follows: First, the bottom-level modules are tested in isolation. Then, these are combined with modules at the next higher level to form complete programs, which are tested in isolation. Next, the programs are combined with modules at the next higher level to form subsystems, which are tested in isolation. Finally, all of the subsystems are combined to permit a system test.

So, if your programmers tell you that they already practice top-down design and top-down testing, beware! Look more closely at what they *really* are doing. For example, could they provide you with a payroll system that provided all employees $100 in hexadecimal or octal shortly after the beginning of the project?

4.2   THE BENEFITS OF THE TOP-DOWN APPROACH

The benefits of top-down design should be immediately obvious. Most problems, whether in data processing or elsewhere, are too complex to be grasped in their entirety. Top-down design provides an organized method of breaking the original problem into smaller problems that we can grasp and solve with some degree of success.

The benefits of top-down testing are not so immediately apparent, particularly in organizations that have followed the bottom-up approach for the past ten or twenty years. These benefits are summarized in the following sections.

4.2.1   Major interfaces are exercised at the beginning of the project

In the brief sketch drawn earlier of the payroll system, Version 1 demonstrated that to a limited extent the edit subsystem could communicate with the update subsystem, which was capable of communicating with the sort subsystem, which in turn could communicate with the various print modules.

In any major information system, one can usually identify subsystems and interfaces between the subsystems. Those interfaces may be implemented in the form of an intermediate disk file, or data passed between CPUs via a telecommunications link, or data passed from module to module through RAM memory. Typically, the interface will be documented by the designer(s) on paper: some documentation of the file layout, the intermodule calling sequence, or something of that nature. Unfortunately, individual programmers may interpret the interface documents slightly differently— especially if they are located in different physical sites, in a large development project. Or the interface document may be blatantly incorrect, a common occurrence with certain information supplied by computer vendors! Or, the interface document may be incomplete, failing to describe certain conditions, exceptions, or special situations.

Thus, the interface between modules and the interface between subsystems are common places for bugs to occur; indeed, a recent study by DeWayne Perry [Perry, 1987] indicates that as many as 40 percent of the errors in an operational system are interface errors. In the bottom-up approach, major interfaces are usually not tested until the very end, at which point the discovery of the interface bug can be disastrous. The presence of the interface bug may require that several modules be recoded; even worse, it often occurs just days before the final deadline— or the day *after* the final deadline!

By contrast, the top-down approach tends to force important, top-level interfaces to be exercised at an early stage in the project, so if there are problems, they can be resolved while there is still the time, the energy, and the resources to deal with them. Indeed, we usually find as we go further and further in the project, the bugs become progressively simpler— that is, the interface problems become more and more localized.

I want to emphasize that interface problems occur not only at the demarcation between major pieces of an application system, but also at the interfaces between the vendor's hardware and your applications, and between the vendor's system software (operating system, database management system, etc.) and your applications. Thus, one of my clients found that Version 1 of an on-line system represented a major test of a terminal with which they had had no prior experience; a new modem; newly installed telecommunication lines; a recently acquired telecommunications system from a major software vendor; a newly acquired database management system from a different software vendor; the hardware vendor's operating system; and several major application subsystems developed locally.

You can imagine the kind of things that were discovered in Version 1: The vendor's terminal worked, but the programming manual for the terminal left out key details that would have caused major problems if their absence had not been detected at the outset. The modem had the nasty habit of dropping bits of data in certain cases. The telecommunication lines actually worked, but the telecommunications monitor gobbled up all available memory in the computer, fragmented the memory into small pieces, and shut down the system because it could not obtain enough big, contiguous chunks of memory. The database management package worked fine, but could only carry out one disk access at a time, a fact which would have caused major throughput problems if it had not been discovered at an early stage. All of the application subsystems had a variety of interface bugs. It was a wonder the client *ever* got Version 1 working at all, but when he did, subsequent versions were produced much more easily.

4.2.2   Users can see a working demonstration of the system

Perhaps the single most important advantage of the top-down approach is that one can demonstrate a skeleton version of a system to a user at an early stage, *before* the programmers have wasted time developing large amounts of incorrect code from fuzzy, inaccurate specifications.

This point brings up one of the most serious philosophical problems in the systems development field today: the myth of the perfect specification, a subject discussed briefly in the previous chapter. This is the belief that if one spends enough time talking to the user, or if one puts a user on the analysis team, or, conversely, if one makes the programmers work in the user department, or if one gets the user to formally sign a contract accepting the specification, and if a few other well-intentioned gimmicks are implemented, then it will be possible to get *perfect* specifications from which we can write perfect code that will make the user perfectly happy.

Humbug! In a few cases, this approach has worked, but it usually is an exercise in futility. First, in any new, sophisticated information system, the user does not know exactly what he wants, and he won't begin to really know what he wants until he begins to see something more tangible than pictures or words on a piece of paper.

Second, communication problems between the user, the analyst, and the programmer are inevitable. The user will explain what he wants in a language that is incomplete, ambiguous, and imprecise. The analyst and the programmer will misinterpret the user's wishes in subtle ways. Even with the improved graphic tools of structured analysis discussed in Chapter 3, misunderstandings still can arise. Furthermore, the less experienced the user and the more complex the system, the more likely the misunderstandings.

Finally, today things often change more quickly than we can develop information systems. Systems whose requirements are specified in 1988 may be scheduled to be completed in 1990; but by 1990, major premises upon which the system was based may have changed. The business will change, the prevailing government regulations will change, the economy will change, the technology will certainly change, and the competition will change. Even the identity of the user may change.

All of these phenomena argue strongly for a top-down approach. Even if the user seems to know what he wants, implement a top-level skeleton first, and look at it. Chances are, he'll want something deleted from or added to the original specifications. In general, it is easier to make changes *before* coding. In many cases, one can avoid the frustrating experience of writing beautiful code, only to throw it away because the user changed his mind![1]

4.2.3   Deadline problems can be dealt with more satisfactorily

Although this book is aimed at managers and their problems, it is not about project management. However, there is at least one aspect of project management that is affected by top-down systems development: missing the deadline. A survey of approximately 200 large U.S. corporations by Capers Jones [Jones, 1986] indicated that the typical systems development project was one year behind schedule and 100 percent over budget. Why? Partly because deadlines reflect political pressures more than a manager's sober, rational judgment. The reason a deadline is January 1 is that someone has insisted that the system must be operational by the beginning of the new year, regardless of PERT charts and computerized estimating models.

Unforeseen events also cause deadline problems. If the bubonic plague (or its more recent variants) strikes the programming staff, the project will be late; if a tornado demolishes the computer room, projects will definitely fall behind schedule.

Yet many of us persist in drawing neater, prettier PERT charts, hoping that users and senior managers will allow us to schedule projects on an entirely rational basis. Also, many of us continue to assume that neither tornadoes nor epidemics will strike.

Thus, when the deadline arrives, the classical bottom-up approach usually leaves us in a vulnerable position. Typically, we find that the design has been completed, most or all of the code has been written, and most, possibly all, of the modules have been tested individually. Unfortunately, when the modules are assembled, they don't work. When the deadline arrives, we are in the middle of system testing, with 20,000 lines of code that don't *do* anything. Try to explain that to a user who doesn't know the difference between a COBOL statement and a football. Even worse, try to explain it to a user who has written a few lines of code in a language like BASIC or dBASE-III— they are

---

[1] An alternative is to use prototyping tools that also can demonstrate a rudimentary version of the system to the user at an early stage. For more discussion of such tools, see Chapter 17.

often under the impression that any amount of code can be written in an afternoon.

Also, try to explain to senior managers who have been getting status reports all along indicating that things are on schedule. Chances are, you've been fooled too. Your programmers probably began telling you on the second day of the project that they were 95 percent finished, and on "deadline day," they *still* are 95 percent finished! Sure, they reached the milestone of "design completed" on schedule, but what does that mean? They reached the milestone of "all modules coded" on schedule, but what does that mean?

When such problems are discovered so late in the project, no amount of threats, cajoling, or bribery will work. It was widely rumored in 1987, for example, that one major software company observed that one of its project teams was falling behind in development of a major new product; management offered the project team a $2 million bonus if they could finish on time. That is surely enough motivation to make any project team work hard; yet, when the deadline arrived, there were reported to be *hundreds* of bugs left in the system, and the bonus disappeared.

Compare these developments with the top-down approach, but be sure to remember that there is no magic, and no free lunch. Whether one works top-down or bottom-up, or middle-out, there will still be deadline problems. The system still may not be finished when the deadline arrives, and the users will still be irritated, even if you never agreed to commit your staff to the official deadline.

However, you will undoubtedly be in a *much* stronger political position than you would with the bottom-up approach, because you will have a skeleton version of the system that performs some demonstrable processing. Of course, this advantage must be viewed in the proper perspective, for if we present a payroll system that produces paychecks in hexadecimal digits, the user is unlikely to be impressed with the effort and might well send the entire project team off to the labor camps in Siberia. Consider the following dialogue, and you will see what I mean.

User:	Good morning. Today's the deadline. Where is my payroll system?
Project manager:	I'm sorry to say that we're not finished.

User:	What? That's ridiculous! We agreed that you'd be finished by January 1.
Project manager:	Actually, *you* agreed that it would be done on January 1. I told you all along that that date was optimistic. However, I *do* have a Version 3 payroll system that works and can be put into operation today.
User:	Version 3? What does that mean?
Project manager:	Well, it's a payroll system that pays everyone by check; it won't pay anyone in cash or by direct bank deposit. And if anyone works double overtime on a national holiday, the system will pay the employee $100 a week. And the system does not validate transactions that *decrease* salary, which means that an employee's salary might accidentally be reduced below zero. But, other than those minor details, the system works.
User:	That's ridiculous! That's unacceptable! I want the whole thing! I asked for the whole payroll system to be working by January 1.
Project manager:	I know, but we didn't make it. In the meantime, you should be able to live with these minor restrictions. We'll have them fixed, and will deliver Version 4 to you in another two weeks.
User:	Grumble, grumble . . . well, I suppose it's better than nothing.

4.2.4   Debugging is easier

One of the advantages of the top-down testing approach involves a technical issue that shouldn't concern you as a manager, but that nevertheless is a factor you should be aware of: The process of debugging is easier when the top-down approach is used.

To explain, the distinction between testing and debugging needs to be defined. Loosely speaking, *testing* is the process one goes through to demonstrate the correctness or incorrectness of a system. It usually consists of supplying known inputs to the program and verifying that the outputs are correct.

Debugging, on the other hand, is the black art of tracking down a bug once its existence has been discovered. The existence of a bug is usually learned from a controlled test procedure; hence, testing and debugging are considered by many programmers to be almost synonymous. But when a production system (e.g., payroll) blows up in the middle of the night, it's debugging that the sleepy maintenance programmer is doing, not testing.

Given that distinction, I argue that debugging is easier in a top-down testing environment because top-down testing tends to be incremental. That is, it usually consists of adding one new module to an existing skeleton of modules, and then observing the behavior of the new system. If the new system misbehaves, common sense tells the programmer that the problem must be located in the new module, or in the interface between the new module and the rest of the system. Indeed, if the programmer becomes desperate, he always has the option of a strategic retreat; he can remove the new module, re-insert the dummy, or stub, in its place, and retreat to his office to contemplate the mystery of the bug.[2]

By contrast, the bottom-up approach tends to be "phased." That is, one usually finds geometrically increasing numbers of modules being combined for the first time, any one of which (or any combination of which) may contain a bug. This problem is particularly evident during system testing, when hundreds or even thousands of modules are combined for the first time, and one of those modules contains a bug that ultimately destroys the entire system. Even worse, a bug in module A combines with a bug in module B to produce a subtly incorrect output that the programmer finds impossible to relate to any single module; or a bug in module A cancels the effect of a bug in module B, thus leading (accidentally) to correct output, until the maintenance programmer innocently fixes the bug in module A at some later point.

---

[2] Meanwhile, the rest of the project team can continue to make progress by adding other modules to the skeleton system. The point of this is that one programmer's bug need not bring the project to a screeching halt. This should not be underestimated.

4.2.5 Requirements for machine test time are distributed more evenly throughout a top-down project

In many projects, the requirement for computer test time rises almost exponentially toward the end of the project. However, the requirement for machine time in a top-down project remains fairly constant during the lifetime of the project. The differences between the two approaches are shown graphically in Figure 4.1.

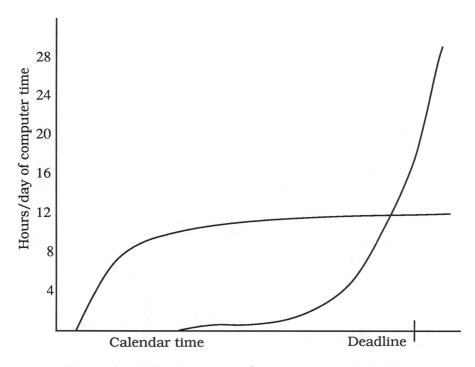

Figure 4.1: **Requirements for computer test time**

You should be able to anticipate the reasons for these two curves from the earlier discussion about top-down development. The bottom-up approach generally does not begin using computer test time until the project is well under way, simply because the approach involves designing and coding most or all of the system before testing begins. Once testing does begin, the requirement for machine time rises rapidly as modules are combined into programs, programs into subsystems, and subsystems into systems.

In contrast, the top-down approach begins using machine time earlier because the project team begins writing code before the design is finished. Normally, the requirement for test time reaches a certain point and then levels off, remaining relatively constant for the project's duration. The reason for the constant requirement for test time is simple: The incremental nature of the testing involves adding one new module to the system each day and running roughly the same set of test data through the system. However, note that this early use of computer time can cause some problems, which I will discuss in Section 4.3.2.

4.2.6   Programmer morale is improved

A minor advantage of the top-down approach—but one that should not be ignored—is that the programmers are usually happier and better motivated. Why? For the same reasons that users and senior managers like the top-down approach: They can see tangible evidence of progress at an earlier stage in the project. The morale boost of seeing an early version of a system is particularly effective in avoiding the "mid-project slump" found in most projects that continue for two or three years.

This boost can be significant. Programmers, for the most part, *do* like to program. They do *not* like to write detailed specifications, they do *not* like to write detailed pseudocode or draw detailed flowcharts, and they do *not* like to become engrossed in the paperwork that is characteristic of the early stages of a typical systems development project. However, when they begin programming and testing—the fun part—they begin to work the 16-hour days on which we have come to depend.

With the top-down approach, programming and testing activity usually begin much earlier in the project, so the programmer begins, at an earlier stage, doing what he really enjoys doing. In addition, he has the tremendous morale boost of seeing a Version 1 system actually work. It doesn't matter that the Version 1 system is trivial and that it only produces hexadecimal paychecks. It is a real system that accepts real inputs and produces real outputs. That progress alone is probably sufficient to motivate the programmer to work 16-hour days to produce Version 2 of the system.

4.2.7   Top-down testing eliminates the need for test harnesses

Finally, there is a characteristic of top-down testing that is technical in nature although it has some management overtones.

The classical bottom-up scheme usually requires the presence of a test driver, or test harness, that is, a program that can read test data from a file, pass the test data to the module being tested, capture the output from the module, and print the output on a suitable output device. Some MIS organizations are disciplined enough to require their programmers to make use of a general-purpose test driver, along with a general-purpose test data generator, but many don't bother. However, in many organizations, each programmer writes a quick-and-dirty test driver for each module being tested.

The top-down approach eliminates the need for drivers, since the existing skeleton system can serve as a natural test driver for a new low-level module being added to the system. On the other hand, the top-down approach *does* require the use of stubs, or dummy routines. Such routines are substitutes for detailed modules that have not been coded yet, and their implementation usually consists of the following:

1.   Immediate exit, with no processing.

2.   Returning constant output; for example, returning $100 in the dummy version of the salary computation module in the payroll system discussed above.

3.   Returning a random number, within some range.

4.   Printing an output message, to inform the programmer that the dummy module was executed.

5.   Executing a timing loop to consume N microseconds of CPU time in a controlled fashion; alternatively, the dummy routine might consume other resources, such as disk accesses. This is useful in real-time systems, where performance issues are important.

6.   Providing a primitive, quick-and-dirty implementation of the *real* function of the module, perhaps coded in a much higher level language.

7.   Asking for help from an on-line terminal (in which case, a human does the work that the module was supposed to do).

Although there is nothing fundamentally wrong with test drivers, dummy routines are usually simpler to code than a corresponding driver routine. In the best cases, the dummy routine consists of one statement: EXIT.[3]

4.3   MANAGEMENT PROBLEMS WITH THE TOP-DOWN APPROACH

Based on the preceding discussion, you might be tempted to issue a memo to your technical staff that says: "Troops! Starting tomorrow, I want all of you to design and test your systems in a top-down fashion!" Or maybe you should send all 300 of your programmers to a one-hour class on top-down implementation, and *then* issue the edict.

As I discussed in Chapter 2, such an approach may lead to confusion. Indeed, even if you ease into top-down implementation slowly, gradually, and diplomatically, you may experience confusion. The troops, even with the best of intentions, are likely to do some silly things in the name of top-down implementation.

What sort of things? Companies vary, but the sort of problems that I have seen include the following:

- A misunderstanding of radical top-down implementation versus conservative top-down implementation

- Lack of sufficient test time

- Lack of hardware for top-down testing

- Staffing problems

- Programmers' fears that changes to low-level modules will propagate to high-level modules

- Common tendency to practice top-down *program* testing, combined with bottom-up *system* testing
- Communication problems in multiteam projects

- Difficulty in visualizing top-down versions

- Difficulty in getting the user involved

---

[3] Also, the dummy routine will often consist of "salvageable" code that will be used in the final implementation, whereas the test driver usually consists of "throw-away" code.

- Unwillingness to renegotiate schedules and budgets

A brief discussion of each of these potential problems follows.

4.3.1 Misunderstanding between radical and conservative top-down testing

You may well be wondering, "What's conservative top-down? What's radical top-down?" The radical top-down approach can be described as follows: First, design the top level module of the system, then *immediately* write the code for that module and test it (meanwhile, the next lower level of modules exist only as stubs). Then design the modules at the next lower level, and *immediately* code and test them. Then design, code, and test the modules at the third level, and so forth.

The conservative approach to top-down implementation consists of designing *all* of the modules at *all* levels, until the lowest-level modules have been completely designed. Then the top-level modules can be coded, and a Version 1 system can be produced. From the experience gained in implementing Version 1, make any necessary changes to the lower levels of design, and then code and test the second-level modules, and so on down to the lowest level.

The radical approach and the conservative approach represent two extreme points on a spectrum. There are an infinite number of compromise top-down strategies that you can select, depending on your situation. You may decide, for example, to finish 75 percent of the systems analysis and design, and then begin top-down coding and testing of those modules that you have designed. Or you might decide to design 25 percent of the system, and then, with 75 percent of the system still fuzzy, start coding and implementing.

There is no single right answer. I cannot tell you whether the radical approach is better than the conservative approach for all possible projects. However, I *can* identify the primary factors that will help you decide just how radical or conservative you will want to be:

- *User fickleness.* If the user has no idea of what he wants or has a tendency to change his mind, opt for the radical approach. Why waste time designing detailed logic that will be thrown away? This is, in essence, the prototyping paradigm discussed in

Chapter 17. On the other hand, if the user knows precisely what he wants, attempt a complete design.

- *Design quality.* Committing the project team to early coding may make it difficult to improve the design later. All other things being equal, I prefer to finish the entire systems analysis and design phase of the project before coding (see Section 4.3.5).

- *Time pressures.* If you are under extreme pressure from users or higher levels of management to produce some tangible output quickly, go for the radical approach. If your deadline is absolutely inflexible—if, for example, it is a case of "you bet your job"—go for the radical approach. If you are not under much pressure, and the deadline is flexible, go for the conservative approach. For a good discussion of real-world techniques of dealing with high-pressure projects, see Boddie's *Crunch Mode* [Boddie, 1987].

- *Accurate estimates.* If you are required by your organization to provide accurate, detailed estimates of schedules, manpower, and other resources, then you should opt for the conservative approach. How can you estimate how long it will take to implement the system until you know how many modules it will contain?

All of this makes sense; at least, it should make sense. The reason that problems have occurred in some MIS organizations is that some programmers, managers, and users have interpreted the top-down approach as a religion, and all three parties tend to interpret that religion differently.

To the user community, top-down means that they should have a fully functional system, with a perfect design, on the second day of the project. The programmers sometimes interpret the religion as an official license to begin writing code on the second day of the project, which unfortunately degenerates into coding without *any* design!

In practice, hardly anyone follows the extreme radical approach described earlier. Most designers instinctively explore at least half of the design before committing themselves to code, even if much of that design activity is subconscious and undocumented. Unfortunately, many projects do seem to follow the extreme conservative approach, and while it may lead to better technical designs, it fails for two reasons: (a) On a large project, the user is incapable of specifying the details of his requirements; and (b) on a large project, users and senior management are increasingly unwilling to accept two or three years of effort by the MIS department with no visible, tangible output. Hence, the movement toward the radical approach.

There are several important things that you, as a manager, should be cautious about. Don't let the users intimidate you into taking a radical approach in situations in which that approach seems inappropriate. Don't let your project management textbooks convince you to follow the conservative approach in developing the perfect design when you know that the user is uncertain about what kind of system he wants. Finally, *don't ever* let your programmers bamboozle you into thinking that top-down implementation means that they are automatically at liberty to begin composing code extemporaneously on the first day of the project.

4.3.2   Lack of sufficient machine time

In some organizations I have visited, the programmers have complained to me (sometimes privately, so that the boss wouldn't become irritated) that they get only one test shot a day. In other words, they have to wait 24 hours to see the output of any test run that they have submitted. While most MIS organizations now provide their programmers with on-line development facilities, there are still a few organizations where the programmers get as little as one test shot a week.

In addition, the programmers sometimes state that they can't get *any* machine time when they need it. As observed previously, the top-down approach requires machine availability earlier in the project life cycle than is customary, causing problems in organizations in which the assumption is always that the programmers do not need machine time until a project has been under way for six months.

In most MIS organizations in which this problem has occurred, the programmers have abandoned top-down testing partially or completely, often without even knowing it. Instead of adding only *one* new module to an existing skeleton and testing the system incrementally, the programmers begin adding *all* of the modules at a particular level (e.g., all of the second-level edit modules in the payroll system described earlier) and testing them *en masse*. In the worst case, the programmers will retreat to the bottom-up approach with which they are more familiar.

So, ensure that your programmers have enough machine time to indulge in the top-down approach, at least for their first few projects, when they may be occasionally tempted to slip back into their old ways.

How *much* machine time should you allocate? Should you expect to use more machine time with the top-down approach than would have been used with the bottom-up approach? The honest answer is: I don't know. You will probably be safe if you allocate roughly as much test time as you would have allocated with your classical bottom-up techniques; and then use the experience of your first few pilot projects (discussed in more detail in Chapter 11) to refine your estimates.

My experience has been that the *amount* of machine time is somewhat less important than the *frequency* of test shots. If the programmer knows that he is going to have only one test shot a week, he is tempted to throw all of his modules into the machine at once and hope that they'll all work. On the other hand, if he knows that he'll get two or three test shots a day, he will be more inclined to follow the incremental approach of testing one new module at a time.

One reason for the inability to predict the amount of machine time needed in a top-down project is that very few projects use *only* top-down implementation. Most organizations use top-down implementation, plus structured design, plus walkthroughs, and so on. Generally, the result is much less machine time. If your programmers write code with no bugs, then they will need a modest amount of machine time to verify that they have no bugs, but they will need no debugging time, and they will need no computer time for recompiling and retesting their programs.

4.3.3   Lack of hardware for testing

Not getting enough machine time for testing is one problem. Not getting *any* machine time for testing is a qualitatively different problem. The most extreme form of this phenomenon occurs in projects that have no available computer hardware during the system development phase. While this is not a very common problem in large organizations adding a new application to an existing inventory of systems running in the corporate data center, it does sometimes happen.

Consider the organization trying to build a large on-line system for a department of end-users who currently do their work manually. In order to carry out top-down implementation, the programmers require access to terminals, modems, local area networks, and telecommunication lines, in addition to the conventional central site hardware. If this is the department's *first* on-line system, the terminals and communications equipment may not exist, and management is frequently reluctant to install the equipment until the last possible moment. Even if they are willing do install the equipment, there may be delays of several weeks or months before it can be ordered from vendors, delivered, and installed.

The result? Bottom-up development, in one form or another. A great deal of application software will be written and tested in a batch environment, or, at best, in a simulated on-line environment, and an attempt will be made, sometimes on the day before the deadline, to interface all of this software with the newly arrived teleprocessing hardware/software.

The reason for management's reluctance is obvious: The teleprocessing and network equipment is expensive, and management is concerned that it will be idle for a substantial portion of the development phase of the project. However, my experience has been that the equipment will be idle anyway while the programmers try to find their bugs. The only question is whether you would prefer to have the equipment installed and idle before the deadline or after the deadline.

Obviously, compromises are possible. If an on-line system eventually will have 1,000 terminals, we could expect to carry out a reasonable form of top-down implementation with three or four terminals and one or two communication lines. If certain pieces of hardware are simply *not* available, then simulator software is better than nothing.

4.3.4   Staffing problems

Some organizations assign a full complement of programmers, designers, and systems analysts to a systems development project on the first day of the project. Sometimes this assignment is the result of contractual and billing procedures, particularly in dealings between a software consulting firm and a separate user organization. Sometimes, however, the problem is more mundane. As a manager, for example, you know that you'll need Fred and Susan in the middle of the project. Unfortunately, if you don't grab them at the beginning of the project, they'll be occupied with something else when you need them. Rather than lose them, you may decide to bring them into your project, even though there is nothing for them to do yet.

The result of this kind of management decision should be obvious. In an attempt to keep Fred and Susan busy, someone will invent some bottom-level modules and hope that they will be needed later. Fred and Susan will then be sent off to code those modules, and the rest of the team will continue to work on the top part of the system.

Subsequent design work may show that nobody really needs Fred's module after all, and that the interface that was specified for Susan's module is completely impractical. That's the risk one runs when combining top-down design with bottom-up design.

Two things should be observed about staffing. First, it is often practical to have several programmer/designers working on the top portion of the system, even if they function only as coders and reviewers (as in a structured walkthrough, discussed in Chapter 9). Thus, Fred and Susan might be very useful as participants in the top-level design, *more* useful, perhaps, than sending them off to code bottom-level modules that may never be needed.

Second, it is a good idea to complete all, or most, of the system's design before trying to figure out how many "Freds" and "Susans" will be required to code the individual modules. Thus, the normal problems of staffing and resource planning often provide a strong argument for the conservative top-down approach.

4.3.5   Programmers' fears that changes to low-level modules will propagate up to the top-level modules

Relatively few programmers object to the top-down approach, but those who do, frequently mention one major concern: Implementing bottom-level modules late in the project may cause problems in top-down modules that have already been designed, coded, and tested.

This concern is usually exaggerated. Yes, the implementation of bottom-level modules may suggest or even require changes to some of the higher-level modules, but this is usually fairly minor. It is *possible* that the implementation of the last bottom-level module will uncover design flaws that will be propagated all the way up to the top of the system, but it's rather unlikely.

If it appears that this may be a serious problem on your project or something that is going to bother your programmers,

then opt for the conservative top-down approach. Finish the
entire design before writing any code. This way, you'll be able to
anticipate almost all of the potential design problems with
bottom-level modules.

At the same time, note that this problem is identical to the
one frequently observed in a bottom-up project. At the end of
program testing, when two major subsystems are linked
together for the first time, we find that the interface isn't right:
subsystem A is passing the wrong kind of data to subsystem B
(usually because someone misread or misunderstood the
interface documentation). Correcting that interface problem
may have a ripple effect all the way down to the bottom-level
modules. My experience has been that problems of this kind are
much worse than the problems discovered with the top-down
approach.

Remember also, many of the problems will come from the
user, and this is an argument for using a more radical top-down
implementation. There is no point in finishing the perfect
design and letting the programmers reassure themselves that all
of the interfaces are proper, only to have half of the entire effort
thrown out because the user changed his mind.

4.3.6   The mistake of combining top-down program testing and bottom-up system testing

This problem is characterized by the following kind of
dialogue at the beginning of a project:

Boss:	OK, troops, let's break the system into individual programs.
Troops:	Right, boss.
Boss:	Fred, you take program one. Susan, you take program two. Charlie, you take program three. And I want all of you to use top-down testing, structured programming, and the rest of that structured stuff.
Troops:	OK, boss.
Boss:	And when you're finished, let's all get back together, and then we'll merge the programs into a system.

As one might expect, this approach has many of the same problems as the original bottom-up approach. Fred, Susan, and Charlie find that their individual programming projects are quite easy, but problems occur when they are reunited. They find that Fred decided to change the interface specifications without telling anyone; Susan's program doesn't work with Charlie's program, and so forth.

In most cases, this problem is the result of a misunderstanding of the top-down concept. Sometimes it is the result of other problems, such as lack of sufficient computer time.

Depending on the size of the project, this combination of top-down program development and bottom-up systems development may or may not be serious. If Fred, Susan, and Charlie are writing small programs that require only a day's effort, then their systems integration difficulties should be manageable. But if this situation occurs with 50 programmers who each spends a year developing his or her individual programs, chaos will reign.

4.3.7 Communication problems in multiteam projects

On very small projects, the programming group is usually broken into smaller teams, each being responsible for a program, or a subsystem, or some other unit of work (e.g., writing the user manual). At that point, Mealy's Law[4] takes over: The eventual structure of the system reflects the structure of the organization that builds the system. For example, if two teams have difficulty communicating with each other because of personality clashes or political problems, then their subsystems will probably have difficulty communicating.

In particular, each team tends to isolate itself from other teams and to develop its own personality. Early integration of the top-level skeleton of one team's subsystem with the top-level skeleton of another team's subsystem is often regarded as a "hassle," and both teams avoid it. As a result, they use the approach discussed in the previous section: top-down program development and bottom-up system integration.

Why is it a hassle interfacing two subsystems at an early stage? Because the interfaces are fuzzy! Team A hasn't defined precisely what data it requires from Team B, and as a result, it's difficult to put the two subsystems into a computer and make them communicate. But that is exactly what the top-down

---

[4] So named after George Mealy, one of the architects of IBM's OS/360 operating system.

approach is trying to accomplish: *forcing* the precise definition of major interfaces and forcing those interfaces to be coded and exercised in a computer to ensure that they work.

In other words, you should *expect* problems in this area. The larger your project, the more problems there will be. Rather than avoiding the problems, you should confront them directly. This is what the top-down approach is all about.

4.3.8   Difficulty visualizing top-down versions

Visualizing system "versions" proves to be a common and serious problem. Many people, especially programmers, have a confused notion of the sequence of implementation in a top-down project, perhaps because they are used to thinking in linear, flowchart terms.

In the earlier example of the payroll system, for example, many programmers think that top-down implementation means the following: Version 1 of the system will do all of the editing, but nothing else; Version 2 will combine all of the editing and all of the update logic (and thus all of the salary computations, tax calculations, and so forth); Version 3 will combine the editing, update logic, and the sorting; and Version 4 will throw in the printing.

It is puzzling that some programmers have had such difficulty visualizing a skeleton version of a *complete* system; for example, visualizing a payroll system that incorporates the top-level logic of the edit, the update, *and* the printing. Regardless of why, this problem does occur and should be watched.

4.3.9   Difficulty getting the user involved

One of the major objectives of top-down testing is to involve the user in the early skeleton versions of the system. If something is wrong with the system from the user's viewpoint, it is better to discover the problem as early as possible. Unfortunately, the user is sometimes too busy to participate in testing early versions of the system. He may say, in effect, "Leave me alone! I'm swamped with work—that's why I need a new system! Don't talk to me until you've got the entire system finished!"

Such a user deserves what he gets, just as a customer who refuses to look at a custom-built house until it's finished deserves what he gets. Unfortunately, the MIS project manager (or the architect) is often blamed even if the customer is wrong.

The moral: Make an extra effort to involve your user in early versions of your system, even if he thinks it's a waste of time. This often means that your early versions will have to emphasize the human interface more than the functionality of the system; that is, you won't be able to get away with hexadecimal paychecks, and you *will* have to worry about the format and layout (and color) of on-line input screens.

4.3.10   Unwillingness to renegotiate schedules and budgets

It's likely that when the user sees Version 1 of his new MIS system, he will want major changes. He may decide that certain functions are essential, even though he never mentioned them in the analysis phase of the project. Features that he previously considered essential are now deemed useless. Still other features of the system may have to be modified drastically.

Thus, it's likely to be a whole new ball game. When Version 2 of the system is demonstrated to the user, the game may change again. Indeed, each version of a top-down system may bring changes to the specification—although the changes should be less and less drastic with each successive version.

Unfortunately, the user, as well as the MIS project manager, sometimes fails to appreciate that these changes require a reevaluation of the timetable, the staffing plan, and the budget for the project. Further, the user may be reluctant to agree to any changes in the project schedule or budget. "Why, these are just small changes," he'll say. "You should be able to work these into the system without any real fuss or bother." Or, if he's clever, your user may say to you, "I thought all of this top-down development stuff was supposed to make it easier for me to get what I want, and easier to make changes. Now you're telling me that you can't make any changes!"

In fact, you *can* accommodate minor changes to the original specifications without changing the schedule or budget; the increased productivity associated with the structured techniques helps you in that respect. But if it's a major change that the user wants, it's obvious that something will have to give.

More important, it's a mistake to let the user think that he can arbitrarily change the specifications for his system without having to worry about the additional time and money it may cost. So you should go through the negotiation process, even if you can accommodate the change with no extra work.

Chapter 5
STRUCTURED DESIGN

Having discussed top-down design, we now turn to a related topic: structured design. We begin with an overview of the technical concepts of structured design, followed by a discussion of the problems you are likely to encounter when implementing structured design in your organization.

5.1 AN OVERVIEW OF STRUCTURED DESIGN

The term *structured design* was introduced to the systems development industry in a landmark article published in the *IBM Systems Journal* in 1974 [Stevens, 1974]. Prior to that article, the various concepts discussed in this chapter were referred to as *modular design, logical design, composite design,* or the *design of program structure.*

The last phrase best describes the idea. What concerns us here is the architecture, organization, and structure of computer programs and of systems of programs. Structure is a concept that people have talked about for years, but have only recently formalized. Structured design is not the same as top-down design. Solving a large, complex problem using top-down design is generally preferable to employing bottom-up design, random design, or no design. However, it does not guarantee creation of a good design. In fact, we can quite easily design a terrible design in a top-down fashion. A good system, in the context of this discussion, is easy to implement, easy to debug, and easy to maintain and modify. A terrible system is one that, for some reason, is expensive to develop and maintain.

This should not really come as a surprise. As discussed in Chapter 4, top-down design does not actually tell us *how* to break a large system into smaller pieces. In addition, it does not indicate what kind of intermodule interfaces are preferable. In general, it lacks the formal guidelines that enable us to design systems so that we can debug, maintain, or modify one module without having to know anything about other modules and certainly without having to modify the code in any other modules.

This is not to suggest that top-down design is *bad.* Indeed, some people have designed very good systems using nothing more than the informal guidelines of top-down design.   There are two reasons for their success: First, top-down design is preferable to using *no* design, which is the common situation in many MIS organizations today; and second, some programmers and designers instinctively produce a *good* top-down design, without realizing that they have done so.

Structured design can be thought of as a collection of five related concepts, two of which are discussed in other chapters in this book.

- *Documentation techniques*— graphic tools that emphasize the structural, or hierarchical aspects of a system rather than the procedural (iterations and decisions) aspects.   These tools, including structure charts and HIPO charts, are discussed in Chapter 7.

- *Evaluation criteria*— guidelines that help us distinguish between good and bad systems at the modular level.

- *Heuristics*— rules of thumb, which are useful when evaluating the "goodness" of a particular design, but which should not be followed religiously.   Tom Parker, in *Rules of Thumb* [Houghton-Mifflin, 1987], describes a heuristic as "a homemade recipe for making a guess.   It is an easy-to-remember guide that falls somewhere between a mathematical formula and a shot in the dark."

- *Design strategies*— strategies that allow the designer to systematically derive good solutions to common types of MIS problems; top-down design could be thought of as one such strategy, although it is less specific and helpful than some of the other available ones.

- *Implementation strategies*— plans that dictate the order in which to code and implement modules, including bottom-up implementation

Lack of space prevents us from discussing all of the technical theory, heuristics, and design strategies in detail; [Page-Jones, 1988] and [Yourdon and Constantine, 1989] may be consulted for additional details.   However, I will illustrate the philosophy behind structured design with a short example and then briefly describe some of the technical concepts.

Put yourself in the position of a management consultant. Suppose that you were asked to render an opinion about the organization chart shown in Figure 5.1. Most likely, you would comment that Vice President A, Manager X, and Manager Y all have trivial jobs, since their responsibility seems to consist solely of managing one subordinate. Being a cynic, you would probably suggest that all of the work in that department is being done by Worker Z, and that all of the managers above Z should be fired!

Similarly, suppose you were asked to evaluate a company having an organization chart like the one in Figure 5.2. Chances are that you would predict trouble: The boss is a prime candidate for a heart attack; at the very least, one would expect him to make many mistakes, simply because he manages too many people.

Finally, suppose you saw the organization chart in Figure 5.3. Each manager supervises an appropriate number of immediate subordinates—a reasonable "span of control"—and the entire organization seems properly balanced. While there may be many other problems in this organization, at least the architecture indicated by the organization chart is realistic.

Of course, all good companies do not require exactly three vice presidents, nor do they require perfect symmetry. Just because Vice President A has two immediate subordinates, we do not suggest that Vice President B must also have two immediate subordinates. But, Figures 5.1 and 5.2 show evidence of structural problems—a *skewed* organization chart— and Figure 5.3 does *not* show similar evidence.

Program structures and system structures can be discussed in a similar way. Figures 5.1, 5.2, and 5.3 might well be structural representations of three different programs of three different systems, since the distinction between programs and systems is largely artificial at this level of abstraction.

Thus, we can make some *structural* criticism of the program/system shown in Figure 5.1. It consists of a top-level "executive" module, which accomplishes its overall function by calling upon three "vice president" modules. Our concern, of course, is with module A. From Figure 5.1, we suspect that it consists of a single instruction, a subroutine call to module X. Similarly, we deduce that module X contains only one instruction: a call to subroutine Y. Also, we conclude that module Y is a one-instruction module that does nothing but call module Z. Hence, module Z seems to be where all the work is done.

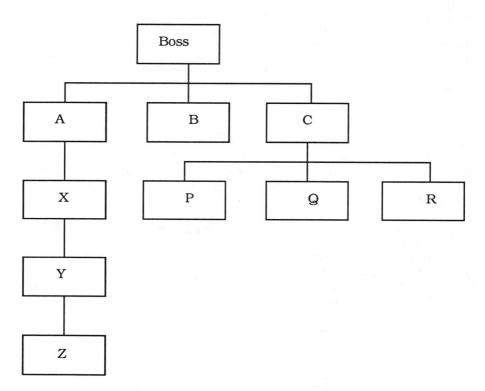

Figure 5.1: **A company's organization chart**

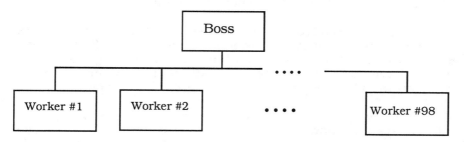

Figure 5.2: **Another company's organization chart**

These deductions must be kept in perspective. Although we suspect that modules, A, X, and Y are trivial, we don't know their importance unless we look at the code. Also, we recognize that there is nothing disastrously wrong with a series of one-instruction subroutines doing nothing but calling a lower-level module. Running such a system on a computer will not cause the computer to explode or halt. It's just that such a structure is— well, what should we call it? trivial? bureaucratic? inefficient? In short, there is probably a better alternative to Figure 5.1.

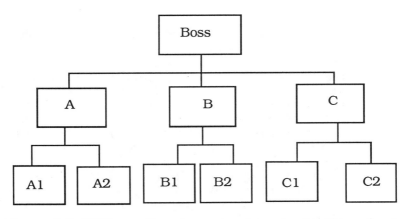

Figure 5.3: **Still another company's organization chart**

Obviously, Figure 5.2 represents the opposite extreme: an excessive span of control. We should be concerned about it in a software environment for the same reason that it concerns us in a management environment: extreme complexity. Our executive module probably has too many nested loops and decisions, and too much management logic, in the sense that it cannot be properly understood by either the maintenance programmer or the development programmer.

What we have just illustrated is a *heuristic*— a rule of thumb that should be used as a guideline, but not interpreted as religious dogma. For example, the heuristic seen in Figures 5.1, 5.2, and 5.3 is known as "span of control," a phrase borrowed from the management field; the structured design heuristic is "a module should not have more than 7 ± 2 immediate subordinates."

Other concepts of structured design are the following:

- *Coupling*— a description of the strength of association between different modules in a system; in other words, coupling is a name for a generally bad characteristic of a system. My colleague Larry Constantine describes coupling as the taffy that sticks modules together, so that an innocent attempt to modify or debug one module might result in the programmer tangling with another module. We can identify design practices that increase coupling between modules (bad news!), as well as those that decrease the coupling between modules (good news!).

• *Cohesion*— a term borrowed from sociology and social psychology describing the strength of association of the elements *inside* a module. The elements of a module should all be strongly associated (highly cohesive) and all involved in performing the same, single task. On a more practical level, cohesion is a way of talking about the rationale that designers use to form modules. We can identify several useful levels of cohesion, some of which are good and others bad. The ultimate objective of cohesion is to show designers how to form good modules, all of whose instructions are essential to the performance of one, and only one, task.

• *Pathological connections*— one of the strongest forms of coupling between modules, occurring when one module refers to the "insides" of another module. Pathological connections can be avoided if a subroutine executes only when it is invoked formally by a superordinate; the subroutine operates only on data given to it by its superordinate; the subroutine receives only those data essential to the performance of its task; and the subroutine delivers all of its outputs, or results, to its superordinate.

• *Transform-centered design*— one of several design strategies that helps the designer to systematically derive good solutions to common types of applications. Transform-centered design requires the designer to study the flow of data through the system as the basis for determining which modules will be required and how they will be organized hierarchically. Other design strategies, such as those proposed in [Jackson, 1975], [Higgins, 1979], [Orr, 1977], and [Warnier, 1976], require the designer to study the structure of the input and output data in order to determine the module hierarchy.

* *Packaging*— a term useful for describing the decisions that the designer must ultimately make to shoe-horn his logical modules into the physical environment provided by the computer hardware, the vendor's operating system, and the programming language. An important precept of structured design is that packaging should be delayed as long as possible, partly because it obscures the basic nature of the design problem, and partly because it leads to gross inefficiencies if completed too early.

5.2   MANAGEMENT PROBLEMS WITH STRUCTURED DESIGN

Even with a reasonable amount of training and study, designers may experience some problems with their first few attempts to use structured design; fortunately, this is becoming less of a problem because nearly 75 percent of the MIS organizations in the United States now report that they are using some form of structured design, and most universities teach structured design in their computer science and MIS curriculum. The most common problems are:

1.   Designer's inability to grasp abstract design philosophies and concepts

2.   Conflicts between the old classical design philosophies and the new structured philosophies

3.   Difficulty enforcing formal design disciplines within small- or medium-sized projects

4.   Complaints of inefficiency

5.   Difficulty defining the proper roles of analyst, designer, and programmer

Each of these problems is discussed below.

5.2.1   Designer's problems grasping abstract design philosophies

The overview presented earlier in this chapter may have made structured design seem like a trivial concept. Don't be fooled. Many of your programmers and designers will find the discipline quite difficult to comprehend. Perhaps this is as it should be: Design *is* hard, and it will never be trivial to design a large system.

Nevertheless, structured design techniques do work, and they can be used by those possessing a reasonable degree of intelligence. This requirement may pose a management problem, however. You may find that using structured design requires more talented people than those currently doing your design work.

This comment is not meant to be snide or cynical. I have no intention of insulting you or your staff. My comment is based on observing several thousand programmers, designers, and systems analysts to whom I have tried to teach top-down design, structured design, and structured programming. Most grasp top-down design and structured programming without too much trouble, but for many, the concept of structured design is incomprehensible.

Part of the problem may be the terminology. Structured design introduces the terms *cohesion, pathological connections, heuristics,* and *transform-centered design,* for example. A more thorough discussion of the subject would add more buzzwords: afferent and efferent modules, temporal and procedural cohesion, among others. Perhaps for this reason we should not be surprised to see designers despair and walk away from structured design!

The terminology poses a dilemma. On the one hand, we don't want to introduce buzzwords in a field already overloaded with them. On the other hand, we *do* need words to describe technical aspects of computer system design never described before, and we do not want to use words that have vendor-dependent meanings (e.g., the word "task" means something different depending on the programming language, operating system, and vendor hardware used). In fact, most of the buzzwords in structured design are not new, but rather have been borrowed from other fields.

Apologies aside, we do expect computer people to have a basic vocabulary. Unfortunately, this assumption may be erroneous, for, during seminars on structured design, a substantial number of designers have asked me, "By the way, what's a heuristic? I've never heard of the word." Providing all programmers and designers with a dictionary definition of the word heuristic, or simply substituting *rule of thumb* or *guideline,* would still not solve the problem. Why? Primarily because most designers and programmers feel an incredible urge to define everything in terms of sacred rules. Even a simple guideline, like span of control, becomes a religious commandment.

Indeed, some MIS organizations insist that all programs have the kind of symmetrical structure shown in Figure 5.3. Thus, the designers in such situations are told that every system *must* contain one top-level module; that it *must* have exactly three second-level modules, whose names will be "input," "process," and "output"; that if the input second-level module has two immediate subordinates beneath it, then the process and output modules must also have two immediate subordinates.

In the same fashion, we find designers who interpret the concepts of coupling, cohesion, pathological connections, and transform-centered design in terms of ultimate good and evil. Hence, modules with low cohesion must be evil, and those with high cohesion must be good. Pathological connections must always be bad, and so forth.

The only advice is the obvious: Hire intelligent people, who will read the current literature on the subject. Send them to conferences, symposia, workshops, or training sessions to learn the techniques. Make them trade ideas with their colleagues, and teach them that structured design is common sense, not a new religion.

5.2.2 Conflicts between design philosophies

Even if your designers understand structured design, your organization may have design standards that seriously conflict with the structured design philosophies discussed in this book and in such books as [Yourdon and Constantine, 1989] and [Page-Jones, 1988]. For example, some MIS organizations have outlawed the use of subroutine calls, PERFORM statements, or procedure calls in Pascal.[1] Clearly, structured design is difficult to implement with these strictures.

More commonly, problems arise in applying the concepts of cohesion, packaging, and pathological connections. The organizational standards may dictate, for example, that every program have a "general-purpose edit module" and a "general-

---

[1] How could this be? Simple. Many of the standards manuals were written in the 1970s, when subroutine calls were grossly inefficient, or simply didn't work. Sadly, the standards manuals have been ignored all this time, and have never been updated.

purpose error routine." While the standards are obviously well-intentioned, structured design would argue against such modules because they represent classic examples of "logical cohesion."[2] Similarly, the organizational standards may require the programmer to develop a "master file control" module for his program, that is, a module that, depending on the nature of a flag passed to it, will either open, close, read, or carry out any of a number of other similar functions on the master file. Structured design would reject that standard, too, on the ground that the module represents a classic example of "communicational cohesion."[3]

As a manager, be aware that many such standards were created at least ten years ago, often for the sake of hardware efficiency, a consideration that is largely irrelevant today (see section 5.2.4). So, what should you do? Be prepared for some conflicts and scrap some of your obsolete standards.

5.2.3   Difficulty enforcing structured design on small projects

After trying it once or twice, your designers no doubt will tell you that a proper application of cohesion, coupling, transform-centered design, and all the rest of structured design, *takes a lot of time.*

To appreciate this, imagine how your designers would react if you asked them to develop a simple sequential file update program of 200 to 300 COBOL statements. Now suppose that you have decided to enforce the following "religious rules" of structured design:

1.   The update program must be broken into modules, no one of which should be longer than one page of a program listing.

2.   All modules must be invoked with CALL statements; PERFORM statements are not allowed.

---

[2] A logically cohesive module contains many similar functions, which is quite different from a module that performs one function. The concern is that the code for those similar functions may become so intertwined (or intertwingled, as Tom DeMarco likes to say) that a subsequent attempt to modify one of the functions will inadvertently damage or destroy another function in the same module.

[3] Communicational cohesion occurs when all elements of one module process the same input and/or produce the same output.

3.   No module is allowed to "remember" anything from one execution to the next. This means that the use of "first-time" switches, or internal state maintenance, is not allowed.

4.   No "manager" module is allowed to do any work; that is, any module that is not at the bottom of the hierarchy must consist only of CALL statements imbedded within loops and decisions.

Actually, these rules are quite reasonable for medium-sized and large projects, but you can imagine how your designers and programmers would squawk if you imposed such rules on a 200-statement COBOL application.

The situation is even worse in some MIS organizations where applications are developed using fourth-generation languages; spreadsheet packages; database management packages such as dBASE-III or Reflex; and such packages as HyperCard on the Apple Macintosh. Because these packages often allow small, simple problems to be implemented in a matter of minutes (well, to be honest, it's often more like an hour!), the programmers don't want to spend time doing *any* design. Instant gratification is the order of the day.

Obviously, only you or the standards department can decide how formal you want to be. If your programmers work individually on small programs that require only a day of work, then many of the principles of structured design will be useful, but you may decide not to enforce them. For medium-sized projects requiring two or three programmers for a few months, some of the formality of structured design is appropriate— and it will prove helpful. On big projects, one should be a fanatic.

Be careful of one thing: Development projects may *appear* to be one-person projects, when in fact they are small pieces of a large, integrated system. Many organizations for years believed in the theory that a big system can be broken into small pieces, each of which can be coded by individual programmers as if each comprised an independent project. While that theory is absolutely valid, we must recognize that the principles of structured design dictate *how* to break a system into small, independent pieces (modules) so that they can later be integrated successfully into a whole system.

Also, consider that the maintenance costs of numerous small programs will eventually add up. Even if it does take somewhat longer to develop a small program with the formality of structured design, it may be worth the effort in terms of easier maintenance.

5.2.4   Complaints of inefficiency

Some designers and managers still think in second-generation terms, when every microsecond was important and each byte of memory was to be cherished as a precious national resource; and today, some designers are building systems on small microcomputers with limited memory, or embedded real-time systems with extraordinarily tight response time requirements. To such people, certain aspects of structured design may be an anathema. For instance, the extensive use of subroutines suggests some inefficiency; the emphasis on highly cohesive modules points to even more inefficiency; and the guideline that data should be passed through a parameter list instead of being placed in a globally accessible area raises howls of anguish from programmers, designers, and managers alike.

Efficiency is essential in some cases, such as in real-time systems or systems with high volumes of transactions, and clearly nobody wants a grossly inefficient system. Nevertheless, we can usually argue that most of the hue and cry about efficiency is irrelevant in today's computer systems.

As a manager, keep the following points regarding efficiency in mind:

1.   In most cases, neither you nor the computer operations manager knows whether or not your computer systems are efficient. More significantly, nobody really cares. If one of your programmers writes a program that consumes one minute of CPU time, for example, does anybody know whether it could have been written so as to consume only 30 seconds of CPU time? Does anybody care?

2.   Efficiency seems to be influenced more by the quality of the programmer than by any specific techniques of design or programming. Recall the Sackman experiment [Sackman et al., 1968] discussed in Chapter 2: Picking a capable programmer can improve the efficiency of your systems by a factor of ten.

3.   Most surveys have suggested that diligent use of structured design adds an overhead of about 10 to 15 percent to the CPU time and memory requirements

of a program. This is a modest price to pay, particularly because recent studies (see, e.g., [Jones, 1986]) indicate that structured design improves development productivity by approximately 25 percent, and reduces maintenance costs by as much as 90 percent.

4. A number of studies have confirmed that the "90-10" rule applies to computer programs, too. That is, 10 percent of the code in a typical system will consume 90 percent of the CPU time. A classic study by Knuth [Knuth, 1971] indicated that 5 percent of the code in a program consumed 50 percent of the total CPU time. Since only a small portion of the code is significant in terms of efficiency, the strategy should be to get the system working, then isolate the inefficient parts, and optimize them. One approach might be recode the critical module in a lower-level language like C, and then use an optimizing compiler.

5. In general, it is easier to make a working system efficient than it is to make an efficient system work correctly. Get the system to operate first. *Then* worry about efficiency.

6. Programmers are notoriously poor at anticipating *which* 5 percent of their code will be inefficient. They frequently blame their efficiency problems on the part of the system they found most difficult to design and code, but the problem usually turns out to be an innocent-looking module that is chewing up 75 percent of the CPU time. This is particularly true when using very high-level languages, for it may not be evident what kind of machine code is generated for a simple, compact high-level statement.

5.2.5 Difficulty defining the proper role of systems analyst, designer, and programmer

An unfortunate side effect of using structured design is the identification of an organizational problem in many MIS departments. Systems analysts spend most of their time talking to the users, and only occasionally do a little design. Programmers spend most of their time writing COBOL statements, and occasionally do a little design. As a result, nobody does any serious design, and the question of who should learn structured design is unresolved.

Both groups should learn structured design, since it is applicable to systems analysis (more on this in Chapter 14), systems design, and program design.

In addition, MIS organizations should consider a new role called the "systems architect." The reasons for this are that a vacuum exists in the design area of most companies, and a majority of the systems analysts and programmers I meet are incompetent to fill the design role without serious changes in the way they perform their jobs.

This is particularly true of systems analysts, many of whom have achieved their current positions after years in the user area of the organization. Thus, while they may be competent in describing the user's business and problem (a crucially valuable skill, to be sure), they don't know a computer from a football.

Other systems analysts may have spent their formative years of their career on the IBM 1401; consequently, they design systems as if they were still working on an IBM 1401. This group, in particular, is guilty of premature packaging— chopping a system into distinct programs at the beginning of the project and dictating that all information will be passed from program to program via magnetic tape files— sometimes disguised as sequential disk files. All of this runs on a mainframe computer with 100 megabytes of memory, capable of holding all of the code in memory at once, and capable of passing all data from module to module through memory.

Meanwhile, the programmers in some organizations have never had the opportunity (or perhaps have never shown the talent) to carry out any real *design* at the architectural level. They expect to be given a complete design, from which they can happily figure out which assortment of COBOL statements will most befuddle the unfortunate maintenance programmer.

Considering these problems, perhaps we do need a new breed of person in our organization. We should distinguish between "business systems design" (talking to the user to find out what he wants), "architectural design" (determining the structure of modules that will solve a well-specified problem), and "procedural design" (developing the sequence of statements, and the decisions and iterations, that will carry out the module's required function).

Chapter 6
STRUCTURED PROGRAMMING

Having addressed top-down design and structured design in the preceding two chapters, we turn now to programming—specifically, to structured programming, the technique often regarded as the first of the structured techniques.

In keeping with the format of the previous two chapters, I will begin with a brief technical overview of structured programming. Most of this chapter's discussion, however, deals with the problems you are likely to have in implementing structured programming within your organization.

6.1 AN OVERVIEW OF STRUCTURED PROGRAMMING

The term structured programming was coined by Professor Edsger Dijkstra in the mid-1960s, and first came to the attention of a significant number of people at a NATO Software Engineering conference in 1968 (see [Dijkstra, 1976]). Since then, the topic has been widely studied and discussed in academic circles. Indeed, most universities now teach structured programming as the "standard" approach to programming.

The concept of structured programming was adopted early by certain sectors of industry as well. IBM, after being exposed to structured programming at that same 1968 NATO conference, introduced the technique on an experimental basis on a project that came to be known as the New York Times system (see [Baker, 1972] for a full description of the project). Finding it a tremendously successful technique, IBM adopted it throughout its own organization and then introduced it to its many customers. Indeed, IBM's influence during the 1970s is one reason why many MIS organizations first became involved with structured techniques.

So what *is* structured programming? From a technical point of view, it could be described as the theoretical basis for all procedural logic—that is, for the kind of logic that we have described traditionally with a flowchart. In the mid-1960s, two

Italian computer scientists, Corrado Böhm and Guiseppe Jacopini proved in [Böhm, 1966] that any procedural logic could be derived from combinations of three basic flowcharts, as shown in Figure 6.1.

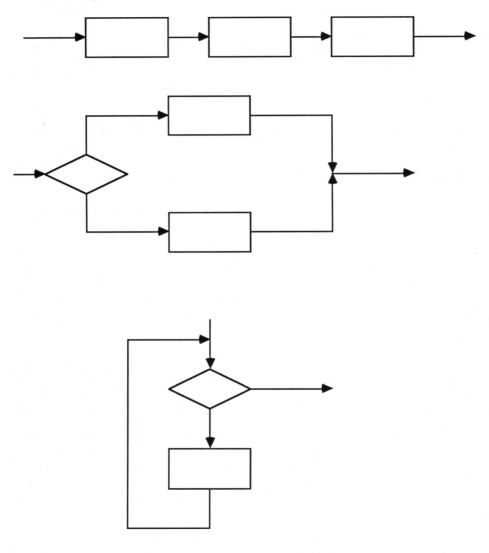

Figure 6.1: **Three flowcharts of structured programming**

These three flowcharts form the core of structured programming. They are popularly referred to as "sequence," IF-THEN-ELSE, and DO-WHILE. Some cynics dub them the holy trinity of structured programming. The discovery that these three are sufficient for any arbitrarily complex logic is profoundly important, just as important as was the engineer's discovery that any form of hardware logic can be constructed from combinations of AND, OR, and NOT gates.

Not only are the three flowchart elements in Figure 6.1 simple, but they also have the desirable property of being "black-box" in nature. That is, they are all characterized by having a single entry point and a single exit point. This feature, too, is profoundly important: It means that we can take any program's flowchart that has been constructed from the three basic forms and examine any part of it as a stand-alone black-box. In contrast, conventional flowcharts wander from page to page to such a degree that neither the development programmer nor the maintenance programmer has the faintest idea of what the logic is supposed to accomplish.

Note that our discussion thus far has been in terms of flowcharts; as we will see in Chapter 7, flowcharts have been abandoned in most MIS organizations. Part of the reason for leading into the discussion of structured programming in this way is that flowcharts are clean and simple: They are language-independent and vendor-independent. In addition, structured programming was developed in this fashion. The Böhm and Jacopini paper that provided the theoretical basis for structured programming used flowcharts, rather than a specific programming language.

However, most programmers obviously *do* use specific programming languages— COBOL, FORTRAN, Pascal, C, BASIC, Ada, and a vast number of less common languages. So, the next obvious question is: What does structured programming mean in terms of specific programming languages?

Quite simply, it means that we should write computer instructions that are direct implementations of the flowcharts shown in Figure 6.1. Obviously, since all programming languages have a variety of simple instructions which can be arranged in a linear sequence, following that guideline should be no problem.

All programming languages also have some facility for making binary decisions, although not all make it easy to program the kind of decision structure shown in Figure 6.1, in which control returns to a common point. What we need is a programming language that implements the IF-THEN-ELSE construct directly. Since we want the ability to build combinations of these structures, we also want a programming

language that allows us to code *nested* IF-THEN-ELSE
structures.

Finally, we want our programming language to give us the
facility to form loops, especially simple loops of the type shown
in Figure 6.1. In languages such as Pascal, Ada, and PL/I, such a
loop is implemented directly with the verb DO-WHILE. In less
formal languages like COBOL, we can use the verbs PERFORM-
UNTIL and PERFORM-VARYING. Older versions of such
languages as FORTRAN and BASIC provided only the special
"counting" loop.

In the more powerful programming languages, we find all
of the verbs with which to implement the flowcharts of Figure
6.1. As Böhm and Jacopini have demonstrated, we don't need
anything else. In particular, the unconditional branching
instruction—the GOTO statement—becomes superfluous. In
languages like Pascal, C, and PL/I, it can be eliminated without
causing anyone significant trouble. Indeed, many introductory
university courses in Pascal do not teach students anything about
the GOTO statement.

As you may be well aware, structured programming is often
described simply in terms of this last point: GOTO-less
programming. As discussed later in this chapter, much of the
controversy surrounding structured programming has been
concerned with the lowly GOTO statement.

To understand why there is such sentiment against GOTO
statements, put yourself in the position of a maintenance
programmer for a moment. Imagine that it's 3 a.m., and you're
sound asleep in your warm, comfortable bed. Suddenly the
phone rings; it's the computer operator telling you that the
WIDGET system has just crashed in the middle of a four-hour
production run.[1] The president of the company has insisted
that the output from the WIDGET system be on his desk by 9
a.m., so you've got to come into work to fix the bug.

Let's further imagine that you did not write the code for
the WIDGET system; it was written by Charlie, who moved to
Afghanistan to join the rebels as soon as the system appeared to
be working. You were assigned the job of maintaining the
WIDGET system, in addition to three other systems, and your

---

[1] In case you don't think this happens, take a look at the statistics in [Lientz, 1980]:
Approximately 9 percent of the typical MIS maintenance budget is spent on "emergency
debugging," and another 12 percent is spent on "normal debugging."

basic philosophy has been to let sleeping dogs lie. As you learned from an older maintenance programmer, the "golden rule" of maintenance programming is, "If it ain't broke, don't fix it." As a result, you are unfamiliar with the code.

Having staggered to work, you have made it very clear to everyone present that you are interested only in finding and fixing the bug, and then returning to your warm, comfortable bed as quickly as possible. This is not the time to get to know the WIDGET system on an intimate basis, and it is surely not the time to carry on long discussions about structured anything.

Let us assume that the computer operator has given you enough information to determine that the system aborted in an area that corresponds to page 123 of the program listing. Turning to page 123, you find the following code before you:

```
SUBROUTINE GLOP
     MOVE A TO B
     X = X + 1
     CALL  FOO(A,B)
     GO  TO  AFGHANISTAN
     .
     .
     .
```

Of course, your first questions are: What does GLOP do? What is its purpose? The ideal situation would be to find that page 123 of the program listing marks the beginning of some recognizable *function*— computing an employee's gross salary, or computing a square root, or converting an ASCII character string to EBCDIC— that would have been finished by the time we reached the bottom of page 123. But such is probably not the case with subroutine GLOP.

Undaunted, you begin reading the code (note that in order to avoid offending anyone, I have included code that is a mixture of COBOL, FORTRAN, and PL/I). The first statement, as you can see, causes the contents of a variable named A to be moved to a variable named B. That seems simple enough, and you might be inclined to shrug your shoulders and move on to consider the next instruction.

However, there are some important things to understand about that MOVE statement: First, you have unconsciously assumed that the MOVE statement will do what it's supposed to do. If you were a paranoid maintenance programmer, you might doublecheck to ensure that the compiler generated the proper object code for that MOVE statement; and if you were *very* paranoid, you might even check the hardware to ensure that it was executing the assembly language instructions properly.

But chances are that you aren't that paranoid. Besides, it's now 3:30 a.m., and all you want to do is find the bug and go home. From the evidence that the computer operator gave you, you suspect that the bug is somewhere in the logic on page 123, and there is no reason to descend to the lower levels of assembly or machine language unless you must.

So, once again, you probably are ready to read on past the MOVE statement. But wait. We have two more things to say about that innocent MOVE: Note that after MOVEing, the computer goes on to the next instruction. Trivial as this point may seem, *that* is what we depend on in order to be able to ignore the details of the assembly language code that actually carry out the instructions of the MOVE statement.

Also, note that you could and probably *should* do some investigating of the MOVE statement. It is reasonable to ask: *Why* are we moving A to B? Why are we doing it now? What is the purpose, the rationale behind using that instruction? Why did Charlie code it?

Assuming that you could answer these questions, you might then examine the next statement. Evidently, the statement increments a variable X by one. Aside from that, it has the same desirable properties as the MOVE statement: Its details can be ignored for the present time. Assume that the instruction can function correctly for the moment, and that, having incremented X by one, the computer will move on to the next instruction.

That instruction, which is a bit more interesting, reads CALL FOO(A,B). Unfortunately, it is not clear what is happening, other than the obvious fact that a subroutine named FOO is being invoked and that two parameters, A and B, are being passed to it.

At this point, you might be strongly tempted to search through the program listing to find out what FOO is doing. Wrong! To become involved in the details of the subroutine is to destroy much of what we have wanted to accomplish by applying the concepts of top-down design, structured design, and structured programming.

The point is that FOO probably carries out some kind of *function*, although its exact nature certainly is not clear from its name. Let us assume, though, that Charlie left a minimal amount of documentation behind, and that you, as the maintenance programmer, are able to discover quickly (without finding FOO in the program listing) that the purpose of FOO is to compute the square root of its first argument, and return the answer in the second argument.

That's all we need to know. At this point, we should *assume* that FOO computes square roots correctly, *just as we assumed that the MOVE statement works correctly.* If you are ultimately unable to find the bug on page 123, only then can you justifiably explore the logic and coding of FOO. In the meantime, it's long past 3 a.m. and common sense dictates that you restrict your attention *solely* to the logic on page 123.

Note that, as with the MOVE statement, you should ask some intelligent questions concerning FOO, namely: Why compute a square root at this point? Does it make sense to compute the square root of A, as opposed to some other variable? Do I really want to store the answer in B? Indeed, answering these questions might uncover the bug on page 123, and this approach is the kind of top-down debugging that I want to emphasize.

Having laid the groundwork, you can now see why the GOTO statement is such a disaster. Immediately after the CALL FOO statement, which you *assumed* would return, you see a statement that says

GO TO AFGHANISTAN

Ho! ho! Probably the last statement Charlie wrote before he departed, but at 4 a.m. the humor is not amusing. Instead of laughing, you find yourself asking the following pertinent questions:

1.   Where is AFGHANISTAN in the program listing?

2.   Why are we going to AFGHANISTAN?

3.   What are we going to do when we get to AFGHANISTAN?

4.   Most important: Will we ever get back to the code on page 123?

Unfortunately, these questions *cannot* be avoided. It may well be that the instructions at AFGHANISTAN are only minor details, but there is no way to know that, and no way to avoid finding out, as you were able to do with the FOO subroutine.

Thus, you must track down the location of AFGHANISTAN in the program listing, a possibly tedious effort in itself. Chances are, AFGHANISTAN is far away (no pun intended) from page 123. For example, suppose AFGHANISTAN is on page 786, making it necessary for you to do three things:

1.   Stick one finger in the program listing at page 123, in the faint hope that you will eventually get back there.

2.   Carefully remember what the "state of the world" is at this point; that is, remember what variables A, B, and X contain.

3.   Turn to page 786.

Imagine the following code on page 786:

AFGHANISTAN.
   X = X+1
   MOVE B TO C
   GO TO MOZAMBIQUE

The second statement looks simple enough, just another case of incrementing variable X. Now, what did X contain when you go to AFGHANISTAN? You tried to remember all of that before you turned to page 786; but at this hour, it's hard to remember very much, so you quickly turn to page 123 (thank goodness you left your finger stuck in the listing) to refresh your memory, and then return to page 786.

But wait! How do you know that the only way that the program gets to AFGHANISTAN is from the code on page 123? In other words, how do you *truly* know what variable X contains when you begin executing instructions on page 786? Indeed, there may be a dozen or a hundred devious paths that eventually lead to AFGHANISTAN.

At 4 a.m., your temptation would be to ignore this unpleasant thought, and therein lies the source of many a bug. If you decide to change that first instruction at AFGHANISTAN to something like X = X+2, it may well work for the particular case you were following (from page 123), but you may have destroyed things for some other, at this point, completely unknown logic path that also ends at AFGHANISTAN. Thus, you might fix one bug and be able to go home, but the "fix" might introduce a new bug, which will bring you back to the computer room tomorrow night.

Indeed, your troubles are just beginning, for, as you can see, AFGHANISTAN executes two relatively simple statements, and then uses a GOTO to disappear to MOZAMBIQUE.

But where is MOZAMBIQUE? Why are we going there? What is the program going to do when it gets to MOZAMBIQUE? Not knowing the answer to these questions, you have no choice but to stick another finger in the program listing at page 786, and turn to yet another part of the listing.

I think you would agree that after finding three or four such GOTO statements, you would be tempted to give up. You've forgotten where you started, you've run out of fingers to stick in the listing to remind you where you've been, and you don't know where you're going, and you're becoming very sleepy.

This scenario illustrates what structured programming is all about, or, to be more precise, it is the *antithesis* of structured programming. By eliminating GOTO statements, especially the wild GOTOs that jump hundreds of pages in the program listing, and restricting ourselves to combinations of the three Böhm and Jacopini forms, the result is code that can be read and understood, literally, from the top down. If we begin reading code at the top of the page and continue reading in a straight-line fashion, by the time we reach the bottom of the page, we have finished doing something.

The result? First, coding in this manner means that the development programmer can understand what he is doing (which our mythical friend, Charlie, probably didn't). Consequently, he can write more code with fewer bugs, thus becoming more productive and more reliable. If the development programmer understands what he is doing, then the code will probably work. As a result, those early morning telephone calls will diminish. If the maintenance programmer *does* get a middle-of-the-night call, it's more likely that he will be able to find the bug in a reasonable amount of time, as well as fix the problem without introducing any new bugs.

So, this is what structured programming is all about. For more details, you and your programmers might want to consult the references on structured programming in the Bibliography.

6.2   MANAGEMENT PROBLEMS WITH STRUCTURED PROGRAMMING

By now, you should be prepared for a section on problem areas. I suggested in earlier chapters that programmers, designers, and systems analysts run into difficulties trying to implement structured analysis, top-down design, top-down testing, and structured design. Why should things be any easier with structured programming?

Actually, things are much better as we come to the end of the 1980s. Approximately 80 percent of the MIS organizations in the United States now report that their programmers are using structured programming techniques on a consistent basis, and the current generation of computer science students are entering the work force with proper training in structured programming. On the other hand, there is a much larger number of college graduates *not* trained in computer science, who are entering the work force as engineers, accountants, salespeople, and hundreds of other professions— in other words, these are the "users" for whom MIS departments build systems. These young men and women have been exposed to BASIC and LOGO all through their education, and most likely have never learned how to write structured code.

In any case, there *are* management problems. You should be prepared for the following difficulties and complaints:

1.   Eternal arguments over the use of GOTO statements

2.   The myth that GOTO-less code is equivalent to good code

3.   Weaknesses in the syntax of some high-level programming languages

4.   Programmers' ignorance of their programming languages

5.   Difficulty in applying structured programming to assembly language

6.   Problems with old-timer programmers' attitude

7.   Complaints of inefficiency associated with structured programming

8.   Conflicts with old programming standards

9.   Difficulty in enforcing structured programming standards

10. Difficulty in using structured programming in a maintenance environment

11. Problems with nested IF statements

Each of these problems is discussed below.

6.2.1   Arguments over using GOTO statements

The discussion in the previous section illustrates the major arguments against using GOTO statements. It's not that I—or that Dijkstra, Wirth, Böhm, or Jacopini—feel that the GOTO statement is inherently evil. It is true that GOTO is a four-letter word, but it really isn't a Communist plot to overthrow capitalism. On the other hand, what concerns me is that the GOTO statement is potentially dangerous and can easily lead to the kind of programming situation described earlier.

Unfortunately, the issue of GOTO statements has become almost a religious one. To say, "I am writing structured programs," is considered equivalent to saying, "I have cleverly managed to avoid writing any GOTO statements in my program."

By itself, that sort of religious mania might not be so bad. Unfortunately, there are times, in the real world, when one desperately feels a need to write a GOTO statement. The major arguments *in favor* of the GOTO statement are as follows:

*   There are times when the programming language makes it difficult, if not impossible, to describe a simple piece of logic without using a GOTO statement. I will have more to say about this in section 6.2.3.

*   Sometimes a judiciously placed GOTO statement will significantly improve the efficiency of a program, compared to the structured version.

*   One can occasionally argue that a GOTO statement is more readable than the equivalent structured code. A good case is the coding for a premature exit from the middle of a loop: Such a case *can* be coded in a structured fashion, but unless the programming language has special verbs such as BREAK or LEAVE,

it requires extra program flags and some clumsy-looking code.

• Similarly, some programmers argue that GOTO statements are a more readable, more comprehensible alternative to nested IF statements. This argument is discussed in more detail in Section 6.2.11.

• Sometimes the programmer simply can't determine how to express a familiar logic in a structured form because he has spent so many years flowcharting and/or coding logic in an unstructured form.

None of this is worth a major battle. If a programmer considers alternative means of coding some logic and believes that a GOTO statement makes the code more efficient, more maintainable, or easier to understand, then using it is probably legitimate. The easiest way of solving an argument here is to submit the code to a walkthrough, as described in Chapter 9; if the programmer's colleagues also feel that the GOTO statement is a better way to code that module, then it is probably OK.

If the concepts of top-down design and structured design discussed in Chapters 4 and 5 have been employed, then the issue of GOTO statements is not so critical. If structured design concepts had been enforced, the AFGHANISTAN situation described earlier in this chapter would not have occurred: Charlie would have been required to design his system as a collection of small, independent, highly cohesive, loosely coupled modules that could each be coded on a single page. Consequently, there would be no GOTO statements jumping from page 123 to page 786, for they would represent pathological connections. If there were a few GOTOs jumping around *on* page 123, the arguments would probably be minimal.

Structured programming, no matter how brilliant, cannot compensate for poor design and poor systems analysis. Proper structured analysis and structured design are of paramount importance; they far outweigh the impact of structured programming.

Thus, don't let arguments about GOTO statements go on for more than a few moments. Do make sure that your programmer knows how to express a piece of logic in a structured, GOTO-less fashion before deciding whether to use the GOTO statement. If all else fails, there is the Ashcroft-Manna technique,[2] described in Chapter 4 of [Yourdon, 1976]. This technique is guaranteed to give a programmer a structured means of expressing *any* logic.

6.2.2   The myth that structured code is good code

Just as there is the belief that GOTO statements are intrinsically bad, there is a myth that structured, GOTO-less code *must* be good; merely by eliminating the GOTO statements from code, one has readable, understandable, perfectly maintainable, error-free code.

Clearly, this is not so. One can *always* write bad code if one tries hard enough. With or without GOTO statements, a programmer can construct obscure, hopelessly inefficient, perverse code. In fact, if a programmer decides that he doesn't like the idea of structured programming, he may deliberately write bad code in order to demonstrate that structured programming is a bad idea.

Programmers commonly write structured code that is the following:

- *Inefficient*— hopelessly so, as illustrated by

```
DO I = 1 TO 3
     CASE I OF
          CASE 1
               A = 13
          CASE 2
               B = 75
          CASE 3
               C = 86
     END CASE
END DO
```

when he could have written

```
A = 13
B = 75
C = 86
```

If that code isn't perfectly clear to you, have one of your programmers explain it to you. Such gross

---

[2] Briefly, the Ashcroft-Manna technique is a deterministic algorithm for converting an arbitrary program into a finite-state automaton.

inefficiencies often occur as a result of a fatal fascination with all the structured programming verbs.

- *Incorrect*— Some programmers write structured code that has more bugs than their previous unstructured code. This is sometimes the result of weaknesses in the programming language (see Section 6.2.3) or the result of the programmer's ignorance of certain features of his programming language (see Section 6.2.4).

- *Obscure*— The coding shown above is a good example of obscure code. Obscure code also commonly results from the programmer trying to squeeze too many levels of nested loops and decisions onto one page of coding. Perhaps the worst offender, though, is one who uses the nested IF statement, which I will discuss in Section 6.2.11.

6.2.3   Weaknesses in high-level programming languages

During the 1970s, one of the most significant problems in implementing structured programming was that many of the common high-level programming languages interfered with the programmer's natural inclination to design and code structured logic. Such a criticism was never really valid with languages like Pascal, C, Ada, PL/I, or Modula-2; however, it was a reasonable criticism with such languages as COBOL, FORTRAN, and BASIC.

New versions of these languages (e.g., True BASIC, COBOL-86, and FORTRAN-77) have added nested IF-THEN-ELSE constructs, DO-WHILE constructs, and the other features necessary for structured programming. Thus, if your maintenance programmers are still maintaining code written in an ancient, vintage-1968 version of COBOL, FORTRAN, or BASIC, you will definitely have problems. Most of the ugly features of a programming language can be hidden by a *preprocessor*, such as METACOBOL for COBOL, or RATFOR for FORTRAN. However, you might be justifiably reluctant to make *any* changes to patched-up, delicate old systems. If this is your situation, structured programming won't be of any help.

6.2.4   Programmers' ignorance of their programming language

There is an even more serious problem than high-level languages lacking structured programming constructs: Many programmers are ignorant of the language features that must be used to write structured code. There is a certain irony to this, particularly with a language such as PL/I. As I pointed out above, PL/I is one of the more suitable languages for structured programming, for it has a DO-WHILE, an IF-THEN-ELSE, and various other powerful features. Most people assume that, since PL/I is a powerful language, PL/I programmers must be powerful programmers. That is, almost everyone assumes that PL/I programmers write good structured code, because, after all, their language makes it so easy.

The trouble is that many PL/I programmers have *never* used a DO-WHILE statement and have no idea how it works. Many of them have never used a nested IF statement and have used a simple IF-THEN-ELSE only on rare occasions. Many of them, you see, are still writing a disguised form of FORTRAN, or COBOL, or RPG, or assembly language in PL/I. One survey of more than a hundred commercial applications at a large automobile manufacturer showed that, in 100,000 lines of PL/I code, there were only *11* DO-WHILE statements, and that in approximately 20 percent of the programs, there were *no* IF-THEN-ELSE statements.

Things are not much better in the COBOL world. Many veteran COBOL programmers I have encountered have never used a CALL statement for invoking subroutines, except possibly to CALL a database management function provided by vendor-supplied system software. Similarly, a majority have never used a nested IF statement and don't understand how a simple IF-THEN-ELSE works. Many have never used the PERFORM-UNTIL iterative statement, and are extremely cautious about using the special "counting" loop, PERFORM-VARYING. And only a few COBOL programmers have any concept of a block structure—that is, a group of statements that can be treated as if they were a block or integral unit.

So, what should we do? Shoot all of our existing programmers and get new ones? The idea is tempting, particularly since most universities now teach programming students how to use those features of the language they need to know in order to write structured code. The real problem is training. The reason most PL/I programmers don't know how to use a DO-WHILE statement is that nobody ever taught them how, and nobody ever suggested that it would be a good idea to use such features of their language.[3]   Similarly, nobody in the 1960s and 1970s taught the majority of today's battle-scarred, veteran COBOL programmers how to use PERFORM-UNTIL or IF-THEN-ELSE or any of the other structured aspects of their language.

So, if you want your programmers to write good structured code, it may be wise to send them back to school to review the fundamentals of their language. It should take only a day or two of their time, and the effort will be repaid many times over.

6.2.5   Difficulty in applying structured programming to assembly language

The reaction of an assembly language programmer to structured programming is fairly predictable: "What does all of this have to do with me? How can I possibly eliminate GOTO statements in an assembly language program? Everyone knows that assembly language programs have to jump around!"

To answer this, remember the basic Böhm and Jacopini theorem: Any procedural logic can be flowcharted in a structured fashion, as a combination of one-in-one-out blocks of logic.   That statement is true regardless of whether we are flowcharting the logic for a payroll system, order entry system, compiler, real-time operating system, or anything else. And it is true whether that logic is eventually coded in COBOL, Ada, or assembly language.

The nice thing about COBOL, Ada, and most of the high-level programming languages is that they *directly* implement the structured flowcharts that we saw in Figure 6.1. In assembly language, we have to hand-compile our structured flowcharts into the primitive instructions that make the machine work.

So, my answer to the assembly language programmer is, "Yes, you have to use branching instructions in your program. But your code should be a direct implementation of well-structured flowcharts; your code should consist of blocks, each with one entry and one exit." In addition, I offer the following suggestions about writing structured programs in assembly language:

---

[3] The same survey mentioned above, in which virtually none of the PL/I programmers used a DO-WHILE, also found that 50 percent of the verbs in the PL/I language had essentially *never* been used. PL/I is such a rich language that most programmers learn only the subset they need to get along, which, of course, is exactly the same phenomenon that one finds in English: Most people use only a few hundred words to carry on their day-to-day conversation.

1.   *Stop using assembly language.* Woodstock and the 1960s are behind us; only mad dogs and Englishmen use assembly language today.   If you must write extremely efficient programs, use a language like C. Remember, optimizing compilers never get tired; human programmers do.   While it is still true that the best human programmer can write an assembly language program that is 5 to 10 percent more efficient than the code produced by an optimizing compiler, such compilers routinely outperform average human programmers.

2.   If your programmers are working on a large mainframe or mini computer, you should consider using macros to implement DO-WHILE, IF-THEN-ELSE, and so on.   Several standard packages are available, for example, on IBM mainframes, and your programmers should be ingenious enough to develop them on other computers if the computer has a decent macro assembler.

3.   Consider using a preprocessor that gives you the ability to write IF-THEN-ELSE and DO-WHILE statements intermingled with ordinary assembler statements.   This is useful if your vendor's assembler does not have a macro capability.

4.   Pester your vendor for a systems implementation language.   IBM's PL/S language is one example, and Control Data's SWL (Software Writer's Language) is another; most hardware vendors have such a language for developing their system software. Alternatively, consider a language like PL/360, described in [Wirth, 1968].   These languages generally provide the structuring verbs, *plus* powerful means of representing data, *plus* the normal assembly language instructions.

5.   Require your programmers to describe their procedural logic in a pseudocode, something that resembles an informal mixture of English and Pascal, *but is structured.*   This pseudocode expression of their logic can serve as a comment preceding the assembly language implementation.   Pseudocode comments may also be placed in the comment field beside each assembly language instruction, but my experience has been that programmers won't

maintain these comments as the code is modified during maintenance.

6.   Ignore structured programming in an assembly language environment.   Put your energy into structured analysis and design.   If your systems analysts and designers follow the guidelines in Chapters 3, 4, and 5, the code within each small module won't be difficult to develop.

6.2.6   Problems with old-timers' attitudes

I discussed most of the common attitude problems in Chapter 2; remember that you *will* encounter some emotional objections, mostly from programmers who have been coding for ten years without ever being told *how* to code.

Many of the negative reactions to structured programming have occurred in MIS organizations that enforced GOTO-less programming with a religious fervor.   If you are prepared to let your programmers stick an occasional GOTO into their code, particularly to compensate for limitations in their programming language, chances are they won't protest quite so loudly.

6.2.7   Complaints of inefficiency

Most of these complaints are similar to the complaints about the inefficiency of structured design.   Most of the answers are the same, too. Rather than repeating the philosophical points made in Section 5.2.5, I will mention only a few points peculiar to structured programming.

Many programmers do think that structured programming leads to less efficient code.   Why?   There are a few consistent arguments:

1.   The IF-THEN-ELSE statement occasionally gene-rates somewhat less efficient code than the programmer could have written with GOTO statements.   Several years ago, the difference in efficiency may have been significant, often a factor of two or more.   Today, the programmer can assume that at worst the IF-THEN-ELSE statement might cost him a microsecond or two, and possibly an extra byte of storage.

2.   A religious interpretation of structured programming may lead to a few extra program flags and switches

(mostly so that the programmer can exit abruptly from the middle of a loop). This may cost a microsecond or two, and an extra byte or two of memory. Big deal.

3. In a few cases, structured programming requires the programmer to duplicate small blocks of code, rather than using a GOTO to jump into the code from several different places (recall the AFGHANISTAN example earlier in this chapter). As a result, the program is slightly larger than it would otherwise have been.

In almost all such cases, we are talking about microseconds of CPU time, whereas the real issue of efficiency involves hours of computer time; *real* efficiency is almost always achieved by intelligent systems design, not tricky coding.

6.2.8   Conflicts with old programming standards

Another potential problem is that the techniques of structured programming may conflict with your organization's programming standards. But if this is true, it probably means that the standards were written in 1968. And if *that* is true, then I guarantee that none of your programmers are reading the manuals. Throw them out.

I will discuss the whole issue of standards for structured systems development in Chapter 12. In the meantime, you may want to examine the sample programming standards for COBOL and PL/I in Appendices A and B.

6.2.9   Difficulty enforcing structured programming standards

An objection relating to standards enforcement is often raised at this point: "Assuming that we have programming standards that are compatible with structured programming, how do we enforce them? How do we ensure that a programmer uses a GOTO only when necessary?"

If, as a manager, you wish to enforce dogmatic standards, there is a simple answer: Build or purchase a standards-enforcing package and insist that all new programs be run

through the package before being put into production.[4]   That
way, you can ensure that nobody uses any GOTO statements (if
that's what you want), that nobody has more than three levels of
nested IF statements (if that's what you desire), and that
everyone has followed whatever other standards you've decided
to enforce.

However, most organizations have "soft" standards or
guidelines which are to be interpreted by the programmers with
a certain degree of common sense.   Thus, we normally see
standards like, "Don't use GOTO statements unless you have to,
or unless you honestly think the code would be more
understandable."

How do you ensure that standards of this type are put into
practice?   Use structured walkthroughs or team programming.
If the entire project team thinks that the code is good code,
then it probably *is* good code, whether or not it has GOTO
statements.   Walkthroughs are discussed in more detail in
Chapter 10.

6.2.10 Difficulty in using structured programming in a maintenance environment

I observed in Chapter 2 that 50 percent or more of the
data processing effort in many organizations today is
maintenance, patching, correcting, and improving existing
programs.   Most, if not all, of these programs were written in an
unstructured fashion.   What relevance does structured
programming have in such an environment?

The advantages of structured programming may influence
an organization to rewrite an old application sooner than would
have been politically possible otherwise.   Also, if large chunks of
code are to be changed or inserted into an existing program, it
should be possible to do such work in a structured fashion.

Many organizations are seriously examining the idea of
"restructuring": converting their unstructured programs into
equivalent structured programs.   The Böhm and Jacopini
theorem provides the theoretical basis for such a conversion,
and several software vendors offer a conversion programs and

---

[4] Even better, get a software metrics package that will analyze your programs, using either
the Halstead or McCabe complexity formulas, and tell you how complex the code is. One
such package is PC-Metric, available from SET Laboratories, P.O. Box 03627, Portland,
OR 97203.

conversion services.[5]   Before you jump at such a solution, though, consider the following problems:

- After five or ten years of maintaining a rotten old program, your maintenance programmers may finally *understand* it; also, they will come to feel a pride of ownership, and they may actively *like* the program, just as parents will sometimes give more love to a handicapped child than to their other children. A restructuring program would rearrange the code so that they probably wouldn't understand it any more. Thus, it is often a good idea to use the restructuring program immediately after (or immediately before) a new maintenance programmer has been assigned the responsibility of maintaining a grungy, old program.

- A restructuring program is usually based on the assumption that the program obeys the legal syntax of the language.   This is not always true, and is particularly invalid for those programs written in COBOL. Programmers have a way of using undocumented, illegal features of the language that should not work, but *do*. A restructuring program would usually upset this delicate balance.

- A restructuring program cannot transmute lead into gold. It cannot convert a truly bad program into a truly good program. If *can* eliminate GOTO statements and "dead" code (code that cannot ever be executed, because the flow of control will never reach it—but which the maintenance programmer is reluctant to throw away), and it will usually improve the organization of the procedural logic. But there is always the chance that it will do nothing more than transform a bad unstructured program into an equally bad structured program.

Another problem is that if you teach your maintenance programmers about structured programming, they will become frustrated if they are sent back to their department to continue patching unstructured rat's-nest code. However, failing to teach maintenance programmers anything about structured programming leads to the converse problem: The first time they are

---

[5] Among the vendors who provide restructuring programs are IBM; Peat, Marwick, Mitchell, which offers *Structured Retrofit*; and Language Technology, Inc., in Cambridge, MA, which offers *Recoder*.

given a *structured* program to maintain, they will be nervous. "What's this?" they'll ask.   "Nested IF statements? And subroutine calls? My God! I can't read any of this!"

Also, the first few structured programs written by your development programmers may be somewhat difficult to maintain.   As I suggested earlier, a structured GOTO-less program is not necessarily a good program; and until your programmers fully understand what they are doing, they may actually write some bad structured code.   Your maintenance programmers will certainly let you know, and you should listen to them.

6.2.11   Difficulties with nested IF statements

The last problem area discussed in this chapter is perhaps the most pervasive one: Programmers seem to have great difficulty writing code of the following form:

```
IF MARITAL-STATUS = MARRIED
    IF SEX = MALE
        IF AGE GREATER THAN 30
            BLAH
            BLAH
            BLAH
        ELSE
            BLAH
            BLAH
    ELSE
        IF AGE GREATER THAN 45
            BLAH
            BLAH
        ELSE
            BLAH
            BLAH
ELSE
    IF MARITAL-STATUS = SINGLE
etc.
```

This is the infamous nested IF. Don't worry if you find it a little difficult to understand; your programmers generally do, too.

Why is the issue of nested IF statements associated with structured programming? Simply because the GOTO statement has been taken away. Previously, your programmers would have written code like the following:

```
IF MARITAL-STATUS = MARRIED AND SEX=MALE AND AGE
        GREATER THAN 30 GO TO X-ROUTINE
ELSE GO TO Y-ROUTINE.
```

Without his GOTO statement, the programmer may find that he is coding more and more IF-THEN-ELSE statements nested inside other IF-THEN-ELSE statements.

Without becoming too deeply enmeshed in technical issues, I offer the following suggestions:

1. Many of the problems raised above are *training* problems, as I observed in Section 6.2.4. Most of your programmers have probably never been taught how the IF-THEN-ELSE statement works. Give your programmers a refresher training class, and most of your problems will go away.

2. Attitude may be part of the problem: Some programmers just don't like the ELSE statement. This is one time when you may want to back off from a dogmatic interpretation of GOTO-less programming, and let them do what they want. Make sure, though, that they know what they're doing and that they are using the GOTO statement because they sincerely believe the code is easier to read. Many programmers who use this argument don't want to admit that they haven't figured out how to eliminate their GOTO statements.

3. Many programmers confuse nested IF statements with something quite different: compound Boolean expressions. Some programmers say, "I don't like nested IF statements because I always get into trouble with statements like this: **IF X NOT EQUAL Y OR Z THEN GO TO AFGHANISTAN.** True, that statement is messy, but it has nothing to do with the problem of nested IF statements. While you're giving your programmers a refresher course on nested IFs, though, you might also give them a short course on Boolean logic. Most programmers sorely need it!

4. Many programmers confuse nested IFs with CASE structures. There are many situations, for example, in which the programmer wants to write

        IF MARITAL-STATUS = MARRIED
            BLAH
            BLAH
        ELSE
            IF MARITAL-STATUS = SINGLE
                BLAH
                BLAH

```
ELSE
      IF MARITAL-STATUS = DIVORCED
            BLAH
            BLAH
      ELSE
            IF MARITAL-STATUS = WIDOWED
                  BLAH
                  BLAH
            ELSE
                  PRINT
                  "ILLEGAL MARITAL STATUS".
```

The significant point is that the example above is not a nested IF, but instead a simple either-or situation. Either a person is married, or single, or divorced, or widowed. We should write this logic in the following way (assuming we are using a programming language that does not support the CASE statement directly):

```
IF MARITAL-STATUS = MARRIED
      BLAH
      BLAH
ELSE IF MARITAL-STATUS = SINGLE
      BLAH
      BLAH
ELSE IF MARITAL-STATUS = DIVORCED
      BLAH
      BLAH
ELSE IF MARITAL-STATUS = WIDOWED
      BLAH
      BLAH
ELSE
      PRINT "ILLEGAL MARITAL STATUS".
```

When a case is written like this, it becomes obvious that we could string *hundreds* of these ELSE-IFs together without making the code more difficult to understand, because we are only thinking about one IF at a time.

5.   Occasionally, there are complaints about the formatting of nested IF statements. Note how the first version of our MARITAL-STATUS example above was indented several spaces for each level; after five or six levels, we run out of room. As I implied, though, this is sometimes a false issue: If the code is written in the ELSE-IF style shown in the second version, there should be no problem.

6.   Programmers sometimes complain that it is difficult to understand more than a few levels of nested IFs. Indeed it is. The problem is that of a human trying

to comprehend a difficult logical statement, *not* of whether the computer can parse a nested IF. Recognizing that the problem is a human one, we can draw on a wealth of experience and studies of human ability to understand complexities. Studies by Noam Chomsky (in the field of linguistics) and Gerald Weinberg (in the programming field) suggest that very few people can understand more than three levels of nested IFs.

7.   If the application requires more than three levels of nested decisions, the programmer should break it into several pieces. That is, separate modules should be written so that they can be comprehended separately and independently. Thus, the example at the beginning of this section might have been coded as follows:

```
IF MARITAL-STATUS = MARRIED
    IF SEX = MALE
        PERFORM MARRIED-MALE-ROUTINE
    ELSE
        PERFORM MARRIED-FEMALE-ROUTINE
ELSE
    etc.
```

8.   Finally, many nested IF problems are an indication that the programmer is unfamiliar with decision tables. The code at the beginning of this section, for example, dealt with at least three different variables: marital status, sex, and age. If we wish to recognize five different kinds of marital status, then there are 5*2*2=20 different combinations of these three variables; and no matter whether the programmer uses GOTO statements or nested IF statements, he has to make sure that the has considered all 20 different combinations. What leads to bugs is the common tendency to forget a few of those combinations or confuse them. Thus, a decision table approach is often the best way to make sure that all combinations are expressed, that redundancies, ambiguities and contradictions have been eliminated, and that the logic is organized in a way that it can be coded trivially. Ask your programmers to draw a decision table for the MARITAL-STATUS problem. If they give you an uncomprehending look, send them back to school for that lesson before you worry about nested IF statements.

Chapter 7
DOCUMENTATION
TECHNIQUES

Up to this point, I have described the most important *technical* aspects of the structured techniques for implementing a series of user requirements: structured analysis, top-down design, top-down implementation, structured design, and structured programming. Now, we can discuss the problem of *documenting* MIS systems produced by these techniques.

You may have noticed that there were few illustrations, particularly technical diagrams, in the previous three chapters. Chapter 5 contained three company organizational charts to illustrate the concept of span of control, and Chapter 6 contained conventional flowcharts to illustrate the basic elements of structured programming. The paucity of illustration was intentional. It is important that the technical concepts of design and programming be understood first, so that the discussion of documentation can build from a solid foundation.

A documentation technique is just what its name implies, and it must not be confused with the concepts of design discussed in previous chapters. A flowchart is only a picture; the act of drawing a flowchart does not ensure a good design. Unfortunately, many systems development professionals confuse this point. When asked whether they are practicing structured design, they say, "Sure! We *must* be using structured design; after all, we're drawing HIPO diagrams and a bunch of other funny-looking charts that we never did before!"

HIPO? What's that? Indeed, what *kind* of documentation are we talking about? It is practical to organize the incredible mass of documentation accompanying MIS development projects into three categories:

- documentation that is traditionally associated with systems analysis

- documentation that describes the *structural* design of a system

- documentation that describes and illustrates the *procedural* design of an individual module of the system, such as that provided by detailed flowcharts.

Some documentation—such as user manuals—will not be influenced by the structured techniques, and it is likely that you will continue using the same form of documentation that you have in the past. However, the structured techniques will probably introduce new documentation methods within your organization, and may cause you to abandon others.

This chapter discusses the impact of structured techniques in each of these areas of documentation and the problems that a manager may have in attempting to implement the techniques. For reasons that will become clear later in the chapter, I begin with the second category.

7.1 DOCUMENTATION TO ILLUSTRATE A SYSTEM'S STRUCTURE

Many organizations have *no* structural documentation techniques. They have narrative specifications, flowcharts, and other bits and pieces of paper. But, in most cases, these classical forms of documentation do little to illustrate the structure or architecture of a system.

For this reason, certain new documentation techniques—introduced in Chapter 5 to illustrate the structured design concepts—have a profound impact within some organizations. For the first time, designer/programmers have been able to *see* the system architecture that they have been designing blindly for years; merely seeing what they are specifying is often sufficient for them to make substantial improvements in the quality of their designs.

The three most important techniques for documenting the structural design are the data flow diagram, the HIPO hierarchy chart, and the structure chart. Each technique is discussed separately.

7.1.1 The data flow diagram

The data flow diagram, or DFD, has also been discussed in the software engineering literature as a "program graph, or a "bubble chart," and is used to show the flow of data through a system. A typical DFD is shown in Figure 7.1.

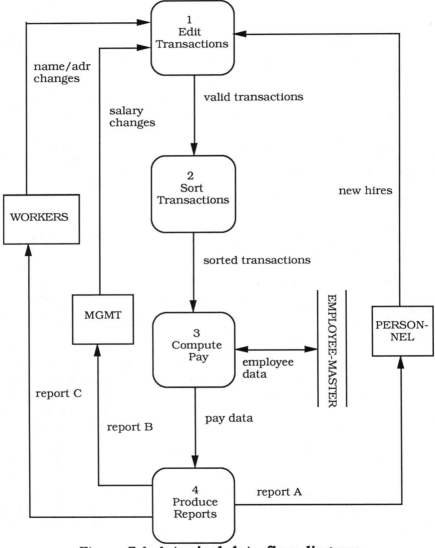

Figure 7.1: **A typical data flow diagram**

    Although described in Chapter 3 as a systems analysis tool, in fact, the DFD was first used as a design tool. Past experience has demonstrated that one of the best ways to create a good design is to translate a conventional narrative English functional specification into a nonprocedural model of the system. Indeed, the data flow diagram is similar to the conventional "system flowchart," except that it does not indicate whether the processing activities shown inside the bubbles will be implemented as modules, programs, job steps, minicomputers, or some other physical form. Similarly, Figure 7.1 does not show whether the data flowing between the processing steps will be implemented by a tape file, disk pack, telephone communication line, or information transmitted through RAM memory. In other words, the DFD is a *logical, abstract* system flowchart.

The DFD is an important tool for the structured design techniques discussed in Chapter 5. In particular, the transform-centered design "cookbook" requires a DFD (which may have been provided by the systems analyst as a result of his interviews with the user) as the first step in what ultimately leads to the systematic development of a good design.

In addition, the system flowchart—a crude, physical form of the DFD—is the most common document that analysts, designers, maintenance programmers, and operations people turn to when they want to see an overview of the current system.

7.1.2   HIPO hierarchy chart

Another documentation concept introduced as a result of the structured techniques is known as HIPO, an acronym for **H**ierarchy, plus **I**nput, **P**rocess, **O**utput. The acronym describes a documentation approach developed and popularized by IBM in the 1970s. Figure 7.2 shows a typical HIPO hierarchy chart, or "visual table of contents" (VTOC).

Another type of HIPO diagram associated with an individual module (i.e., with one of the individual boxes in the VTOC) is discussed in Section 7.2. The diagram shown in Figure 7.2 is intended primarily to illustrate the overall architecture of a system, specifically which modules are subordinate to others, just as in a company organization chart.

The analogy between a company organization chart and a HIPO hierarchy chart is a fairly close one. The HIPO diagram in Figure 7.2 does not show the precise sequence in which modules will be executed, nor any detailed decisions or loops, nor any of the detailed processing steps that take place inside any given module. Since it does provide a good overview of a large system, it is often a useful document for discussions between the user, systems analyst, manager, and programmer. However, many MIS organizations have found that it is difficult, if not impossible, for one document to serve the needs of such a disparate group.

7.1.3   Structure chart

A variation on the HIPO hierarchy chart is known as a structure chart; an example is shown in Figure 7.3. The structure chart conveys much of the same kind of information as the HIPO chart of Figure 7.2; many of the differences are cosmetic. Note, for example, that the lines connecting the various modules in Figure 7.3 are drawn in a "tree-structured" fashion, rather than in the horizontal and vertical manner that characterizes Figure 7.2. Note also that connecting lines terminate in an arrowhead, whereas those in a HIPO chart do not.

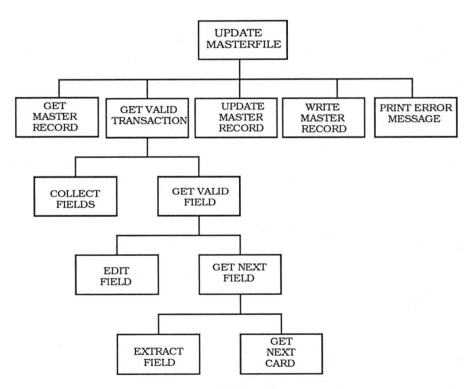

Figure 7.2: **A HIPO hierarchy chart**

Significantly, the structure chart shows occasional procedural detail without becoming bogged down in detail. Figure 7.3 shows the presence of some loops and some decisions that the designer believed were sufficiently important to be shown. Such procedural details could be included with HIPO, too, but the "official" version of HIPO (as documented in [HIPO, 1974]) does not include this information.

Perhaps more important, the interfaces between the modules are shown on the structure chart itself. Figure 7.3 shows the inputs and outputs associated with all of the modules. In contrast, the HIPO hierarchy chart of Figure 7.2 does not show the interfaces between the modules. Some organizations suggest using an "input-output table," a separate document that lists in a tabular fashion each module's inputs and outputs. Other organizations advise that such details be shown on the document that describes the contents of the individual modules— that is, on the detailed HIPO diagram discussed in Section 7.2. I disagree with these variations, and strongly prefer showing the interfaces directly on the diagram, as shown in Figure 7.3. This puts all of the crucial information about the system components, and the interfaces between those components, right in front of the reader's face.

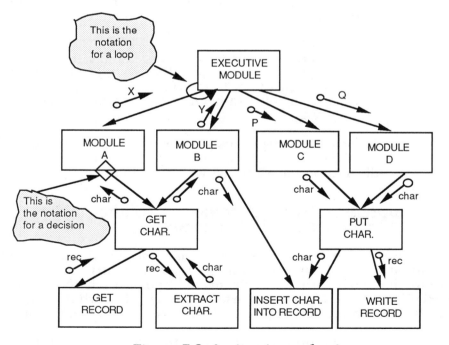

Figure 7.3: **A structure chart**

Many people do not even realize that this is an issue. They draw HIPO hierarchy charts, as in Figure 7.2, and never think about the interfaces until they begin writing the code.   Even then, they may not think about the interfaces formally. All of the system's data may be defined in, and available from, the DATA DIVISION of a COBOL program or equivalent forms of global data in other programs, for example, blank COMMON in FORTRAN. As a result, the interfaces are often not defined formally, but evolve as the code is written.

This is wrong! Wrong, wrong, wrong! To ensure that this critically important interface information is not ignored, designers have found it advantageous to show the intermodule interfaces on the same diagram— on the same sheet of paper, or CRT display screen— as the hierarchical picture of the system. The danger exists that this extra information will clutter the diagram to the point of unreadability, but not if you follow these rules:

- The designer should record the highest level *aggregate* of data being passed between two modules. If module A passes an entire database record to module B, simply write "database record" on the structure chart; do not write the names of all 178 fields in that record.

- If the diagram becomes cluttered, usually the design could be improved.   One of the signs of a good design is a clean set of interfaces with relatively few distinct forms of data being passed between any pair of modules.

- In fact, those designers who draw structure charts of the form shown in Figure 7.3 generally find that the diagram is not cluttered with too much detail.

7.2   DOCUMENTATION TECHNIQUES TO SHOW A SYSTEM'S PROCEDURAL DESIGN

The documentation techniques discussed in the previous section are useful for illustrating the overall structure of a system, but they provide little or no information about the detailed procedural design of each module. So, what impact have the structured techniques had on detailed documentation?

For a few organizations that use the techniques, nothing has changed. The programmers still write detailed flowcharts and detailed narrative specifications for each module. Serious efforts are made to keep this documentation up to date during the maintenance phase of the project, and the maintenance programmer is reasonably confident that the flowcharts resemble the code that he or she is maintaining.

However, not many organizations are continuing to work in this fashion. Although management standards, contractual obligations, and other external pressures may dictate that the detailed flowcharts be produced, they are rarely useful. Programmers will tell you that the reasons are threefold: They never draw the flowchart until *after* the program is working (making it probable that the flowchart shows what the programmer *thinks* his code is doing rather than what his code really *is* doing); flowcharts are not kept up to date during the maintenance effort because it's too much trouble; and, as a result, the maintenance programmers know that they're wasting their time if they look at the flowcharts.[1]

Most MIS organizations that use structured programming have abandoned detailed flowcharts completely. What is substituted? For those organizations that use structured techniques, the answer quite often is: *nothing*. The logic is simple. The structure charts or HIPO diagrams provide an overall picture of the system. If the design has been carried out according to the principles of structured design, it should be possible for the maintenance programmer to maintain or debug one module without having to know anything about the detailed contents of any other module. If the code has been written according to the principles of structured programming, it should be possible to read the code without any comments. In this context, comments could be regarded as an apology for bad code. In any case, there is no point in maintaining the fiction that detailed flowcharts are accurate. Better to have *no* documentation than incorrect documentation that breeds a sense of false security.

Even though such an argument may make eminently good sense, it is considered radical in some MIS organizations. Many such organizations still require some detailed design documentation before the programmer is allowed to write the

---

[1] Some important research carried out by Professor David Scanlan at California State University in Sacramento indicates that students strongly *prefer* flowcharts as a way of learning and understanding complex algorithms for the first time (see [Scanlan, 1987]). This suggests that the main reasons for the contempt shown by "real-world" programmers for flowcharts are (a) they are tedious to draw, and (b) one can't be sure that the flowchart is an accurate representation of code written by someone else. Both of these problems can be solved with automated flowcharting tools, which are widely available for PC-based workstations.

code, and that documentation may be kept in archival files for a period far exceeding the lifetime of the original programmer!

For those who wish to continue to maintain some degree of detailed flowchart, but who are disillusioned with detailed flowcharts, three different types of documentation techniques have gained popularity: pseudocode, detailed HIPO diagrams, and Nassi-Shneiderman charts. Each of these techniques is discussed next.

7.2.1   Pseudocode

Among other terms, pseudocode is also called "Computer Esperanto." In Chapter 3, I referred to it as Structured English. Pseudocode could be defined as "narrative documentation" constructed from combinations of simple, imperative sentences, written in English, containing a single, transitive verb, and a single, nonplural object; IF-THEN-ELSE and DO-WHILE statements of the nature discussed in Chapter 6; and appropriate extensions to structured programming, such as the CASE construct.

An example of pseudocode is shown in Figure 7.4. The example illustrates a general characteristic of pseudocode: It is reasonably well organized and precise, and yet informal enough to be intelligible to both programmers and nonprogrammers. Since it does not require a flowcharting template, pseudocode can be written quickly and easily, and it can be maintained using any word processing system. Thus, it can be kept up to date more readily than a detailed flowchart or HIPO diagram (which means that there is more of a chance that it *will* be kept up-to-date).

There may be another, more significant, advantage to pseudocode: It may be possible to translate the pseudocode logic *mechanically* into object code. Pseudocode compilers are beginning to appear in PC-based CASE workstations (see Chapter 19 for more details on CASE tools); and one could regard new languages like HyperTalk (the underlying programming language for Apple's hypertext HyperCard on the Macintosh) as an executable pseudocode language. The reason this is important is quite simple: It guarantees that the pseudocode *will* be an accurate representation of the actual program. Further, if any subsequent modifications are made during the maintenance phase, they could be made directly to the pseudocode, thus avoiding the problem of obsolete, inaccurate documentation.

MASTER-FILE-UPDATE:
1.   DO WHILE there are more transactions or more
      master records
      a.   IF the master account number is equal to the
            transaction account number
            1.   Update the master record from the
                  transaction record
            2.   Write the updated master record
            3.   Get the next valid transaction record
            4.   Get the next master record
      b.   ELSE:
            1.   IF the master account number is less
                  than the transaction account number:
                  a.   Write the master record
                  b.   Get the next master record
            2.   ELSE
                  a.   Print an error message
                  b.   Get the next valid transaction
2.   Close the transaction file
3.   Close the master file

Figure 7.4: **An example of pseudocode**

Programmers who code in Pascal, Ada, PL/I, or other
powerful high-level languages often remark that the pseudocode
is so close to the real code that it is a waste of time to bother
with it. There is some truth to this. However, remember that a
human reader (who may not be a professional programmer) does
not require the same degree of precision as a compiler.
Pseudocode seems to represent a nice compromise between
precision and informality.

Those who program in COBOL have mixed opinions about
the usefulness of pseudocode. On the one hand, pseudocode is
sufficiently close to COBOL that one wonders whether it provides
any useful information. On the other hand, pseudocode does
allow the programmer to express some structured logic that may
not be directly implementable in COBOL (e.g., REPEAT-UNTIL,
CASE, and BREAK constructs).

For programmers coding in FORTRAN, BASIC, assembly
language, and other primitive programming languages, pseudocode definitely is of value. First, it allows the programmer to
think in a structured fashion, which his real language does not
allow him to do. Second, it provides a convenient basis for
hand-compiling the real assembly language code, in an almost
mechanical fashion. And third, it provides an easy-to-read overview of the procedural logic for the maintenance programmer.

I must admit, however, that some of the concerns about detailed flowcharts are also valid for pseudocode. For example, how does the maintenance programmer know whether the pseudocode approximates real code? How can we ensure that the pseudocode is updated whenever the real code is updated? If pseudocode is easier to write, maintain, and update, it is *more likely* to be kept accurate and up-to-date than are equivalent hand-drawn flowcharts. But there are no guarantees that this will occur; the only long-term solution, as discussed above, is compilable, executable pseudocode.

7.2.2   Detailed HIPO diagrams

Another form of detailed documentation is known variously as a detailed HIPO diagram, a functional HIP diagram, or an IPO diagram. An example of a detailed HIPO diagram is given in Figure 7.5. Note that it can be cross-referenced to the HIPO hierarchy chart in Figure 7.2.

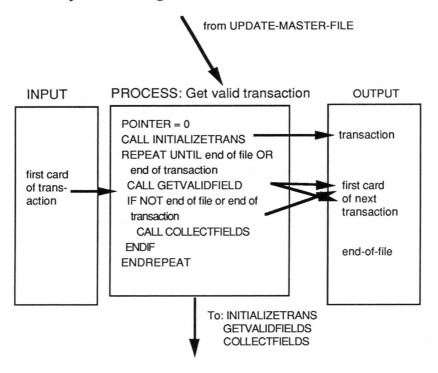

Figure 7.5: **A detailed HIPO diagram**

Detailed HIPO diagrams show the relationship among inputs, processing logic, and outputs of a module in a highly graphic way. That feature is both a blessing and a curse: The diagram can be used as a means of conveying information to users, managers, systems analysts, and programmers. On the other hand, because it is a graphic modeling tool (as evidenced by IBM's providing HIPO templates, HIPO coding pads, and a detailed manual on how to use HIPO, with specific emphasis on techniques for drawing the fat arrows in Figure 7.5 such that they don't cross), a HIPO diagram requires a nontrivial amount of artwork. What are the chances that a detailed HIPO diagram will be updated if there is a change to the module's code at three o'clock in the morning? Indeed, what are the chances that the real code *ever* bears any resemblance to the detailed HIPO diagram? Generally, there is a good chance that after the programmer had put considerable time and effort into developing his detailed HIPO diagram, he found, while writing the code, that he had to change some aspect of the procedural design, whereupon he conveniently "forgot" to redraw his detailed HIPO diagram.

Thus, there is serious concern that detailed HIPO diagrams will degenerate in the same manner as do detailed flowcharts. Several MIS organizations have abandoned detailed HIPO diagrams for this reason.

Finally, note that the central process portion of the detailed HIPO diagram is essentially the same as the pseudocode discussed earlier. The information shown in the input portion and the output portion of the detailed HIPO diagram could be shown on the hierarchy chart or structure chart discussed in Section 7.1. Thus, I conclude that there is nothing really essential in the detailed HIPO diagram that could not be obtained with other techniques, and the extra artwork involved in detailed HIPO diagrams poses serious questions of maintenance.

7.2.3   Nassi-Shneiderman diagrams

Figure 7.6 illustrates a third method of describing the detailed procedural logic within a module. This technique is known as a Nassi-Shneiderman diagram, in honor of the two men who first published their ideas on the subject. On occasion, the diagram in Figure 7.6 is referred to as a Chapin chart, or simply an N-S diagram.

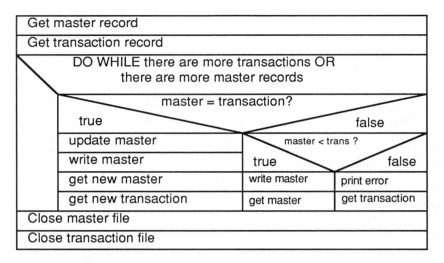

Figure 7.6: **A Nassi-Shneiderman diagram**

Indeed, structured flowchart is an appropriate term. As we can see, Figure 7.6 is similar to a conventional flowchart, except that it has no arrows. Moreover, the three basic ideographs of Nassi-Shneiderman diagrams correspond to the three basic constructs of structured programming. The simplicity of N-S diagrams is appealing, and several organizations have adopted the diagrams for this reason alone. However, many programmers have observed that an N-S diagram is really just "pseudocode with some boxes around it." If that is the case, why not simply write the pseudocode?

7.3   DOCUMENTATION ASSOCIATED WITH SYSTEMS ANALYSIS

A typical MIS project requires a vast amount of additional documentation: feasibility studies, cost/benefit analyses, documentation for the operations staff, user manuals, data dictionaries, and so forth.

Much of this documentation will remain basically unchanged by the introduction of structured system development techniques. However, as we have seen in Chapter 3, the most significant product of the systems analysis phase, the functional specification, has been altered significantly by the introduction of structured analysis.

Also, the documentation tools used for structured analysis are similar to those used for structured design and for structured programming. In fact, such techniques as DFDs, state transition diagrams, and pseudocode were introduced first in the design and programming field, and years later became tools of structured systems analysis.

This similarity of documentation has one advantage that should be emphasized: *consistency*. The documentation produced by structured analysis can be carried straight into the design phase of the project with little or no change, which means that we can minimize the danger that the design will drift away from the specification. In contrast, it used to be common to see a conventional narrative specification translated into a systems design that accomplished slightly more than, slightly less than, or at least something different from, the requirements stated in the specification; and, in the same fashion, the code would accomplish something different than the requirements stated in the original design document.

7.4   MANAGEMENT PROBLEMS ASSOCIATED WITH DOCUMENTATION TECHNIQUES

The primary problem with introducing new documentation methods is the danger that they may suffer the same fate as detailed flowcharts. You should be prepared for this problem, particularly if you decide to adopt the use of detailed HIPO diagrams, Nassi-Shneiderman diagrams, or even pseudo-code in your organization.

In particular, you should assume that your programmers and designers may not keep the HIPO hierarchy charts or structure charts up-to-date. My experience has been that programmers and systems analysts can usually be browbeaten into redrawing at least the high-level structure charts and data flow diagrams whenever a change is made to the design, since the overall design changes much less frequently than the detailed logic within a module. But I have also heard bitter complaints from programmers who resent being forced to redraw a complicated diagram like that in Figure 7.3, just because one interface has been changed or one new function has been added to the system.

I believe there is only one solution to this problem: *automated support for diagramming.* As will be discussed in Chapter 19, PC-based CASE tools now make it possible to create and maintain DFDs, ERDs, STDs, structure charts, and flowcharts and the accompanying narratives. It is generally true that it takes the same amount of time to create the first version of a diagram with a CASE tool as it would have taken by hand; subsequent changes and revisions, though, can be accomplished trivially with the CASE tools. Without automation, I believe that you are kidding yourself, as a manager, if you expect your technicians to produce complex graphic-based documentation and keep those graphics up-to-date.

There are three other problems you should be prepared for when introducing new documentation tools: (a) religious interpretation of the "rules" for drawing the diagrams; (b) the myth that the use of the documentation techniques is equivalent to the act of design; and (c) the myth that acquiring a CASE tool will give one the instant wisdom to know what kind of documentation needs to be developed.

The problem of religious interpretations seems to be most acute in the case of HIPO, although I have seen similar problems with N-S diagrams and DFDs. Some organizations have formulated stringent standards about the way HIPO diagrams should be drawn, thereby creating a tendency to draw diagrams to satisfy the standards manual, rather than to illustrate a computer system.

The second problem concerns me more. Occasionally, when programmers are asked if they use structured design, they respond: "Oh, yes, we're using structured design. We're drawing lots of HIPO diagrams." Implicit in this statement is the assumption that *drawing* a HIPO diagram is the same as *doing* a design.

You should make sure that your programmers and systems analysts understand the distinction between documentation conventions and design principles. Many programmers, for example, would argue that the structure chart shown in Figure 7.3 is bad. Imagine the following dialogue, which I have actually had with various programmers from time to time.

>   Manager: What do you think of this structure chart
>   in Figure 7.3?
>
>   Charlie: I don't like it . . . it's bad.
>
>   Manager: Why? What's wrong with it?

Charlie: Well, the diagram shows a level-two module calling a level-six module, four levels beneath it.

Manager: What's wrong with that?

Charlie: That's not the way they do it in HIPO.

Manager: So what?

Charlie: I just don't like it. I think it would be a better design— at least it would *look* better— if some additional "dummy" modules were introduced at levels three, four, and five, so that we could maintain the convention of a module calling only modules that are one level beneath it.

The problem in this conversation is that Charlie has a certain belief about the way the diagram should look; apparently, the form and symmetry of HIPO appeal to him.   While this response is acceptable, it is bothersome that Charlie's feeling about the preferred form of a *picture* leads him to conclude that the *design* in Figure 7.3 is bad. In fact, it isn't bad: There is nothing wrong with a high-level module calling another module much, much lower in the hierarchy.

Chapter 8
CHIEF PROGRAMMER TEAMS

Chapters 8 and 9 discuss some of the organizational concepts that have been introduced into the MIS community along with structured programming, structured design, and structured analysis.

This chapter treats the Chief Programmer Team Organization, or CPTO. It could have been a very lengthy chapter, but my experiences during the past ten years suggest there is not much point. Most MIS organizations in the real world are *not* using the CPTO concept and have no intention of doing so in the foreseeable future.

However, there are a few organizations—especially small software and consulting firms—that are implementing modified forms of the chief programmer team approach; it does remain as a practical model for organizations that want to "leverage" the talents of their superstar programmers.

As in the previous chapters, I will begin by providing a brief overview of the CPTO concept. In addition, I will point out the reasons why large MIS organizations will probably not even attempt to implement the concept.

8.1   THE MOTIVATION BEHIND THE CPTO CONCEPT

Much of the motivation for the chief programmer team has been discussed in previous chapters. It can be summarized as follows:

- a growing awareness of the Peter Principle

- a realization of the vast differences in the abilities of programmers

- a realization of the communication problems that are inherent in large, classical programming organizations

The Peter Principle, as you may recall, suggests that in most organizations, people are promoted until they reach their level of incompetence. There is an important corollary to the Peter Principle, too:

> *After a certain period of time, all positions in a company are filled by people incompetent to perform them.*

Thus, in the computer field, we find that good junior programmers become senior programmers; good senior programmers become systems analysts; good systems analysts become project leaders; and good project leaders are promoted into the upper echelons of MIS management, and possibly into general management positions.[1]

This phenomenon is one of the major motivations for the CPTO concept. Programmers have an understandable desire to earn more money and gain more stature in their organization—and these goals can usually be attained only by moving into management. (Another alternative is to become an independent consultant, but that has its own risks, which many would rather avoid.) Of course, once a programmer reaches the level of project leader, he considers it beneath his dignity to write code; even if he would *like* to indulge in doing a little coding, he doesn't have the time.

The chief programmer team concept is one solution to this dilemma. The title of *chief programmer* is analogous to that of chief scientist or chief engineer in other disciplines—a master of his or her craft with great skill and many years of experience. If such an attitude could be created, the programmer who is dubbed chief programmer would feel honored to be recognized as a master craftsman; moreover, he would have a tangible incentive if his organization accorded an equivalent salary and status as provided to high-level managers.

What kind of salary? How about $100,000 per year? In some cases, it might be more appropriate to pay $250,000 or even $500,000 a year. You can imagine that such a salary would have quite an impact on programmers' acceptance of the Chief Programmer Team Concept![2]

---

[1] A good case in point is John Reed, the current CEO of Citicorp.

[2] I have difficulty dealing with numbers like these, because my first real programming job paid $3.00 per hour, which I considered an *enormous* increase over the $1.35 hourly wage I had been earning washing dishes in the MIT dormitory cafeteria. The first and second editions of this book were published in the 1970s, before salaries were so drastically affected by runaway inflation. However, the general notion of "superstar" salaries has now become so widespread that half-million dollar salaries are not beyond the realm of imagination.

The second major motivation behind the CPTO concept is the recognition that there is an order-of-magnitude difference in the abilities of programmers. As pointed out in Chapter 2, Sackman's experiment suggests that talent among *experienced, competent* programmers could differ by as much as a factor of 25.

If so, a simple strategy comes to mind: Why not fire the majority of mediocre programmers and hire a few hand-picked superprogrammers to do all the work? When we consider the number of secretaries, clerks, managers, and other support personnel that could also be eliminated by this wholesale removal of the "Mongolian hordes," it seems quite a bargain to pay our chief programmer a mere $100,000 per year.

Although seemingly rational, this argument has three problems. There are *very* few such talented superprogrammers; those few are choosy about where they work and will usually shun the boring, medium-sized MIS organizations; and finally, most organizations would not consider paying a salary of $100,000 per year to a programmer even if it *is* rational to do so. There are some exceptions, of course—the personal computer hardware/software companies like Apple, Microsoft, Borland, and Lotus—but that doesn't help the potential chief programmer who writes COBOL programs for the Amalgamated Cement Company in Dry Gulch, Montana.

Why does an organization refuse to pay $100,000 to a programmer who can turn out the same amount of work as 25 programmers whose salaries are $30,000 each? The answer is that senior management simply cannot understand the concept because their company is not in the computer business. For example, the American Widget Company is in the business of making widgets; their computer department is a necessary evil, existing only to print invoices, paychecks, and other such documents. Senior management might be able to understand paying $100,000 a year to their chief widget designer, but the notion of paying such a high salary to someone in their MIS department would be unthinkable.

As a result, senior management is also unimpressed with the third motivation of the CPTO approach: the recognition that communication problems between programmers become unmanageable on large projects. Although organizations with projects involving only three or four programmers do not recognize this as a problem, the communication problem becomes apparent in projects involving a hundred programmers. For these projects, the meetings, memos, interface documents, and standards manuals are nothing more than futile attempts to maintain some semblance of communication.

The individual programmer's habit of taking the initiative whenever he has the opportunity is one reason for the difficulty. In a typical project, each programmer is given a module to design, code, and test. However, the interface between his module and the rest of the system probably has not been defined very precisely. As a result, each programmer takes the initiative to define his interfaces more precisely, or he makes some minute changes to the defined interfaces. With twenty or thirty programmers making such independent design decisions, the project becomes chaotic.

With a chief programmer team, the communication problems are reduced because far fewer people are required on the project. In addition, the chief programmer makes all of the critical design decisions, directing the other programmers on the project, determining the interfaces to their modules, and enforcing these decisions.

With this approach, one person sees the overall picture at all times. In contrast, in many conventional projects, *nobody* really understands the whole system. In addition, the chief programmer approach means, at least in theory, that the subordinate members of the team do not have to talk to each other to find out what is happening. Thus, instead of $N \bullet (N-1) \div 2$ lines of communication between the N programmers on the project, we find that there are only $(N-1)$ lines of communication.

8.2   THE HISTORY OF THE CPTO CONCEPT

Some organizations believe that they have been using the chief programmer team concept for years. Indeed, I often visit organizations whose MIS managers tell me, "Oh, yes, we've been doing this for quite some time . . . Charlie, here, is our resident superprogrammer." In most cases, Charlie turns out to be a slightly better than average programmer, but no superstar. Also, the *team* characteristic of the CPTO approach (discussed later in this chapter) is usually missing completely.

On the other hand, many of the computer manufacturing organizations and some software consulting firms have *truly* used the chief programmer team concept for a decade or two. The smaller computer firms, for example, have known for quite some time that they could compete with IBM, Burroughs, and the other mainframe companies only if they could develop operating systems and compilers with small teams of two or three geniuses.

Using two or three people to develop an operating system would have been an interesting suggestion for IBM during its development of OS/360 in the mid-1960s. IBM has frequently become involved in massive system development projects with hundreds, if not thousands, of programmers, and has seen firsthand some of the problems discussed in previous chapters. Thus, it is not surprising that IBM took the lead in formalizing and articulating the concepts that other computer vendors have been using unofficially for years.

IBM's first experiments with the CPTO approach involved work on the NASA Manned Spacecraft System in the mid-1960s. The next experiment—more formal and more widely discussed—was the famous New York Times system discussed in [Baker, 1972]. Since then, IBM and other organizations have implemented a substantial number of CPTO projects. The stories of the early superprogrammer projects are fascinating, but not germane to this book. If you are seriously interested in the CPTO approach, I recommend that you read [Aron, 1976], [Baker, 1972], [Brooks, 1975], or [Mills, 1973].

8.3   THE NATURE OF THE CHIEF PROGRAMMER TEAM

So far, I have referred rather loosely to such labels as superprogrammer, chief programmer, and chief programmer team. To become more precise, let's define who these people are and identify what functions they perform.

Let's look at the last of these first. Based on the terminology used in [Brooks, 1975], we can identify ten different types of people who might comprise a chief programmer team:

- the chief programmer
- the copilot
- the administrator
- the editor
- the secretary
- the librarian
- the toolsmith
- the tester
- the language lawyer
- the programmer

I will discuss each of these team members individually in the following subsections. All of these tasks involve separate and specific skills, although multiple tasks can be grouped and performed by a single person.

8.3.1   The chief programmer

The chief programmer is also called the "surgeon" by Fred Brooks, who describes the role this way in [Brooks, 1975]: "He needs great talent, ten years of experience, and considerable systems and application knowledge, whether in applied mathematics, business data processing or whatever."

From the comments already made, we can assume that the chief programmer is an excellent designer; is familiar with the features of operating systems, database packages, structured programming, and structured design concepts; and is capable of coding ten to twenty times faster than the other programmers in the organization. To put these qualifications into perspective, IBM's Joel Aron reported in [Aron, 1976], "Of the 2,000 programmers on the NASA project, only a handful would qualify as chief programmers." Other organizations have suggested that only one out of two hundred programmers is qualified to be a chief programmer. One authority in the field has suggested, perhaps facetiously, that there are only a dozen or so chief programmers in the entire world.

In addition to being a superbly gifted technician, the chief programmer personally defines the functional specifications for the system. Not only must he be conversant with the user's application, but he must also be able to express it in a form intelligible to the user. Of course, many managers argue that a superprogrammer is unlikely to be able to do both well, which is one reason why Brooks and IBM argue that there are so few people qualified for the job. In other words, merely being a super *coder* is not enough to be considered a chief programmer.

Not only does the chief programmer define the functional specifications, but he also personally designs the entire system: He writes all of the critical code in the system (including the top-level modules, and some of the more complex modules in other parts of the system), and he may even write *all* of the code.

In addition, he is responsible for writing all of the documentation for the system—user manuals, data flow diagrams, data dictionaries, structure charts, Nassi-Shneiderman diagrams, narrative descriptions, and anything else that may be required. Clearly, the chief programmer must have a good command of the English language, a capability that one finds sorely lacking in most programmers.

Finally, the chief programmer is responsible for supervising the other specialist members of his team. Thus, the chief programmer must have supervisory capabilities, although that part of his job does not occupy much of his time.

Our chief programmer, then, is a truly marvelous person: a combination of manager, superprogrammer, superdesigner, technical writer, and systems analyst. You can appreciate why there are arguments that such people— if there *are* any such people— deserve a salary of $250,000 per year!

8.3.2   The copilot

The term *copilot* appears in Brooks' discussion of chief programmer teams. More common in IBM literature is the phrase "backup programmer."

The copilot is generally an apprentice chief programmer, although he may be (or may have been) a chief programmer on other projects. His purpose is to serve as the chief programmer's alter ego. He shares in performing the design work and knows the code intimately. In addition, the copilot researches alternative design strategies and serves as a sounding board for the chief programmer's more farfetched ideas.

Another important function of the copilot is to act as insurance. If the chief programmer should be forced to leave the project, the copilot would probably be able to take charge. Less dramatically, we could imagine the chief programmer phasing out of a project during the final stages, leaving the copilot to finish the last few detailed modules. (Note that with a top-down approach, the copilot would not be left with the unpleasant job of system testing at the end of the project.)

On the negative side, I make the following observation: If it is hard to find *one* chief programmer for a project, it will be all that more difficult to find two such highly talented people for a single project.

8.3.3   The administrator

The administrator is the member of the team responsible for worrying about money, budgets, allocation of computer time, and other tasks requiring paperwork and interfacing with the bureaucracy of the surrounding organization. This function is most important in projects in which there are substantial legal, contractual, or financial dealings.

Interestingly, most organizations would refer to such a person as the "project manager"; and yet, in the Chief Programmer Team Organization approach, this person is *subordinate* to the chief programmer. Such an approach has been used in other fields, but it is considered novel, indeed, radical, in most MIS organizations. The usual reaction is,

"What? You're suggesting that the project manager should report to some programmer who makes all the decisions? You've gotta be kidding!"

8.3.4 The editor

As mentioned, the chief programmer is responsible for generating all documentation for a project. Since he actually writes the documentation, the greatest possible technical accuracy and clarity are ensured.

However, an editor can make grammatical corrections to the chief programmer's rough drafts, provide references and bibliographies where appropriate; and, perhaps most important, oversee the mechanical aspects—word processing, desktop publishing, etc.—of producing the documentation.

8.3.5 The secretary

Normal clerical duties of typing, filing, and so forth, are carried out by secretaries, just as in any business operation; however, a formal chief programmer team is assumed to have two secretaries: one to handle tasks associated with the project administrator and one to assist the editor.

8.3.6 The program librarian

The program librarian maintains the technical records of the project: source program listings, data dictionaries, CASE-generated DFDs, etc. This aspect of the chief programmer team was widely adopted in the 1970s, when a great deal of manual effort was required. While it is still a useful and popular concept today, it is less important because of the widespread availability of automated tools for organization and administration of project data.

8.3.7 The toolsmith

The toolsmith provides any specialized program development tools that the chief programmer requires. These might include specialized utility programs (such as disk-to-printer programs of a variety not provided by the vendor); catalogued procedures and JCL; macro libraries; and any text-editing, file-editing, or debugging tools. In many conventional projects, such tools exist as part of a general-purpose library. On the other hand, the chief programmer may feel that he needs some special utilities. Also, because the tool-building aspect of the project may only be a part-time job, the toolsmith might be able to serve more than one chief programmer team.

8.3.8   The tester

Basically, the tester develops data that can be used for module and system testing. The tester may develop some of his test data from the functional specifications, without regard to the code; other data may be developed *after* the tester has seen the code. In addition, the tester may develop test harnesses, dumps, traces, and other special testing/debugging packages.

Some CPTO projects assign the testing function to the copilot, while others ask the user to develop test data. In a large project, though, generation of test data and test utilities can be a full-time job, requiring certain talents and psychological makeup found only in a full-time tester.

8.3.9   The language lawyer

The language lawyer is the expert in various detailed parts of the systems development environment: the operating system, the database management system, compilers, JCL, and so forth.

The language lawyer exists to answer the following sort of questions: "What really happens— at the assembly language level— when I execute a MOVE CORRESPONDING statement in COBOL?" or, "Does the current version of the operating system *really* implement the XYZ system call correctly?" or, "What's the fastest way of zeroing a table in assembly language on the Widget computer?" These are things that the chief programmer might be expected to know, particularly such static information as the fastest way to zero a table on a specific computer. Much of the information, though, is dynamic: It changes with each new release of the vendor's compiler or operating system. Also, it is usually buried in the small print in the appendix of some manual, if it exists at all.

Thus, while the chief programmer is probably resourceful enough to be able to find the answers to questions of the sort posed above, he prefers to draw upon the knowledge of the language lawyer.

8.3.10   The programmer

On small- to medium-sized projects, there may be no need for a programmer because all of the coding may be done by the chief programmer. On medium- to large-sized projects, the programmer writes code that has been specified and possibly designed by the chief programmer

8.4   MANAGEMENT PROBLEMS WITH THE CHIEF PROGRAMMER TEAM

The problems with the chief programmer team can be summarized as follows:

1.   Chief programmers are hard to find. Many organizations make the mistake of assuming that their most senior programmers are chief programmers, whereas they probably are not. Other organizations are fooled into believing that their programmers are superprogrammers, perhaps because they know more obscure instructions in the programming language than some of the other programmers. Many organizations find that they have some programmers who can code quickly, but who cannot document, carry on a reasonable conversation with the user, or supervise other people. Such supercoders are not chief programmers.

2.   It is difficult to convince organizations to compensate the chief programmer properly. Some organizations claim that they offer dual career paths, but such claims are usually vacuous.

3.   Even with appropriate pay and fringe benefits, it is difficult to convince a chief programmer to work for a boring company— and most large companies are indeed boring! Why should a chief programmer waste his time writing yet another payroll system on a run-of-the-mill mainframe in RPG-III when he could be working on a state of the art application for a smaller, more glamorous firm with the latest technology in hardware, software, and productivity tools?

4.   Organizing a chief programmer team so that it fits into the organizational structure of most companies is awkward. Theoretically, the chief programmer is in charge of the chief programmer team. But where does that leave you, the project manager? Are you willing to be replaced by a 28-year-old superprogrammer?

5.   The chief programmer team concept is hard to reconcile with the classical view of the systems analyst. Theoretically, the systems analyst would be subordinate to the chief programmer, the opposite of the political structure in most organizations. Indeed, the purist CPTO approach suggests that there is no need for systems analysts at all, since the

chief programmer can carry out that function.   So what do we do with our systems analysts?

6.   Finally, it is difficult to introduce the CPTO concept into an organization that currently employs hordes of less than superprogrammers.   What does one do with them? Fire them? Let them die of old age?

These questions are not easy to answer, and ironically the people who must provide the answers are often those whose empires, political stature, and jobs are threatened by the CPTO approach.   As a result, the majority of MIS organizations I have visited have abandoned the concept.   A few others have given their senior (and possibly mediocre) programmers the new title of Chief Programmer, thus deluding themselves into thinking that they have successfully adopted the CPTO concept.

Several organizations have adopted those aspects that can fit into their current method of doing business, particularly the program librarian concept and the structured walkthrough concept.   Structured walkthroughs are discussed in more detail in Chapter 9.

So, if you meet someone who says that his organization is practicing the chief programmer team approach, chances are that the organization has introduced walkthroughs and program librarians and labeled the result a chief programmer team.

An alternative to the chief programmer team is the "egoless team"; this is discussed in Chapter 9.

Chapter 9
STRUCTURED WALKTHROUGHS

In Chapter 8, the chief programmer team was discussed, a concept that could have a major impact on the organization of programmers in your company. This chapter discusses another such organizational concept: *structured walkthroughs.* One of the more important activities of a systems development organization, structured walkthroughs can be an extremely important activity for *any* group of programmers, whether or not they work in teams.

What is a walkthrough? Why are walkthroughs usually associated with programming teams? Where did the term originate? These questions are discussed in this chapter, which begins with an overview of the technical concepts and proceeds to a discussion of the problems you are likely to encounter when implementing the techniques in your MIS organization.

9.1   EGOLESS TEAMS

Before discussing the notion of "walking through a program," we need some background. The original application began with Gerald Weinberg's classic, *The Psychology of Computer Programming,* [Weinberg, 1971].

Weinberg's work introduced into the computer field such phrases as egoless programming, programming teams, democratic teams, egoless teams, adaptive teams, and even programming families. One can draw analogies with efforts in other industries (e.g., such automobile companies as General Motors, Volvo, and Saab) to establish teams responsible for well-defined areas of production. The idea also has been greatly influenced by such psychological theories as transactional analysis ("I'm OK, you're OK").

The purpose of teams in the programming field is primarily to change programming from "private art to public practice," as Baker and Mills put it (see [Baker, 1973]). Or, to slightly paraphrase Weinberg, the intention is to change programs from private masterpieces to corporate assets. There is a growing recognition that many programmers have been working *alone* throughout their careers and that they have been more interested in the personal, intellectual pleasure of writing programs than in seeing the programs work for the user.

A programming team, if it is successful, creates an environment in which everyone feels free to discuss and critique everyone else's programs. This environment is necessarily *egoless* and discussions about individual programs are formalized in a walkthrough.

Many other aspects of egoless teams are sufficiently radical that the concept has not yet gained wide acceptance. For example, experience with egoless teams indicates that different people will emerge as the natural leader at different stages of the project. One team member may dominate during the design phase of the project, others may dominate during coding, while still others may take the leadership position during the testing and debugging phases.

Another characteristic of the egoless team is that nobody is really in charge—nobody is the boss, in the traditional sense. This feature generally makes outside management somewhat nervous ("Whose rear end are we going to kick if the project comes in behind schedule?"), although that problem can sometimes be circumvented by nominating one team member as the spokesperson for the group. The absence of a formal boss may also be difficult for certain team members to handle, for they may be accustomed to and prefer an authoritarian manager who tells them what to do.

Note also that the egoless team may not have any superprogrammers. If it did, we would probably call it a chief programmer team. However, as observed in Chapter 8, most companies don't have a superprogrammer anyway, so the egoless team is perhaps the best way to effectively use the large number of average programmers that a company may employ.

Obviously, the mere act of putting three or four people into a project does not make them function as a *team*. Implicit in the concept of a team is the notion of working closely together, reading each other's code and other technical products, sharing responsibilities, knowing each other's idiosyncrasies (both on a technical and a personal level), and accepting a group responsibility for the product. If this attitude can be instilled, the effect is synergistic: Five people working together on a team may produce twice as much as they would working individually.

Here is another comparison between the chief programmer team and the egoless team: If you have a superprogrammer in your organization, the chances are that he's not egoless. He's very good, and he's happy to tell everyone just how good he is—destroying the democratic flavor of the team, especially when it comes to walkthroughs. You may find that the chief programmer wants to review all of the code by himself, rather than making it a group activity. This sort of one-on-one confrontation between an individual programmer and the chief programmer is hardly likely to be egoless.

Many feel that egoless teams will predominate in the future. In organizations in which such a concept has been implemented successfully, the results have been impressive, and the programmers will tell you that they would never revert to the old, classical project organization. On the other hand, some MIS organizations have found that they simply cannot implement the concept: There are too many psychological problems, too many personality clashes, and too many political problems.

In summary, then, it seems that the concept of true programming teams, or families, will probably suffer the same fate as the chief programmer team concept. I will not discuss it further in this book, but I recommend that you read [Weinberg, 1971], as well as [Semprevivo, 1980] and [Thomsett, 1981], if you find the idea interesting.

If egoless teams are a failure, why am I addressing them, especially in this chapter? The reason is simple: About the only aspect of the team concept likely to be implemented in the typical organization is that of a walkthrough. Walkthroughs approximate team programming and are one of the first steps toward establishing programming teams.

9.2   TYPES OF WALKTHROUGHS

Most discussions about walkthroughs concentrate on code; that is, people sometimes think that the only purpose of a walkthrough is to examine a program listing. In fact, there are a surprising number of different types of walkthroughs, including:

1.   *Specification walkthroughs.* As the name implies, the primary purpose of this type of walkthrough is to look for problems, inaccuracies, ambiguities, and omissions in the system *specification*. Such a walkthrough would presumably consist of the user, the senior systems analyst, and one or more analysts on the project, and would involve examining the DFDs, ERDs, data dictionary and other documents produced by the structured analysis approach discussed in Chapter 3.

2.   *Design walkthroughs.* The purpose of this walkthrough is to look for flaws, weaknesses, errors, and omissions in the architecture of the design

before code is written. This walkthrough might involve the user, certainly the systems analyst, and the senior designer (or chief programmer), and probably all of the other designers as well. The documents used for this walkthrough would be structure charts (or HIPO diagrams) and detailed design documents such as pseudocode, Nassi-Shneiderman diagrams, or flowcharts.

3.   *Code walkthroughs.* A code review includes the programmer who wrote the code, the other programmers on the team, and, possibly, a few programmers from outside the team as well as the designer of the module.

4.   *Test walkthroughs.* This walkthrough's purpose is to ensure the adequacy of the test data for the system. It is *not* intended to be a forum for examining the output from the test run. Attendees include the programmers on the project; the tester, if such a person exists (recall the discussion in Chapter 8); the systems analyst; the designer; and perhaps the user, if he can be enticed to join the fun.

Specification, design, and test walkthroughs are not new; they are usually called "reviews" in most organizations. Unfortunately, the very phrase *design review* terrorizes analysts and designers, evoking images of a formal political ritual, in which users, analysts, and programmers spend an entire day yelling at each other and insulting each other's ancestry while the big bosses from the user and programming departments sit in the back of the room smoking cigars and taking notes. Or, the phrase may connote a political ritual of another kind: a dull meeting convened to rubber-stamp a design that nobody understands.

The point is that design and specification reviews tend to be formal and somewhat political. Of necessity, they tend to be global in their examination of a design. Because of the number of people involved, they can be convened only occasionally, and since it is such a hassle getting the design review committee together, one feels obliged to make a formal presentation, complete with flip charts, overhead transparencies, and 35mm slides, of the entire design.

By contrast, walkthroughs tend to be more informal and local in nature. The people who participate in the walkthrough may meet three times a week, or even three times a day, quietly discussing small parts of the design, specification, or code. As a result, a great deal more is usually accomplished.

It is important to note that walkthroughs take place in the order presented in this chapter. It is extremely unpleasant to discover in a *code* walkthrough that there was an error in the specifications or that the design is unacceptable to the rest of the team. By the time design begins, the team should have uncovered the major weaknesses in the specification; by the time coding starts, the team should have discovered the major problems in the design.

9.3   OBJECTIVES OF A WALKTHROUGH

The objectives of a walkthrough should be explicit. The major objective, of course, is to find errors: an omission, a contradiction, or a logical error of any kind. Happily for all of us, walkthroughs are quite successful in this respect: The number of errors in production systems decreases by as much as ninety percent in organizations that use walkthroughs diligently.

Another major objective is to look for weaknesses or errors of style. The walkthrough will usually point out major efficiency and readability problems in the code (e.g., cryptic data names), modularity and cohesion/coupling problems in the design, and fuzzily stated requirements in the specification. Naturally, arguments will arise in this area of style—what appears reasonable to one person will not necessarily seem reasonable to another.

There are other less tangible objectives of a walkthrough. For example, the mere threat of a walkthrough tends to improve the quality of the code, design, specifications, or test data. Clearly, one does not want to look foolish in front of one's peers. At the coding level, this phenomenon sometimes translates into something more obvious: The other members of the team may be unwilling to walk through anything other than structured code developed in a top-down fashion.

Also, team reviews or walkthroughs serve as a consciousness-raising session for everyone. Not only do the junior people learn techniques from the senior people, but the senior people often get new ideas and insights from the junior people. Weinberg has made a further observation: He claims that for a junior programmer, one year working as part of a team that practices walkthroughs is equivalent to two years of working alone.

Frequent walkthroughs minimize the chance of having to throw work away if someone is forced to leave the project. In conventional projects, we usually find that a half-finished program is worthless if the author leaves, because a new programmer or systems analyst finds it impossible to figure out what the original programmer was doing; hence, he throws the half-finished code away, and starts over.

9.4   WHEN SHOULD A WALKTHROUGH BE CONDUCTED?

The guidelines for scheduling walkthroughs are simple: A walkthrough should be conducted as frequently as possible, so that *small* pieces of work (code, or design, or specification, or test data) are reviewed. However, a walkthrough should be scheduled only when the author is ready. One of the worst things you can do as a manager is to legislate walkthroughs at arbitrary times, such as every Friday afternoon, or after every hundred lines of code, or after every seven bubbles in a data flow diagram.

The scheduling of a specification walkthrough or design walkthrough is fairly well determined by the states of document development. When a unit of documentation—a DFD or structure chart—is available for review, a walkthrough should be scheduled. As an example, a code walkthrough could be held at any of the following stages:

- before the code is entered into the computer

- after the code is entered into the computer, but before it is compiled

- after the first compilation

- after the first clean compilation

- after the first test case has been executed successfully

- after the programmer thinks that *all* test cases have been executed successfully

There are both advantages and disadvantages to scheduling walkthroughs at each of these stages. Conducting a walkthrough can be relatively unpleasant, for example, when the source document consists only of an illegible, handwritten coding sheet. Each sheet of paper probably contains only ten or twenty lines of code, requiring the reviewer to turn the pages constantly to see what the program is doing. Furthermore, the reviewer sorely misses symbol tables, cross-reference listings, and other helpful aids that the compiler or assembler normally produces.

On the other hand, a walkthrough scheduled for this same time-frame takes advantage of the earliest opportunity for code review. Delays sometimes occur in keying and compiling a program, and the team may wish to ensure that the code is correct before wasting a day, or as much as a week, waiting for it to be entered into a computer. Thus, some MIS organizations conduct their walkthroughs after the code has been keyed, but before it has been compiled. The source document is usually a simple printout.

It is much more common, though, to conduct a walkthrough *after* the program has been compiled. At that point, the reviewers are working with a more legible document, with more information on each page, and with the symbol tables, cross-reference listings, and other helpful information that the compiler provides as a matter of course. Some people argue that the walkthrough should not take place until the programmer has produced a clean compilation without syntax errors. In most cases, this makes sense *if* your organization has reasonably good turnaround time for compilations (e.g., with an on-line development environment). Obviously, you must strike a balance here: While you don't want to waste the entire team's time looking for syntax errors when they can be found easily by a compiler, neither do you want the author of the program to spend several days compiling and recompiling his program repeatedly to rid it of subtle, difficult syntax errors.

It is usually a bad idea to delay the walkthrough until the programmer has begun testing his program, and it is *definitely* a bad idea to wait until the programmer thinks he has finished all of his testing. First, much time has probably been wasted with the programmer looking for his own program bugs. The *team* could have spotted the bug more quickly. In addition, ego problems may arise if you wait too long before having a walkthrough. For example, if one of the team members suggests that the code be revised to make it more readable, the author of the program is likely to become defensive. He has invested time and energy, psychic as well as physical, and his is not strongly interested in listening to someone else's suggestions about rewriting the program.

Another reason to hold a walkthrough early in the project is that finding bugs in a program has a positive psychological effect on the team. Many organizations contend that the more bugs found in a walkthrough, the more successful the walkthrough has been.

On a personal level, a programmer generally doesn't mind spending an hour or two reviewing someone else's code if he finds a bug or two. He feels that his time has been well invested. However, if he spends an hour reading through the code and does *not* find a bug, he could think that he's wasting his time. He may become sloppy in subsequent walkthroughs, thinking that there won't be any bugs in *any* code that he walks through.

9.5   CONDUCTING THE WALKTHROUGH

In many cases, walkthroughs are so informal that one cannot really say that they are "conducted." The programmer takes someone else's code home in the evening, curls up in front of a roaring fire with a bottle of wine, and spends a pleasant evening looking for bugs.

In more formal circumstances, there is usually a prescribed pattern to the walkthroughs; that is, they tend to be more "structured." What follows is an abbreviated set of guidelines to be modified as you see fit. For more details, see [Yourdon, 1989b] or [Freedman and Weinberg, 1980].

- A coordinator, who may be the chief programmer, chairs the meeting and sees that order is maintained. This implies, of course, that the meeting is sufficiently large and formal, and that the personalities are disparate enough that order does have to be maintained. The coordinator also schedules the walkthrough, reserves a conference room, distributes materials, and so on.

- The author generally makes a presentation of his product (the specification, the design, or the code) to the reviewers.[1] During this overview or presentation phase, general comments and questions may be entertained, but specific questions ("How does your system handle an XYZ transaction?") should be deferred.

- Following the general discussion, the author walks through the product in minute detail, reviewing each piece. This walkthrough is usually not done with specific test cases. Instead, it is based on a logical argument of what the code or design will do at various stages.

- After the general walkthrough, members of the reviewing audience may ask to walk through specific test cases. This process continues as long as anyone can think of situations in which the behavior of the product is suspect.

---

[1] There are varying opinions regarding the author's presentation. Some people feel that if the product requires an overview presentation, something must be wrong with it. It should be possible for the reviewing audience to understand it without any help. Others give a different argument. An overview presented by the author has the danger of brainwashing the reviewers into making the same logical errors as the author, and they will overlook the same bugs in the product that he did. Thus, some people feel that the author should *not* make a presentation, but should be present only to answer questions from the rest of the group.

- The coordinator normally resolves disagreements if the team is unable to reach a consensus. Such disagreements might include questions of style, efficiency, or interpretations of the specification. These can continue interminably if they are not stopped by the coordinator.

- Additional walkthroughs may be necessary to review corrections and changes to the code. It will usually be evident whether a second walkthrough is required, and the team should be able to reach an agreement in this area relatively quickly. Many organizations require that the team take a formal vote to determine the need for a second walkthrough.

The above comments may give you the impression that at more formal walkthroughs, no one is allowed to speak unless he had raised his hand and received recognition from the coordinator. Such is usually not the case. Walkthroughs tend to be rather informal, give-and-take sessions among peers who need little outside supervision to maintain order.

9.6 OTHER ASPECTS OF WALKTHROUGHS

Every organization conducts its walkthroughs somewhat differently. How your programmers and systems analysts conduct their walkthroughs will depend on their personalities and their surroundings. However, the following suggestions are useful in most MIS organizations:

1. Have your people schedule their walkthroughs in advance—a day or two ahead is usually sufficient. If possible, have them distribute appropriate materials (DFDs, data dictionary entries, program listings, structure charts, etc.) to the participants a day or two in advance as well, and encourage private reviews prior to the public walkthrough. Many of the bugs and problems are trivial and need not take up the time of the entire group.

2. Make sure that you, as the manager, stay out of the walkthrough; keep other big bosses out, too. You may be curious about the walkthrough mechanism, and you may wish to sit through one after your programmers and analysts have had an opportunity to become used to the technique. However, you should be aware that your presence, especially

during the first few walkthroughs, will probably be extremely inhibiting.

3.   See that proper notes are kept during the walkthroughs, not only of bugs but also of suggested changes and improvements to the product. Such suggestions tend to be forgotten, and if the author was not enthusiastic about the suggested improvements, he is *very* likely to forget about them.

4.   Create a proper attitude for the programmers and analysts. Make them see that it is good to find bugs. Impress upon them that *everyone* in the team is responsible for any bugs remaining after the walkthrough: the author who put the bug into the product *and* the people who failed to find it in the walkthrough. Make them all sign the walkthrough report, especially if they are convinced it is correct. Then, when the system has been implemented, call *all* of them into the computer room in the middle of the night when an undiscovered bug blows up the program during a production run!

5.   Make sure that your people understand that the major purpose of the walkthrough is error *detection*, not error *correction*. If the solution to a bug can be demonstrated quickly and easily to the author, no harm is done, but it is a disaster to see half a dozen programmers and analysts dash to the blackboard and begin arguing about the correctness of a fix they have each just invented for a bug. It is sufficient to let the author know that the bug exists. Let *him* decide how to fix it.

6.   Keep the walkthroughs short and sweet. An hour is long enough, and ninety minutes is probably the absolute limit. Studying someone else's code, design, or specification is mentally fatiguing, and one's attention begins to wander after an hour. Also, don't schedule multiple, consecutive walkthroughs. Finally, a nice touch is to have coffee and donuts (or beer and pizza) if your budget, or personal finances, allows it.

9.7   MANAGEMENT PROBLEMS WITH WALKTHROUGHS

As you can anticipate, there can be problems with the walkthrough concept.   Perhaps the first problem occurs in the management area: Some MIS managers are not convinced that walkthroughs are a good idea.

Some managers, for example, argue that it's a waste of time to tie up so many people to examine a technical product. "Six technicians sitting in a room for an hour!" a manager will exclaim. "How can that possibly be cost-effective? Chances are that they spend most of their time talking about football or sex!" If you hear this complaint from other managers in your organization, you should have these four answers:

1.   It would probably take the author considerably longer to find the same number of bugs. After all, if the author puts bugs into his program or specifications, then he will undoubtedly create test data that repeat the same logical errors.

2.   Some bugs would *never* be found by the author. It's worth a few hours of effort by the team to find such bugs. Otherwise, they will be discovered at a later stage in the development of the system (e.g., systems analysis errors detected during the coding phase) or, even worse, after the system has been put into production, at which time, the bugs are *much* more expensive—both to find and to correct.

3.   There is no other reasonable way of ensuring that the style of the product is acceptable, reflecting a proper implementation of the principles of structured analysis, structured design, and structured programming.

4.   Case studies such as those discussed in Chapter 2 confirm that walkthroughs are a highly productive technique available to the organization.

You should also be prepared to answer the managers in your organization who are convinced that all testing and debugging should be done by the computer. Again, there are some fairly standard arguments that you can use:

1.   Machine time is cheap compared to the cost of people, but turnaround time in some MIS organizations is terrible. If your programmers have

to wait for more than 15 minutes to get a program compiled, they won't be very productive while they're waiting for output.

2. The machine will only find bugs that the programmer exposes through his test data. Again, the author of the program tends to unconsciously select test cases that will demonstrate that this program *works*, not that it has a bug.

In some cases, it may be preferable to let the computer find the bugs. If the turnaround time is acceptable, it usually makes sense to let the author of the program find his own syntax errors with the assistance of the compiler; similar trivial errors in a specification or design can be detected by today's CASE tools. It may also make sense to let the programmer eliminate the more trivial logic errors in his program, but be careful not to wait too long for a walkthrough, or the author will become too egotistical about his code.

Still another common viewpoint is that junior programmers and systems analysts should not be allowed to participate in walkthroughs. Many managers feel that reviews should be conducted only by the chief programmer or the project manager. Your response to this suggestion should be one or all of the following:

1. The possibility of ego confrontations increases with a one-on-one situation, particularly between the programmer and his superior. The team environment has a mitigating effect on the clash of egos.

2. The chief programmer or project manager is too busy to give the product a thorough walkthrough and probably will skim the code, looking only for obvious errors.

3. Even if the chief programmer spends a significant amount of time, he is only human and can make mistakes. Subjecting the product to a team walkthrough increases the chances that *someone* will find the bug (although it must be admitted that some time may be wasted as a result of *everyone* finding some of the bugs independently).

4. To paraphrase the old proverb, "Out of the mouths of babes (and junior programmers) come pearls of

wisdom." Junior programmers often have refreshingly different approaches to design and systems analysis problems. Analysts as well can contribute equally refreshing ideas in the areas of coding and design.

Finally, management is likely to be concerned about the possibility of ego and personality problems. The programmers in their group may have very strong personalities, and the concept of a walkthrough may be viewed as an open invitation to fisticuffs. Here are some replies to this concern:

- Arguments of this sort are healthy. Since personality conflicts exist anyway, why not get them out into the open and resolve them?

- A strong coordinator should be able to mediate most ego conflicts, and prevent arguments from dominating the walkthrough.

- Many conflicts can be avoided by establishing standards at the beginning of the project. This point is discussed more fully in Chapter 12.

- Almost all arguments can be avoided by disallowing discussions of style and restricting the walkthrough to an exercise in finding errors. This limitation is unfortunate, but it is better than having no walkthrough at all.

- Ego problems are easier to cope with if the review comes after a small investment of time has been made, not after the author has spent six months developing what he considers to be a perfect product.

As you might expect, not all of the objections to walkthroughs come from the management community; the programmers and analysts create a few problems of their own. You should anticipate the following problems when implementing walkthroughs:

- *Attitude problems.* Some of your programmers and systems analysts will be unwilling to cooperate. If they can't be convinced to participate in the walkthrough approach after a few months of practice, you have two alternatives: Fire them, or put them in a corner to work by themselves. If you

choose the latter approach, I strongly recommend
that they be forced to maintain their own work.

- *Inexperience at giving or taking criticism.* Many
  programmers and some systems analysts seem to
  have had little exposure to the group dynamics
  involved in walkthroughs. Indeed, one often finds
  that certain people are attracted to the data
  processing field because they find it easier to deal
  with machines than with people. If you find this to
  be a problem, give your technicians some training in
  interpersonal skills.

- *Unenthusiastic reviewers who don't try hard enough
  to find bugs.* Everyone knows about the programmer
  or systems analyst who is overly critical in a
  walkthrough; he makes his presence known. But,
  we sometimes overlook the person who sits quietly
  in a corner and never says a word. To repeat a point
  made earlier, it is important to make *everyone* feel
  responsible for bugs. It may help to give the quiet
  programmer a call at 3 a.m., asking him to come
  into the office to help track down a bug that he
  didn't bother trying to find in the walkthrough.

- *Walking through too much at one time.* Watch out
  for this one. Your programmers and systems
  analysts will sometimes try to spend an entire day
  walking through several thousand lines of code, or
  several dozen data flow diagrams. Anything after the
  first 90 minutes is likely to be a waste of time, unless
  you allow a significant opportunity for a coffee break.

- *Fear that walkthroughs will be used to judge
  performance.* This problem can be serious,
  particularly in programming. It's a paradoxical issue,
  since everyone knows that programmers are not
  paid solely on the basis of their performance (as
  pointed out in Chapter 8, no one is willing to pay
  $250,000 for a superprogrammer). So why should a
  programmer care if a few bugs are found in his
  program? On the other hand, you can appreciate his
  fear. In response, you should do two things: First,
  stay out of the walkthrough, especially if the
  programmers view you as an ogre rather than as a
  friend. Second, impress upon everyone that the
  product, not the person, is being reviewed.

- *Arguments over style.* There is no magical way to prevent programmers and systems analysts from arguing over such things as the merits of nested IF statements, or the way arrows and bubbles should be drawn in a data flow diagram. However, you should recognize that arguments over style are sometimes interminable. The best thing to do is to leave the team alone. Although team members may waste a considerable amount of time at first, sooner or later they tire of such arguments and will learn to discipline themselves. An alternative is to establish standards to which everyone can adhere, but self-imposed discipline is much more effective than externally imposed standards.

Chapter 10
WHICH TECHNIQUES TO IMPLEMENT FIRST

We have discussed structured analysis, top-down implementation, structured design, structured programming, chief programmer teams, structured walkthroughs, and structured analysis. In this chapter, I will address questions frequently asked by MIS organizations exposed to all of the structured techniques for the first time: Which techniques should we implement first? Should we start with structured programming? Or would it make more sense to begin with structured design? Or should we jump in with both feet and try all of the new techniques at once?

There is no single right answer to these questions. What's right for one organization may not be right for another. From what you've seen thus far in this book and from your knowledge of your own MIS organization, *you* have to decide what would be best. Nevertheless, there are at least half a dozen issues that you should consider when deciding which structured technique(s) to implement first.

10.1 IMPLEMENTING ALL OF THE STRUCTURED TECHNIQUES AT ONCE

Some organizations can execute such a feat. After reading about the techniques or getting a presentation from a vendor or consultant, they decide to use all of the structured techniques at once. As you might expect, this plunge is more likely to happen in the smaller MIS organizations and software shops with only a half-dozen or so programmers, and is *not* very likely to occur in the larger organizations.

Sometimes, an organization will decide to try all of the structured techniques on a single pilot project, as discussed in the next chapter. Even in such a limited situation, however, experimenting with several new techniques at once often leads to chaos.

The reasons are obvious. Structured programming, structured design, and structured analysis are not simple concepts, and a lot of concentration is needed to make them work correctly. If the programmers and systems analysts are trying to implement walkthroughs *and* chief programmer teams, as well as adjusting to other organizational changes, it will be difficult for them to succeed with any of these techniques.

10.2   TECHNIQUES INVOLVING ORGANIZATIONAL CHANGE

As suggested in Chapters 8 and 9, some organizations will find it difficult to ever implement chief programmer teams, librarians, and walkthroughs. Even if you can, you'll probably find it more difficult to introduce one of these as the first structured technique. Usually, it is easier to introduce first a relatively innocuous *technical* concept, like structured programming, which neither threatens anyone's empire nor conflicts with current organizational philosophies.

Similarly, you may have trouble introducing structured analysis as the first structured technique in your organization, especially if your department engages solely in programming and implementation, while an entirely different department carries out systems analysis. In addition, while most users react favorably to data flow diagrams and the other documentation tools described in Chapter 3, a hostile user organization may reject these new tools for political reasons— or they may simply decide that they don't like looking at pages filled with bubbles and boxes. Some users may not be willing or able to conceptualize their requirements by looking at the abstract, pictorial models that structured analysis generates; for such users, the concept of prototyping discussed in Chapter 17 may be appropriate.

Once you've demonstrated that structured programming, top-down implementation, and structured design are good ideas, then you will probably be in a strong enough political position to say to the boss, "The last three structured techniques that I introduced to the company have turned out to be winners. Why not gamble a little now, and let me try something like structured analysis?"

Again, I'm not suggesting that you *must* follow this tack. Your top management may be more intrigued with the organizational aspects of the structured techniques and uninterested in such seemingly trivial technical concepts as structured programming.

10.3   USING STRUCTURED CODE ALONE

Earlier in the book, we discussed the point that structured coding is a solid idea and probably a significant improvement over the coding approach currently used by your programmers—but that it's not enough, alone, to solve all your problems. If your design techniques are poor—if your designers are still creating large, sloppy modules that are strongly "coupled" to other equally large, sloppy modules—then the best coding won't help. In fact, even if you're using structured design, you may be in trouble.   You may be creating brilliant solutions to the wrong problems, becasue of weaknesses in the analysis effort. Structured design *and* structured analysis are crucial for structured coding to have any value.

Grasping this point is important because if you introduce the structured techniques with great fanfare and promises of spectacular improvements, then the first technique you bring into the organization had better demonstrate spectacular improvements.   But, if you try structured programming alone, you might not achieve such overwhelming improvements.   My recent experience with a few projects involving only structured coding has been that the initial gains in productivity and reliability will seem quite impressive, but the long-term maintainability of the system may not be very impressive at all. For a good example of this, see [Plauger, 1976].

Consequently, it may make sense to begin with structured design or structured analysis; and when either is working properly, *then* introduce structured coding.   Once you've overcome the objections, battles, and problems associated with structured analysis or design, introducing structured programming will be almost trivial.

10.4   USING TOP-DOWN DESIGN AND IMPLEMENTATION FIRST

As I discussed in Chapter 4, many of the advantages of the top-down approach are political. Compared to classical approaches, the method allows you to demonstrate something to the user at an earlier stage, to survive deadline crises more gracefully, and to manage (and schedule) computer test time requirements better.

These benefits are very noticeable to the user community, senior management, and the computer operations staff.   For this reason alone, some MIS managers have decided that using the top-down approach is a good way to introduce the structured techniques within their organization.

However, this strategy can backfire. As mentioned in Chapter 4, many programmers view top-down implementation as an invitation to start coding *before* they have done any real design. Especially on your crucial first few projects, beware of this danger.

10.5   CONDUCTING INFORMAL WALKTHROUGHS

Informal walkthroughs are a good way to start implementing the structured techniques because you can't expect an individual programmer or systems analyst to understand and implement any of the other structured techniques by himself. By forcing everyone to talk about their specifications and designs and their code in a low-key, nonthreatening fashion, you can maintain quality control when you most need it.

This point needs emphasizing. If you send all 30 of your programmers to a class about structured programming, they will grasp 30 different versions of what the instructor says; I can attest to this from personal experience! They will write thirty different kinds of structured programs, some good, some mediocre, some downright bad. If nobody looks at the code, you will never know who truly understands structured programming.

If you begin by establishing an environment in which everyone's code, design, and specifications are exposed to public discussion, then you will ensure that a relatively uniform version of top-down implementation, structured design, and structured programming can be implemented.

You may conclude that walkthroughs by themselves are not significant enough to deserve being the only technique introduced within your organization; you may decide to introduce walkthroughs together with structured programming, structured design, or structured analysis. Once again, *you* have to make the decision.

Chapter 11
CHOOSING A PILOT PROJECT

Most organizations consider a pilot project to be a formal experiment in the use of one or more of the structured techniques. Indeed, being an experiment is its primary virtue. If structured programming is a bad idea, it is preferable to discover this fact in a low-cost, low-risk experimental project. If the pilot project confirms that structured programming is the best thing since the invention of peanut butter, then the success of the project provides the political leverage for introducing structured programming throughout the organization.

There are other benefits too. A pilot project is a good way for people to learn the structured techniques, and learning by doing is almost always preferable to learning from a textbook, seminar, or videotaped training course. In addition, the programmers who work on the pilot project can be used to "seed" subsequent projects as the structured techniques begin to be implemented on a larger scale.

Not every organization feels that it needs a pilot project. A small MIS organization whose members have all been exposed to the structured techniques in depth, *at the same time*, may decide to formally adopt the techniques without any experimentation. However, most large organizations are unable to change this swiftly, and a pilot project may be politically necessary to convince programmers and project managers to try something new.

Hence, the idea of pilot projects is good, although there are good pilot projects and bad pilot projects; a bad pilot project is sometimes worse than none at all. This chapter offers advice on the characteristics of a good pilot project.

11.1   A GOOD PILOT PROJECT SHOULD BE OF A REASONABLE SIZE

Some organizations make the mistake of trying the structured techniques on too small a project, such as a two hundred statement program. In most cases, such a tiny pilot project won't be very convincing. First, some overhead is involved in the new techniques, especially if the organization adheres to the guidelines of structured design and structured programming in a formal, "religious" fashion. Also, by the time a programmer figures out how to use structured design and structured programming on his 200-statement problem, another programmer could have finished designing, coding, and testing the same job, in elegant style, using classical methods.

However, there is a more fundamental objection to the use of the new techniques on small pilot projects. Most of the techniques of structured analysis, structured design, structured programming, top-down design, and structured walkthroughs are intended as a means of dealing with *complex* data processing systems. They are not needed on small problems, for we can use conventional techniques on small problems as we have since the 1950s and 1960s. Bluntly, anyone can write 200 lines of code and eventually get them to work, and if he has had a lot of practice doing such jobs, anyone can write a 200-statement unstructured program faster than a programmer can finish his *first attempt* at writing those 200 statements in a structured fashion.

So, choose a medium-sized system as your pilot project. A project involving three to six person-months is reasonable, but interpret "medium-sized" within the context of your organization; it might be larger or smaller than what I have suggested.

11.2 THE PILOT PROJECT SHOULD BE USEFUL, VISIBLE, AND LOW-RISK

Implementing an on-line chess-playing program as your pilot project will not be effective because nobody will use it (except during their lunch hour), and nobody will care whether it is better or worse than a classically-developed chess program. It is preferable to choose a project whose output will be visible to the organization, and whose success will be appreciated by the organization. Ideally, the pilot project should be one that your organization was planning to implement anyway.

On the other hand, your pilot project should *not* be critical to the success or the solvency of your organization. The project might fail, and using the structured techniques for the first time on a risky, highly critical project may destroy both the project *and* the reputation of the new techniques. The structured techniques might turn out to be too much for the programmers to cope with, especially if they are already coping with unreliable hardware, difficult customers, tight schedules, and internal politics. If the project does fail, the failure may be blamed on the structured techniques, even if the real reason for the failure was something entirely different.

However, sometimes you might not have an alternative. If you are in charge of a project that appears doomed, you may decide to gamble on the structured techniques with the hope that they will produce a miracle. I know of one or two MIS organizations that have been forced into this position, and, luckily, they have succeeded. But it's a risk that you should avoid if you can.

The ideal pilot project might be the redesign of an existing system that is so old, patched, and difficult to maintain that everyone agrees that it should be scrapped and redeveloped. Your new structured version will probably be a success, giving you the added advantage of having something with which to compare it. Selecting an existing system for redesign using the structured approach also provides you with a safety valve; even if the structured version fails, you can probably survive by continuing to use the old system.

11.3   THE PILOT PROJECT SHOULD BE MEASURABLE

One of the purposes of the pilot project is to demonstrate the virtues of the structured techniques to the rest of your organization. This objective strongly implies that you should measure various aspects of the pilot project, such as the following:

- the number of lines of debugged source code generated per programmer per day in the pilot project (but beware of the Hawthorne Effect). Alternatively, you might want to measure function points; see [DeMarco, 1982] or [Jones, 1986] for more details.

- the number of bugs found after the system was put into production, and how those bugs were distributed.

- The efficiency (memory, CPU time, etc.) of the structured product compared to the older, equivalent, unstructured version.

- The amount of time spent on walkthroughs, and their efficiency as a defect-removal method.

- The amount of time spent in the analysis phase using structured analysis compared to the amount of time traditionally spent in the analysis phase.

These few categories may prove sufficient, or you may decide to turn the pilot project into a full-scale research project. The point is, hard numbers will usually convince the rest of your organization to believe the success of the pilot project.

One potential problem in measuring the pilot project is that you may not have any other figures in your organization for comparison. Many MIS organizations today have no idea how productive their programmers are, how many bugs exist in their production systems, or how much effort they are spending on maintenance. As a result, it becomes difficult to determine whether the pilot project is substantially better or worse than the classical methods. One solution is to compare the results of your pilot project with figures that are reported in the literature—case studies that are reported regularly in *Datamation, Computerworld, IEEE Transactions on Software Engineering*, etc. Unfortunately, true comparison is difficult because every organization measures these factors differently.

For this reason, however, many organizations feel that the ideal pilot project is the redesign of an existing system. With some investigation, one can usually accumulate relevant statistics about the current version of the system—development time, number of bugs discovered during the past N years of maintenance, number of maintenance programmers assigned to the system, and, of course, the amount of CPU time and memory consumed by the current system. Hard statistics can be collected regarding CPU time and memory requirements of the new system, along with maintenance and reliability of the new system, and these help convince skeptics about the merits of the structured techniques.

Chapter 12
DEVELOPING STANDARDS FOR THE STRUCTURED TECHNIQUES

The subject of standards eventually arises in any discussion of the structured techniques. The purpose of this book is not to provide you with all the standards you will need in your organization; you can obtain those from some of the textbooks listed in the bibliography or from various consulting firms that specialize in structured systems development. However, I will offer some brief advice on when and how such standards should be developed.

First, keep in mind that many of your standards won't be affected by the introduction of structured analysis, etc. Many large MIS organizations already have an immense collection of standards, many of which are unrelated or only peripherally related to the issues of structured programming, walkthroughs, and the other techniques. One of my clients, for example, even has a standard that determines the colors of standards manuals: Systems standards manuals are green, programming standards manuals are blue, operations standards manuals are yellow, personnel standards manuals are red, and so forth. Presumably, the structured techniques would not upset this scheme!

Even in the areas of systems analysis, systems design, and program design, many of the conventional standards can remain unchanged. Your organization probably has standards that dictate the use of disk packs and file names, and the paperwork to be completed for a mainframe production job is given to the computer operator. I estimate that 90 to 95 percent of this can be left intact, much to the relief of your standards organization!

Perhaps only a few aspects of your standards manual should be scrapped:

1. Scrap dogmatic rules outlawing isolated programming statements, especially COBOL standards that outlaw PERFORMs and nested IFs.

2.   Scrap any emphasis on the microsecond-levels of efficiency, unless they are posed as informative guidelines.   Large portions of some MIS organizations' standards manuals are concerned with the relative merits of COMP-2 versus COMP-3 data representation in COBOL, and the relative efficiencies of obscure string-handling statements in PL/I. As emphasized in previous chapters, concern about efficiency at this level is usually irrelevant. Moreover, such comments typically become obsolete after a year, because the compiler vendor releases a new version with different (and hopefully better) operating characteristics.

3.   Scrap most of the sections concerning "packaging." If your standards dictate that systems *must* be broken into job steps or partitions in a certain way, and that data *must* be passed between job steps on a certain type of intermediate file (disk or tape), you should probably rewrite the standards in the light of the packaging concepts of structured analysis and design, or eliminate the standards altogether.

In the following sections, I make some additional suggestions about standards.

12.1   WHEN STANDARDS SHOULD BE DEVELOPED

A few organizations make the mistake of trying to develop a whole new standards manual before they have any experience with the structured techniques. Indeed, the members of the pilot project may wish to develop a few informal standards for themselves, mostly so that they won't waste time quibbling over details in their structured walkthroughs. But these would be quite different from a formal set of standards issued by a standards department.

The cardinal rule to follow is don't develop standards until a pilot project has been completed. The reasoning here should be obvious, since you can't really tell what kind of standards will be appropriate until after you have tried the structured techniques. For example, how can you tell whether nested IF statements are good or bad until your programmers have tried writing a few of them?

12.2   HARD STANDARDS WILL PROBABLY BE IGNORED

As suggested in earlier chapters, some MIS organizations interpret the guidelines of structured programming, structured design, structured analysis, and the other techniques as religious rules. These rules have a nasty habit of showing up in the standards manual.

Thus, some standards manuals contain the following kinds of statements:

- *All* walkthroughs must be between 30 and 60 minutes.

- *Every* programmer must have a walkthrough of his code on a weekly basis.

- GOTO statements will not be allowed under *any* circumstances.

- The span of control of a module must *never* exceed seven.

- The specification of the user's requirements may not commence until a model of his current system has been *completely* and *totally* specified.

It may be possible to force programmers and systems analysts to follow these dictatorial rules for a while, but sooner or later, they will fall into disuse, just as all previous sets of hard standards did.

12.3   SUMMARY

From the preceding comments, you can anticipate the approach I favor: a modest set of style guidelines, combined with frequent walkthroughs.

It is intriguing that many of the MIS organizations that have developed structured programming standards have been able to express all of their guidelines in ten or twelve pages. Furthermore, many of the managers indicated that a deliberate effort was made to keep the standards to a restricted length to ensure that the programmers would actually read them. By way of example, Appendixes A and B contain suggested structured COBOL and structured PL/I programming standards.

The factor that will determine the success or failure of your standards is the *walkthrough* concept discussed in Chapter 9, and treated in greater length in [Yourdon, 1989b]. Indeed, one could argue that if the walkthrough concept is successfully implemented, no programming standards are needed. Certainly, hard, rigid standards would not be needed.

This point has to be emphasized, particularly in the MIS organizations that have fallen in love with their standards manuals. What is the purpose of standards in the area of program design and coding? Presumably, they ensure that programmers will turn out *good* programs. But goodness must ultimately be judged by a human being—typically the maintenance programmer who is called upon to make such judgments at 3 a.m., when he is looking for a bug. Similarly, what is the purpose of standards for functional specifications? It's not to keep the members of the standards department gainfully employed. On the contrary, their purpose is to ensure that systems analysts and users can communicate.

My point is simple: If a team of programmers reads through the design and code for a system and honestly thinks that it is good, then it *is* good, regardless of what the six-volume standards manual may state. If the team thinks that the program is bad, then it *is* bad, even if the author of the program scrupulously obeyed all of the rules, all of the do's and don'ts of the standards manual. Similarly, if a team of systems analysts and users decides that a set of functional specifications is understandable and correct, then, in my opinion, strict adherence to standards—especially those pertaining to the format and style of the specification—is secondary.

Chapter 13
IMPACT ON SCHEDULING, BUDGETING, AND PROJECT CONTROL

One of the issues frequently raised about the structured techniques is their effect upon classical project management: classical estimating, scheduling, budgeting, resource allocation, and project control. Implicit in this concern is the assumption that the structured techniques will render everything that you have learned as a project manager useless.

The primary purpose of this chapter is to reassure you that most of the knowledge and experience you've gained in this area is still valid. Specifically, the chapter addresses the effect of the new techniques on estimating and scheduling activities, and on milestones as they are classically understood and on the kind of milestones that are used in structured projects.

13.1   THE EFFECT ON ESTIMATING AND SCHEDULING

I must admit a large degree of cynicism in this area because I have watched the way most MIS managers estimate a project and determine when it will be finished—it is still what my colleague Tom DeMarco calls "backwards wishful thinking." That is, they find out when the user absolutely, positively *must* have the system, and then they schedule backwards to see when the coding should begin, etc.

There is, of course, a great body of knowledge on scheduling resources for systems development projects; these include Barry Boehm's classic *Software Engineering Economics* [Boehm, 1981] and Tom DeMarco's *Controlling Software Projects* [DeMarco, 1982]. And much of the available knowledge on estimating formulas and models has been incorporated more recently in PC-based estimating programs.

Nevertheless, I remain a cynic. In my experience as a consultant, I have too often seen that people cannot devise reasonable estimates because they are overwhelmed by their egos or by political pressures, or (more charitably) they are working on a type of systems development project they have never before experienced.

For example, Charlie, the project manager, has just been placed in charge of developing a new on-line order entry system to be run on a Brand X computer with a Brand Y database management system and a Brand Z telecommunications monitor; and all of this is going to be built with programmers that Charlie has just hired. The only kind of order entry system that Charlie has worked on before was a smaller, simpler batch system that ran on a Brand W computer, using a different programming language and different programmers. How is Charlie going to develop an accurate estimate?

In many cases, Charlie doesn't have to devise a schedule because the schedule is determined for him. Part of the assignment is "Get this system up and running by the first of January!" Charlie does an obvious interpolation between where he is now and where he must be by January 1: "This is April 1, and I have four programmers, and I've got to be finished by January 1. That means that I'd better have the design done by June 1, and I'd better start coding by July 1 . . . and . . . and . . . ."

You may not agree with this assessment. You may have your own method of estimating and scheduling development projects, in which case I congratulate you and suggest that you keep your method secret, guarding it as carefully as you would a winning technique for betting on the stock market or the horse races.

But *I* don't know how to estimate projects on a scientific, rational basis if (a) the deadline is determined in advance, and (b) I have no database of previous projects from which to base a current estimate.

I do know, however, that you have been estimating and scheduling your projects in some fashion—and you should continue in the same way with the use of structured techniques, with the possible exception of applying a "fudge factor" to the estimates. For example, your present scheme might involve asking five or six programmers for an estimate of the time required to code and test a certain module. Then you might toss out the high estimate and low estimate, and compute the arithmetic mean of the remaining estimates. Then you might add a "fudge factor" of 50 percent to cover unforeseen circumstances. With the structured techniques, there is a good possibility that you will be able to eliminate the fudge factor after the first few projects.

The effect of the structured techniques on your actions should be fairly minor, but the effect on your results will be dramatic: The chances are good that you will be able to meet the schedule and the estimates that you make. With your current projects, you add 50 percent to your estimates just to be safe, and yet probably find that your project is still three months late. With the structured techniques, you should probably still add 50 percent to the estimate, *but then you will meet the schedule as estimated.*

Consider this idea for a minute: *Why* are your current projects three months late? Aside from totally unforeseen catastrophes, what is the cause of the schedule slippage? It is usually not the time required to design the system, nor the time required to write the code. Most of the slippage occurs during that nebulous time called "system test and integration." That category, which you probably never scheduled in a properly con-servative fashion, is the one that will be decreased significantly with the use of structured development techniques.

Lest you think that I am being unnecessarily cynical, let me reassure you that I, too, make an honest attempt at scheduling and estimating the systems development projects in which I am involved. How? Probably the same way you do: by breaking the system into small pieces (modules), each of which is assigned to an individual programmer or to a small group of programmers. Then I ask each programmer or group for an estimate, and I adjust the estimate up or down based on my knowledge or their past performance, and any other available data. I then add all of the estimates from all of the program-mers, throw in another fudge factor of two (i.e., doubling the estimates supplied by the programmers), and *voila!* I have the overall estimate for the project.

With the structured techniques— especially structured analysis and design— this process is more accurate. Both structured analysis and structured design favor the development of smaller modules. Also, the techniques favor highly *independent* modules so that the overall effort required for the project can be more nearly approximated by the sum of the individual parts. In the past, the estimates tended to be based on larger modules whose completion was more difficult to estimate accurately and on modules that tended to be more *dependent* on one another (a fact that often wasn't discovered until late in the project— the systems integration phase).

13.2   THE EFFECT OF STRUCTURED TECHNIQUES ON CLASSICAL MILESTONES

In the past, systems development projects have been characterized by these recognizable milestones:

- request for system received by MIS department

- approval to begin system study received

- system study completed

- specification for new system completed

- specification for new system accepted

- computer systems design for new system completed

- detailed module design completed

- coding completed

- unit test completed

- system test completed

- acceptance test completed

- system in production

Each milestone served as an opportunity for various members of the organization to gather and review the status of the project. If the milestone had been achieved on schedule and within the budget constraints, everyone assumed that the project was proceeding according to plan.

With the structured techniques, many of these classical milestones will disappear. How many will disappear depends on whether you elect the conservative top-down approach or the radical top-down approach (recall the discussion in Chapter 4). If you elect to follow a conservative approach, all of the milestones up to and including "detailed module design completed" will remain the same.

If you elect to follow the radical approach, only the first two milestones listed above will remain the same, up to and including "approval to begin system study received."

Sooner or later (sooner if you follow the radical approach, later if you follow the conservative approach), you should expect to see the influence of the structured techniques on your milestones: An integrated pattern of specification and design and coding and testing will emerge.

With the structured techniques, therefore, you may expect that some analysis and design will be occurring all the way up to the day before the deadline. You can even expect your programmers to write code until the day before the deadline. These events would have caused ulcers had you been following the classical approach because you would have expected such coding efforts to be followed by several months of that ill-defined activity known as system test and integration.

13.3   MILESTONES AND THE STRUCTURED TECHNIQUES

If many of the classical milestones will be eliminated with the structured techniques, what new milestones will take their place? If you recall the discussion of Chapter 4, the answer should be obvious: The milestones correspond to the delivery of various *versions* of the system. The first few milestones will be the same as they are in the classical approach: We are usually required to produce a systems study and detailed statement of requirements; and, in a conservative approach, we may also need to produce a detailed design of a proposed new system. Then milestones can be expressed as versions. What gives the structured approach such a tremendous advantage over the classical approach is that each version can be defined by a definite date of implementation and by its features and capabilities.

For example, the simple payroll system in Chapter 4 could have the following set of milestones, if we assume a slightly conservative approach:

January 1	request for new payroll system received
February 1	approval to begin system study received
March 1	system study approved
April 1	specification for new system completed
May 1	version 1 of payroll system demonstrated to user
June 1	version 2 of payroll system in operation
July 1	version 3 of payroll system in operation
August 1	version 4: the final version in operation

The advantage of the version milestones is that they are tangible. For instance, from Chapter 4, we recall that Version 1 would not hire or fire anyone, could not give anyone a salary increase or decrease, paid everyone $100 per week, withheld $15 per week in taxes, and paid everyone with a paycheck printed in hexadecimal. Since Version 1 can thus be defined in terms of such tangible characteristics, it should be obvious by the specified deadline whether or not Version 1 works.

This last point is critical. With the classical method of project management, a typical milestone would be described as "detailed module design completed." But what does this mean? How do we know exactly what has been accomplished? How do we know that some design problems have not been postponed, to be discovered at some later milestone?

It is interesting to observe what happens at each milestone of a structured project. When the deadline arrives for Version 1, for example, the system may not be working. In the case of our simple payroll system, that means that the programmers will still be unable to produce a hexadecimal paycheck for $100.

"But that's not fair," the programmers will complain. "Actually, we're done—it's just that there's this one little bug that's preventing us from getting the right output."

To which the project manager will reply, "Too bad! You're not done. You didn't meet the deadline."

The programmers will cry, "We're 99.7 percent done. All we have is one last bug. And we think the bug is in the compiler."

The manager will respond, "Too bad! As far as I'm concerned, Version 1 either works, or it doesn't work. Evidently, your system is incapable of producing hexadecimal paychecks for $100, so it doesn't work!"

At which point, one of the programmers might say, "But that's not fair! *My* module works just fine! It's Fred's module that is causing all the trouble!"

To which the manager might state, "I don't care whose fault it is. Version 1 does not work. Therefore, the entire project is behind schedule."

The version approach to milestones is *extremely* powerful. If you carefully define your versions, particularly in terms of completed modules on a structure chart, the rate of progress is much more evident at a much earlier stage in the project than it used to be.

13.4   SUMMARY

To summarize the effects of structured techniques on estimating and milestones:

1.   Prepare your estimates as you always have;

2.   Expect that the first few milestones— perhaps through the end of systems analysis— will be much as they have always been; and

3.   Eliminate the rest of your milestones, and replace them with *versions* of a top-down systems implementation.

Chapter 14
WHAT CAN GO WRONG?

So far, this book has addressed the myriad little problems that you will encounter when you begin to implement structured programming, structured design, structured analysis, and the other structured techniques. But on a larger scale, what disasters should you expect? What major failures await you? On a philosophical level, *what can go wrong*?

None of the structured techniques are magical. Structured programming will not make it possible for you to walk on water. Structured design will not improve your sex life. Structured walkthroughs will not reduce the number of cavities in your children's teeth. Top-down implementation will not make it significantly easier for you to get along with your boyfriend/girlfriend/husband/wife/lover/mistress, cat, or dog.

Having said that, we are still left with the question: *What* might go wrong? I think you should be prepared for four major problem areas, each of which is discussed below.

14.1 POLITICAL PROBLEMS

Virtually all of this book has been written with the assumption that you are a manager working in a rational environment, that you supervise rational programmers and systems analysts, and that you work with rational users. A further assumption is that everyone in your MIS organization agrees that it would be desirable to develop maintainable, reliable software in an economical fashion.

Unfortunately, these assumptions are not valid in some organizations. You may encounter an irrational user who refuses to discuss his requirements with you. More likely, you work in an environment in which deadlines, schedules, and budgets are dictated from higher levels, and the opportunity for estimating, or even negotiating, is absent entirely.

If your organization has had a history of failures and overruns, you may not be able to invest the substantial time required to carry out proper structured analysis and structured design before you rush into the coding phase of your project.

It may be possible in such cases for you to introduce a "quiet revolution": Begin using structured walkthroughs, structured programming, structured design, and structured analysis without a fuss, and possibly even without telling anyone that you're doing it. Then, when people eventually ask you why your project was successful, you can tell them. Ideally, the MIS function will become increasingly visible in your organization, and senior management will make the investments that are necessary to perform your job properly.

14.2   PERSONNEL PROBLEMS

Almost everyone who has been in the data processing field for ten years or more has fond memories of "the good old days." Those were the days, the old-timers will tell you, when everyone knew how the compiler, the operating system, and even the hardware worked. This knowledge was necessary because one had to patch and modify all three on a day-to-day basis in order to get any work done. Those were the days when people worked throughout the night, slept in the computer room, and operated their own programs. Those were the days when men were men, when computers were *really* computers.

Naturally, these stories are exaggerated, but they contain some truth, too. In particular, the memories suggest that, back then, people lived to program, while today, people program to live. For a majority of computer programmers and systems analysts today, their jobs simply occupy them from nine to five and enable them to pay the rent and buy four color televisions.

Something happened to the personality and mentality of the data processing profession as a whole as we moved to the ultrasophisticated on-line, real-time, fourth-generation and fifth-generation machines of the 1980s. The profession began to attract people who, regardless of their race, creed, color, or university degrees, are *clerks*. They think like clerks, they talk like clerks, and they approach computer programming and systems analysis with all the enthusiasm of a sleepy civil service clerk who knows that he is just one year away from retirement.

For many years, I ran a company that trained some 250,000 programmers, designers, and systems analysts around the world. I met many of these people personally in seminars that I conducted, and was surprised by the number of them that have *never* read any computer articles or even opened a copy of *Datamation* or *Computerworld*; have never heard of ACM, IEEE, DPMA, ASM, or any other professional organizations; can't spell or pronounce the name of Dijkstra, Wirth, or Boehm; aren't aware of the structured techniques and wouldn't be interested if somebody showed them.

When such programmers and systems analysts are *forced* to learn structured programming, structured design, top-down implementation, and structured analysis, a frighteningly large number of them are unable to learn them. It is literally all they can do to write programs in the helter-skelter fashion to which they have become accustomed. To suggest that they should introduce some organization, some common sense, some *structure* into their work is beyond their ken.

If it appears that I am taking potshots at *your* organization, I apologize; yours may be one of the few organizations with good programmers and good systems analysts. My experience has been that small organizations—especially those that *must* make a profit on a year-to-year basis to survive—usually have good systems analysts who are still sufficiently competent technically to write their own programs. Conversely, large, stagnant, conservative organizations that survive by inertia, by *being*, without necessarily making a profit, tend to attract incompetent programmers and somnolent systems analysts; unfortunately, that description fits a lot of big banks, insurance companies, government agencies, and even some of the major manufacturing organizations.

If it seems as though I'm damning the entire profession from a lofty perch, I apologize again. However, it discourages me to meet programmers who have been programming in COBOL for ten years and who have no idea how a PERFORM statement works, but who are considered among the brightest in their organization!

14.3   TIME DELAY PROBLEMS

Even if your programmers and systems analysts are of average intelligence, you may run into another problem. It can easily take two or three years for the effect of structured techniques to be felt in your organization. On a global scale, structured programming was introduced in the 1965-68 era, discussed widely in the literature during the 1969-73 period, and hailed formally in 1973 by *Datamation* as the greatest invention since the advent of the subroutine. Yet there are still MIS organizations that do not use structured programming.

The reasons for this lapse vary from organization to organization, but a familiar pattern exists. First, nobody in company X heard about structured programming and structured analysis for a long time because they were all too busy working on current projects. Nobody had read *Datamation*, even though subscriptions are free; nobody would ever dream of paying real money to subscribe to the *IEEE* journals. Nobody had attended any professional software conferences, nor have they talked to any of their counterparts in other companies.

When they did hear about structured analysis, they weren't quite sure how to react. Probably one of their vendors brought it to their attention, and everyone suspected that it was a plot by the vendor to sell additional computer hardware or consulting services. After a while, perhaps someone decided to set up a committee to study the relevance of the structured techniques to their organization. The committee, as you might expect, studied the matter for a full year before producing its report.

Once the committee decided that the structured techniques were a good idea, someone else made a copy of a technical article on the subject for each of the programmers and systems analysts, attaching a memo that read, "The boss thinks this is a good idea." The programmers ignored it for several months. Another memo circulated, which dictated, "The boss wants everyone to use structured programming and structured analysis from now on."

At that point the programmers began writing their own interpretation of structured code, and the systems analysts began drawing crude data flow diagrams. It didn't work; they didn't like it. So they ignored structured programming and structured analysis again, knowing that the boss never looked at their work anyway.

Having seen that the effort was getting nowhere, someone then decided to take a more organized approach. The brighter programmers and systems analysts were sent to a training course, or given a book to read, or plunked in front of a videotape machine. A pilot project was attempted, and when it achieved only mediocre results, a second pilot project was attempted.

Because a pilot project was eventually successful— *very* successful— standards were developed, meetings were held among all the project managers, and structured programming and structured analysis were officially declared to be good things. Everyone was told to organize and train their project teams, so that the structured techniques could be used in earnest.

Some project managers demurred: They were in the middle of a critical project, and they couldn't afford to rock the boat with newfangled ideas. "*Next* project," they promised, "we'll start using structured analysis." Other project managers objected to using the structured techniques for various political reasons outlined throughout this book.

Meanwhile, *some* managers actually did begin using the structured techniques on a large-scale three-year project. But no results were immediately forthcoming. Besides, the unconvinced managers didn't want to believe the possibly favorable results until the *end* of the project.

How long does it take to implement structured techniques in an MIS organization? I have seen a few organizations implement them overnight, but most of the larger ones take anywhere from *five* to *ten* years to change their culture, to spread the ideas through the organization, and to really see measurable results. Meanwhile, during that transitional period, they must somehow continue suffering with bugs, low productivity, and maintenance headaches.

14.4   MAINTENANCE PROBLEMS

The final problem has been mentioned several times already: Even with all of the structured techniques discussed in this book, you still have to maintain the programming garbage accumulated over the past ten or twenty years. It has been estimated that there are approximately 100 billion lines of existing code around the world; that code is not going to disappear overnight.

I don't have to tell you how difficult it is to maintain an IBM 1401 AUTOCODER program on an IBM 3081, especially when the program listing and the source code for the 1401 program were lost long ago and only a patched object module exists. Some organizations have hundreds of such rotten, old "bug-infested" programs.

If you are one of those unlucky managers who is stuck with the maintenance of a thousand work-years of unstructured code, there is not much that I can do for you, other than offer you a lot of sympathy, and one last little bit of advice: If you don't start *now* to write your new systems in a structured fashion, you will be in the same position ten years from now— if not worse.

Chapter 15
THE IMPACT OF PERSONAL COMPUTERS

During the mid-1980s, personal computers began proliferating throughout the corporate environment. By 1990, it is estimated that approximately 50 percent of the white-collar workers in the United States will have access to a PC (though not necessarily one on their desk). The arguments about whether or not personal computers are beneficial and whether or not users are making productive use of them are beyond the scope of this book. However, the subject is moot since users are getting the machines regardless of what anyone in the MIS organization thinks.

Many MIS professionals and managers will argue that the end-users can accomplish many useful tasks with a personal computer, but also that they can get themselves into terrible trouble. I share that opinion so emphatically that I recently authored a book entitled *The Perils of Personal Computing* [Yourdon, 1985].

The purpose of this chapter is not to explore in great detail all of the ways that users can wreak havoc with personal computers, but rather to explore the subject in the context of software engineering and structured techniques. Is structured analysis irrelevant in an organization where the end-users have their own personal computers? Should users learn structured analysis on their own?

15.1 CLASSIFICATION

Before proceeding, we should remember that not all end-users are alike. Members of the MIS community, myself included, often forget this point, and it is a crucially important one when we begin discussing the things that the user will do with (or to) his computer.

One way of differentiating among users is by level of experience. Roughly speaking, there are three important categories: the rank amateur, the cocky novice, and the veteran. The rank amateur has never seen or touched a personal computer and is frightened that he will somehow break it if he does something wrong. He will need help simply learning which end of a floppy disk should be inserted into the disk drive. The cocky novice, on the other hand, is someone who successfully created a small spreadsheet using Lotus 1-2-3 or Excel, or who managed to put his address book on a computer using dBase-III. From these successful experiences, he has concluded that he can tackle the accounting application in his organization, which involves functions and data elements a thousand times more numerous and complex than his "toy" programs.

There are also a few legitimate veterans, although professional programmers and systems analysts may not like to admit that they exist. End-users who have been project team members on large systems development projects in the 1970s and 1980s may be in a good position to build a well-structured system on an IBM PC or Apple Macintosh. Also, there are people who majored in computer science, but who wound up working in the organization's marketing department ten years ago. Finally, there is a generation of children beginning to enter the job market with an increasing amount of *general* computer literacy: it is estimated, for example, that a child born in 1980 will have written ten thousand lines of code (most of it atrociously unstructured) by the time he or she graduates from high school in the late 1990s.

Generalizations are also possible about the reaction of end-users to personal computers based on their age and job category, even though a generalization can be wrong in any individual case. Indeed, because generalizations may be *dangerously* wrong, it is important to realize that all users are different. It is clearly wrong to assume that all users are illiterate about computers; it is also wrong to assume that all managers are opposed to personal computers (because, according to the generalization, male managers don't know how to type, and female managers don't want to type because it is demeaning).

So, the first question that should be asked when anyone in the MIS organization wants to know how the quality of systems will be affected by widespread distribution of PCs is: *What kind of users are we talking about?* What do they know? What are their attitudes towards personal computers? What are they willing to learn? Are they willing to learn lessons that the MIS organization has learned slowly and painfully over the past twenty years, or do they want to start all over again?

15.2   THE DANGERS OF PERSONAL COMPUTING

In most cases, personal computing has brought tremendous benefits to the user community. MIS personnel occasionally remark that the typical personal computer is only used for one hour a day (so what?), or that it is used only to maintain the end-user's calendar and diary; but there are far more stories of users accomplishing important and useful tasks with their own computer. Users have a strong sense of power when they discover that they can build their own applications quickly, and that they can control the way the systems are run, rather than having to depend on a centralized MIS empire that they often regard as dictatorial and unresponsive.

However, things don't always work as well as the personal computer advertisements on television would have you believe. Although many users have not yet discovered them, the following problems typically occur when *real* systems are developed by amateurs or cocky novices on a personal computer:

- *Lack of testing.* Most users don't write their own BASIC programs, but they do create complex applications using spreadsheet programs and such fourth-generation languages as dBase-III or PC-Focus. In many cases, they don't even spot-check the results of the spreadsheet calculations to ensure that they are correct; nor do they test to ensure that their request for a report of "all customers in Wyoming except those over sixty-five and those who are left-handed, but not the ones who have brown eyes in Montana" produced what it was supposed to produce.

- *Proliferation of local databases.* The MIS community has spent the past twenty years dealing with the problems of fragmented "local" files. Many would argue that we now understand the problem and know how to solve it, but that it will take another five to ten years to implement the solution. Now we have users creating their own databases without any supervision from the MIS organization. A user with a 40-megabyte disk (which will soon be replaced by 100-megabyte disks and then by gigabyte-sized optical disks) can store an incredible amount of data; if every user in every department starts using this potential, the problems of redundancy, synchronization, and data integrity can be staggering.

- *Backup and security.* The majority of end-user databases are not backed up on a regular basis, nor are there backup copies of many critical application programs. Confidential information is stored on floppy disks or hard disks that are easily accessible to anyone who wanders through the office while the user is away from his desk. Again, the MIS organization has only begun to deal with this expensive, difficult problem on the large mainframe computers, and it is not at all clear that most users have any awareness of the problem.

- *The lack of documentation.* Since most users don't write "real" programs in BASIC or PASCAL, we don't have to worry about program documentation. But they *do* build systems by creating their own databases and writing programs in fourth-generation languages, or by purchasing commercial packages which have to be customized or "configured" to meet the user's special needs. In many cases, none of this information is documented; nor are the operating procedures documented; nor are the interactions between the new personal computer and the existing user organization documented. When the user is transferred to a different job, or retires, quits, or is fired, all of this "informal" information will be lost—a problem which, once again, the MIS organization has dealt with many times before.

- *The difference between a program and a system.* Many users believe that they are using a personal computer to improve the productivity of some *local* activity within their own microscopic area of work, such as by automating a calculation that would otherwise be done manually. Inevitably, though, they begin to use their new computer power to add new functions, or change their interfaces with other departments, or cause other departments to change their way of operating simply because of the *speed* with which they can now do their work. Hence, what begins as a local activity (which could be thought of as a program) inevitably ends up as a modification, or perturbation, of a *system.* But users don't usually think in terms of systems, nor do they have modeling tools naturally available to them to study the impact that their changes will have upon an existing system.

15.3 STRUCTURED TECHNIQUES AND PERSONAL COMPUTERS

Thus, users with personal computers *do* need to learn about the structured techniques discussed in this book. Some of the users need to learn about all of the techniques, and *all* users need to learn about some of the techniques.

All users should learn about the system life cycle discussed in Chapters 2 and 3 of this book. They should learn that there are two distinct activities— analysis and design— even if the programming part of their work is trivial. They should learn the importance of testing and should hear dozens of ugly, gut-wrenching disaster stories to impress upon them how easy it is for their organization to lose millions of dollars because of a misplaced semicolon or a sloppy piece of Boolean logic.

When the user is building a system with a database (for instance, a customer database, a personnel file, or a product file), he should be given an introduction to the data modeling portion of structured analysis; he should learn how to think of his database in terms of *objects* and *relationships*. He should also learn about the messy and boring operational issues of backup, security, recovery, audit trails, and redundancy of data.

For example, many personal computer users find that organizing a customer list is one of the first things they do with their new machine. A customer is an entity, something about which we store data. One attribute of a customer is his name; another is his address. But many first-time users unconsciously develop a model in which "customer name" is a single, indivisible unit of information consisting of the person's title, first name, and last name. If the customer list is implemented in this fashion, then all the components of the customer's name will be stored, retrieved, and manipulated as a single, atomic chunk of information.

Similarly, we might imagine the user defining the city, state, and zip code portion of the address as if this material were one indivisible unit. This method may be acceptable for the user's initial applications, and one can imagine the user laboriously entering thousands of customer names and addresses. With such PC-based database packages as PFS:File and dBase-III Plus, the data entry would probably take place by responding to a series of prompts from the computer. Thus, a typical dialogue between the user and the database package might look like this:

CUSTOMER NAME: Mr. John Q. Smith
ADDRESS: 123 Main Street
                         Snarkville, New York 10297

Six months later, it may become painfully obvious that the customer's zip code has to be treated as an individual unit so that the mailing list can be produced in zip code sequence for bulk mailing at the post office. Also, the customer's first name has to be accessed by itself so that the user can write a form letter that begins, "Dear X," with X being the customer's first name. Because of the original conceptual model of the data, and because of the implementation of that conceptual model, it is now virtually impossible to use the thousands of customer names that have been typed into the computer.

When the user is going to implement his own system (whether on a mainframe or a PC), he should learn the concepts of structured analysis presented in Chapter 3, regardless of whether the system is going to be implemented in COBOL, BASIC, or some higher-level (fourth-generation) language. Normally, the user needs between two and five days of classroom lectures and workshops to absorb the details of the structured analysis modeling techniques and to become adept at developing models.

15.4   SUMMARY

As MIS professionals have heard over and over again, ad nauseum, today's personal computers have more power than the most powerful mainframe on earth twenty years ago. The personal computer that I am using to write this book, for example, has five megabytes of internal RAM memory; this is considerably more than most mainframe computers had in the 1960s.

But we MIS people built large, complex systems in the 1960s! We built systems that landed the first man on the moon, automated the stock exchanges, and provided on-line, real-time airline reservation capabilities around the world. And we learned, gradually and painfully, that the only way we could accomplish this was to treat large, complex problems with a great deal of respect. It is fair to say that many organizations began using structured techniques and other software engineering techniques out of fear— fear of the consequences of an information system that fails.

So why should users, with their super-powerful PCs, be any different? They too are building large, complex systems— even if those systems do run on a small machine that sits on a corner of the desk. They too are creating systems whose failure could have disastrous consequences for themselves and for their organization.

Here is an analogy. When the Model-T Ford was introduced to society, it suddenly became obvious that we "users" had the power and the freedom to travel from place to place under our own control; no longer were we at the mercy of the steam locomotive, with its fixed schedules and its centralized management. But does that mean that we allow everyone— everyone with the money to buy a car— to run amok, driving around wherever and whenever they want? Obviously not. A driver's license must be obtained (by satisfying some test that indicates a minimum capability), and then the "rules of the road" must be obeyed on an ongoing basis.

The same should be true, in my opinion, with personal computers in large organizations.

Chapter 16
FOURTH-GENERATION
LANGUAGES

Just as we speak of generations of computer hardware that have been developed over the past thirty years, it is now fashionable to speak of generations of programming languages. Fourth-generation languages have attracted considerable attention in the 1980s, and many MIS professionals wonder how the structured techniques are and will be affected by the use of these languages.

For perspective, we should characterize the first three generations of popular computer programming languages:

- *First generation*— machine language programming, in which the programmer had to be familiar with the binary one's and zero's that formed individual machine instructions. This most primitive form of programming was used primarily in the 1950s, when most of us had never heard of computers, and when many of us had not yet been born.

- *Second generation*— assembly language programming, in which the programmer could use symbolic codes to describe machine instructions (for example, LOAD, ADD, and SHIFT) as well as symbolic codes to refer to machine addresses. This generation began in the early 1960s and continues to be used in a few maniacal MIS organizations even today. However, it began to be replaced in most organizations in the early 1970s.

- *Third generation*— the conventional compiler-oriented procedural languages such as COBOL, FORTRAN, and PASCAL. These languages are significant because they allow programmers to deal with abstractions: Programs can be organized with DO-WHILE and IF-THEN-ELSE constructs, even if there is no single machine instruction available for carrying them out. Complex data elements can be manipulated without much regard for how those elements will be stored and manipulated within the computer hardware. Third-generation languages still predominate most MIS organizations.

16.1   CHARACTERISTICS OF A FOURTH-GENERATION LANGUAGE

In the late 1970s and early 1980s, a new kind of programming language began to emerge; examples are FOCUS, NOMAD, MAPPER, ADR/IDEAL, MARK V, RAMIS, and such languages as PC-FOCUS and dBASE-III Plus for personal computers.

These fourth-generation languages, or 4GLs, usually have the following features:

- *Convenient facilities for defining and creating a database.* The database may be a simple file structure, or, with some of the more sophisticated 4GLs, the user may have the ability to create a relational database. The user is given a facility for defining the data contents of each record; for example, he can indicate that his new customer file should consist of records with fields "first-name," "last-name," and "street-address." In most cases, the user specifies the maximum size of each field; and in many cases, he can indicate the field type (e.g., alphabetic, numeric, date, logical, etc.) and perhaps even a range of permissible values. Similar facilities allow the user to add and delete records from his database.

- *The languages are usually implemented as interpreters rather than compilers.* With third-generation languages, the user/programmer writes a program, perhaps consisting of several hundred statements, then compiles it. If an error is detected, he must correct the original source program and recompile before the program is executed. Once he begins executing the program, he may discover errors, and then the process of revising, recompiling, and executing the program must be repeated. However, with an interpretive language, each statement can be examined and executed as soon as it is entered into the computer. Thus, trivial syntax errors can be corrected when the information is still fresh in the programmer's mind; run-time errors can also be corrected more easily, often with the ability to continue the execution of the program from the point where the error was detected. The problem with interpretive languages is that they are typically between ten times and one hundred times slower than compiled languages. This was a major problem in the 1960s and 1970s, and generally made interpretive languages impracticable; whether it is still a problem in the late 1980s and early 1990s is a subject that will be discussed below.

- *"User-friendly" features.* Even though COBOL was originally intended as a language for "ordinary" people, it quickly became evident that its syntax is so complicated that only a professional programmer would be able to use it; the same is true of FORTRAN and even BASIC if one wants to write more than two or three lines of code. In contrast, the fourth-generation languages typically make a more serious effort to use English-like words rather than the cryptic abbreviations for commands. The user-friendliness is also augmented by the 4GL's tendency to assume default values for tedious details that the nontechnical user often doesn't want to worry about. A common example is report formats: Many users don't want to bother specifying such details as the placement of page numbers, and column headings. The 4GLs also provide extensive "help" facilities (which is possible partly because of the interpretive nature of the language) so that a befuddled user can ask for guidance on his CRT screen, rather than having to grope through a manual that may not be easily accessible.

- *Most details of report generation are handled automatically.* As mentioned above, this feature contributes significantly to the user-friendliness of the 4GLs. However, most of the 4GLs also have provisions for customizing reports, so that a finicky user can place page numbers and headings and arrange the format and layout of the report in whatever manner he wants. For customizing, the user usually has a menu of choices that he can select and change at will, a method considerably simpler and more appealing than programming the same information in COBOL.

- *Ad hoc inquiry facilities.* One reason for building a database is to permit ad hoc inquiries: The user wants to inspect a single record in the database, or perhaps all records that match certain criteria. Or perhaps the user simply wants to browse through the database, unsure of exactly what it is he wants to find. Again, this facility is provided in a format that is command-driven with English-like commands, or menu-driven, in which the user makes his choices in a simple, convenient format. The same task can be done in COBOL, but requires the user to (a) find a programmer, (b) describe what records he wants to retrieve, (c) wait for the programmer to write a program in COBOL, (d) wait for the program to be compiled, and then perhaps revised and compiled again, and (e) wait for the programmer or the operations department to run the program and produce results, which may show the user that he really wanted slightly different selection criteria for his retrieval.

16.2   ADVANTAGES OF FOURTH-GENERATION LANGUAGES

There is no shortage of information about the benefits of fourth-generation languages. Language vendors and industry gurus praise the 4GLs in all of the popular computer magazines and journals. The primary advantages are the following.

1.   *4GLs can increase the productivity of the programming phase of the project by a factor of ten.* Obviously, this increase can be significant. It may mean that a six-month project can be done in two weeks, and that a two-week project can be done in a day. Because of this fast turnaround, all of the details about the project are still fresh in everyone's mind, so that problems and misunderstandings can be resolved more quickly— in contrast to the typical three-year project that the MIS organization carries out, in which everyone involved at the beginning of the project has disappeared by the time the program testing is finished.

2.   *4GLs avoid "reinventing the wheel" on trivial programming matters.* In a typical third-generation programming environment, a substantial amount of time is spent coding the details of file definitions,

record layouts, report formats, and so forth. Inevitably, each programmer duplicates much of the work that another programmer has done the day before. With the 4GLs, all of this specifying is either done automatically or with simple commands that require little duplication.

3.   *4GLs can vastly improve the productivity of program maintenance.*   Many maintenance changes to an existing computer program require little or no systems analysis or design.   Such changes merely reflect the user's need to make a small change to the format of a report or to one of the calculations in the program ("Hey, we just heard that the sales tax was increased to 9 percent yesterday. We better change the program before we enter any invoices today!"). If such programming details can be accomplished ten times more quickly than would be possible in a COBOL environment, then the user can do it himself, rather than waiting for the MIS organization.

16.3   DISADVANTAGES OF FOURTH-GENERATION LANGUAGES

Companies that develop and market fourth-generation languages don't like to talk about the disadvantages of their products, nor do consultants who make their living by preaching to senior management that an "instant solution" to the applications backlog now exists.   But there are some important disadvantages.

1.   *Improvements in the programming process, but not the systems analysis process.*   The programming phase occupies only about 15 percent of the development time and resources of a typical project. Hence, improving that activity by a factor of ten may not really accomplish much, unless the user's requirements are so well known that no formal systems analysis is necessary (which is often the case for maintenance programming).   But for a complex system involving many different users or different groups of users in different geographical locations, the systems analysis activity is still the most difficult and time-consuming part of the project.

2.   *Incompatibility with existing databases.*   For a new system, the user/programmer sometimes has the

ability to create a new database that is compatible with, or even created by, the fourth-generation language. Often, though, the new system must use an existing file or database which may not be accessible by the 4GL. There may be a facility for translating, or "importing," the current database into the format required by the 4GL, but even this step may be awkward. If the new system updates the database, then it has to be translated back, or exported, to its original form (and meanwhile, other users may have been updating the original copy of the database).

3. *Performance and efficiency issues.* As mentioned, the fourth-generation languages are interpretive, which makes them approximately ten times more costly in terms of CPU cycles (and, in many cases, at least ten times more costly in terms of memory requirements and other hardware resources). In addition, some of the newer 4GLs use artificial intelligence technology to permit "natural English" interactions with the user, placing a heavy burden upon the computer. In some environments, efficiency is not a concern (e.g., the personal computer environment, where the user has full access to his machine and a limited volume of input transactions). In some mainframe environments, though, the centralized computer facility may not be able to handle the processing requirements of several hundred users simultaneously running 4GL programs. Also, a 4GL program that was easy to develop may not be suitable for a high-volume application, like on-line order entry or airline reservations, when fast response time is critical. Obviously, this problem will be mitigated by faster and more powerful hardware, which we can expect to see for the next several years. The real question is whether the user's demands and expectations will grow more quickly than the hardware technology advances.

4. *Inadequacies in the language itself.* As mentioned, fourth-generation languages attempt to be user friendly and to relieve the user of many of the details of programming, such as the format of report layouts. Not all are successful. What the language developer thinks of as user friendly may not appear very friendly at all to the users in your organization,

especially when the user does something wrong:
many 4GLs produce unintelligible error messages—
verbose, with lots of detail, but unintelligible
nonetheless—that leave the user shaking his head in
bewilderment.

16.4   CONCLUSION

The discussion above is not intended to discourage you
from using a fourth-generation programming language; in the
proper environment, they can be a powerful tool. Indeed, their
greatest application is in the area of maintenance where so many
of the programming activities are trivial, and could often be
accomplished directly by the user.

On the other hand, 4GLs are not going to provide an
instant solution to the problem of building large, complex
systems. We must still invest a considerable amount of time and
energy modeling the user requirements and then use structured
design to model the hardware and software architecture of the
entire system. *Then* we can use a fourth-generation language to
implement the system, if that language is appropriate for the
machine, the database, and the operating environment.

Chapter 17
APPLICATION PROTOTYPING

In the past few years, there has been strong interest in the concept of prototyping of information systems—that is, using a combination of high-level languages, "screen painters," database facilities, and report generators to enable the systems analyst to build a mockup of a proposed system.

Some MIS professionals feel that the prototyping approach is an alternative to the "paper" models described in the earlier chapters of this book. Indeed, some argue that the growing availability of such prototyping tools may have rendered the structured techniques obsolete. Not so. Prototyping tools are a useful and important *complement* to the structured techniques, not a replacement for them. In some cases, the prototyping tools can minimize the extent of detailed, paper-based systems modeling, but it is dangerous and downright wrong to conclude that the structured techniques have been rendered useless by the introduction of prototyping tools. The rest of this chapter discusses the reason for this conclusion.

17.1   THE MOTIVATION FOR PROTOTYPING

There are three major motivations for using prototyping tools. The first has to do with improving communication between users and systems analysts. While it is almost universally agreed now that the classical functional specification fails to facilitate meaningful communication between user and analyst, some MIS organizations have found that data flow diagrams and the other related tools of structured analysis have failed, too. The latter communication problem has sometimes been caused by a failure to introduce the diagrams to the users properly and to train the user community adequately in their use. Nevertheless, despite the best efforts of the systems analyst, sometimes the users refuse to look at such abstract paper models. In other cases, the user willingly looks at the diagrams, but is unable to comprehend them. If this is the case, the prototyping approach offers an alternative: a working model of the system that uses real terminals (or PC workstations) and supposedly real inputs and outputs.

Another reason for the popularity of prototyping tools is the ease and quickness with which a prototype can be constructed and revised. A prototype of a small- to medium-sized system might be constructed in days, while the equivalent paper model created by the structured analyst might require weeks. If the user wishes to change the prototype either because the prototype reflected the analyst's misunderstanding of the user's requirements, or because the user wanted to explore some different scenarios, the change can be accomplished within hours or even minutes. With the paper model approach, the change could require days, and as discussed earlier, the user might have difficulty visualizing the consequences of the change while viewing an abstract model.

Part of the problem is that the paper model approach of structured analysis and structured design has been conducted almost universally on a *manual* basis, using nothing more sophisticated than paper and pencil. In Chapter 19, I will discuss automated CASE tools, which allow system models to be composed on a personal computer workstation and modified at will. Early results from the use of such automated tools show that the productivity of the systems analysis process can be improved by approximately 30 percent just by automating the drawing and revising of diagrams and supporting textual material. Automation could thus significantly reduce the frustration that users feel while waiting for the model to be developed.

Such user frustrations have also been the result of early versions of project management methodologies that first embraced the use of structured analysis. Specifically, several methodologies emphasized the importance of developing "current physical" models of the system that the user intends to automate. Unfortunately, this process can be time-consuming and wasteful, and it does not provide the user community or senior management with any tangible evidence of progress. In the worst case, a nervous systems analyst can spend forever modeling the user's current physical system because it is nonthreatening and easy to accomplish without any creativity. In such an environment, prototyping is obviously an attractive alternative. However, many current project methodologies (including that described in the current edition of *Managing the System Life Cycle* [Yourdon, 1988]) now de-emphasize the need to model the user's current system and suggest that, wherever possible, the systems analyst begin modeling the essential characteristics of the user's new system.

A final reason for the popularity of prototyping is that it highlights the human interface, by letting the user play with alternative screen formats and report layouts. While not necessarily illuminating the important functions and stored data elements in the system, the facility makes prototyping an attractive approach for many users, especially those who will actually be performing data entry queries at a terminal.

17.2   THE PREMISES IN A PROTOTYPING ENVIRONMENT

For a prototyping approach to work successfully, one has to assume that the following conditions are true:

- *There is only a single user, or at most a small group of users who are "localized" in the sense that they work in the same organizational group and within the same physical location.* It is far less likely that prototyping will be used on a project with diverse users in different organizational groups and different physical locations.

- *The data model exists or can be easily created.* This assumption is safe in an environment where (a) the user wants a new system that will interact with an existing database, and (b) the MIS organization has already developed an information model of that database, complete with data dictionary definitions, entity-relationship diagrams, and so forth. For a completely new system with a completely new database, it may still be possible to derive the information model fairly quickly and create a data dictionary that can serve as the foundation for the prototype.

- *The application is small to medium in size.* With the power of some prototyping tools and with the power of fourth-generation languages that may eventually be used to implement the "production" version of the system, the term *medium-sized* may have to be redefined in many MIS organizations. A system consisting of fifty thousand lines of COBOL may be considered large in a classical environment, but only medium-sized in a prototyping and/or a fourth-generation language environment. Nevertheless, most MIS organizations would not use prototyping tools to develop a complete prototype of a system that will eventually consist of five million lines of COBOL, though it may be advantageous to prototype some parts of the system. Similarly, prototyping would not be used in a system requiring only 500 lines of COBOL code.

- *Everyone agrees that the prototype is only a "toy" system and that it is intended as nothing more than a model of the production system.* As Bernard Boar points out eloquently in [Boar, 1984], a system developed with prototyping tools almost always lacks some features that are essential for a "production" system: backup, recovery, extensive error-checking, audit trails, and performance engineering— that is, appropriate "tuning" to make the system operate with adequate efficiency for high volumes of input transactions.

17.3 THE DANGERS OF PROTOTYPING

From this discussion, it should be evident that there is an intrinsic difficulty with the prototyping approach: The users and the systems analysts may not agree on the basic premises discussed above, or even worse, they not even discuss *any* premises. Obviously, an opportunity exists for frustration, disappointment, and disillusionment ("so prototyping turned out to be just one more panacea that didn't deliver the miracles it promised," mused one discouraged MIS director to me recently) for both users and systems analysts.

Specifically, the problems that MIS organizations have encountered with the prototyping approach are as follows:

- *The prototype is put into full-scale production.* During World War II, several "temporary" buildings were constructed, often at great haste, with flimsy wooden materials and thin tin roofs; one of the more common examples is the ubiquitous Quonset hut. I lived in a Quonset hut six years after the end of World War II; nearly twenty years after the war, I observed that some of the administrative offices in my college were located in similar "temporary" World War II buildings. No doubt there are parts of the world where such buildings continue to be occupied today, more than forty years after the fighting came to a halt. I fear that the same phenomenon will occur with MIS systems built with prototyping tools, especially when the prototype is deceptively "real" and is being built for a user desperate to automate some portion of his business *now*. The problems may not be apparent in the short term, but the long-term consequences of a "toy" system without backup, recovery, and audit trail facilities could be devastating.

• *The prototype may be thrown away.* In order to avoid the problem described above, the prototype *should* be thrown away and replaced with a properly designed and implemented production system. But if the prototype is thrown away, then there will be no model of the requirements of the system, a disastrous state that is characteristic of most, if not all, MIS systems today. A new approach, known as *evolutionary prototyping*, may solve this problem: The prototype is never thrown away, but is gradually "fleshed out" until it has all of the operational characteristics required of the system, *including* backup, recovery, etc. See [Connell, 1989] for more details on the practicality of this approach.

• *The prototyping approach eliminates the idea of essential/logical models.* By definition, a set of prototyping tools provides a *specific* implementation environment for building a "toy" system; we assume that the prototyping environment is compatible with the implementation environment that will be used for the production system, *from the user's point of view* . For example, the production system will use the same kind of terminal, with the same human interface as the prototype. But, the systems analyst and the user are brainwashed into exploring *essential* system requirements within the physical constraints of the hardware/software technology provided by the prototyping environment. Thus, it is likely that with the prototyping approach, no one will develop an essential model of the system, nor will anyone seriously consider alternative implementation technologies, such as different human interfaces (e.g., if you built your prototype in an IBM PC environment, what are the chances that you would seriously investigate the Macintosh human interface?), or different man-machine boundaries (e.g., a distributed system with PCs and a mainframe, rather than a minicomputer).

- *The prototype may be regarded by the user as wasted time.* If the prototype is thrown away and replaced with a separately developed production system, someone in the user community may complain, "Why did we waste so much time building the prototype if it was going to be thrown away?" The problem is usually that the user did not understand at the beginning of the project that the prototype was never intended as anything but a model. This problem is often exacerbated by the fact that the production version of the system takes much longer to build than the prototype.

17.4   CONCLUSIONS AND COMMENTS

Although the previous section dwelled on the problems and dangers of prototyping, you should not conclude that prototyping is a bad idea. It should be regarded as a tool that can be used well, used poorly, or used in circumstances where it was never intended to be used. A superbly crafted tool in the hands of a mediocre technician will not accomplish much, and, in fact, could do much harm. Conversely, a brilliant technician can accomplish miracles even if the available tools are mediocre and primitive.

Two other points should be considered about the concept of prototyping:

- For a large system, it makes a great deal of sense to develop two or three levels of high-level data flow diagrams, together with appropriate data dictionary entries, entity-relationship diagrams, and so on, to get a feeling for the major subsystems that will eventually be built. Then, any one of those subsystems could be implemented with the prototyping tools available to the organization. In this sense, it is obvious that the structured techniques can co-exist with the concept of prototyping.

- The top-down implementation techniques discussed in Chapter 4 could be regarded as an alternative form of prototyping; the difference is that the early prototypes—that is, the early versions of the system—are constructed from real code that should continue to be used in the final production system. As we saw in Chapter 4, there are several factors that influence the project manager's decision to follow a radical top-down approach or a conservative top-down approach; thus, it is possible that the project team could begin coding their first version of the system on the first day of the project. In such an environment, the only difference between the top-down implementation approach and the current prototyping approach is the sophistication of the programming tools: The top-down approach will typically involve a third-generation programming language like COBOL, whereas the prototyping approach is more likely to involve fourth-generation languages supported by sophisticated on-line screen painters, etc. Nevertheless, it is important to recognize the philosophical similarity between prototyping and top-down implementation.

Chapter 18
DATA MODELING AND OBJECT-ORIENTED DESIGN

The purpose of this brief chapter is to put to rest a debate that has raged throughout some parts of the computer industry since the late 1970s: the debate between advocates of information modeling and object-oriented design (known variously as "those database fanatics" and "those Ada fanatics") and advocates of structured analysis and structured design (known variously as "those function-modeling fanatics" or "those guys who draw bubbles").

The fundamental problem is that neither group understands the other, or acknowledges the possible importance of a different viewpoint on the subject of systems modeling. The data modeling group argues, "Model the essential *information* within an enterprise—the functions are simple and will fall into place naturally." The structured analysis group seems to be arguing, "Model the functions and the flow of data between the functions—the database is straightforward and will fall into place naturally." Meanwhile, a third group, largely ignored by the first two groups of religious zealots, consists of people building real-time systems—people for whom the time-dependent behavior of the system is the most important aspect of systems modeling.

Once the analysis phase of the project is finished and systems design is underway, the schism often continues. "Use the data as a guideline for deciding how to partition the system into smaller pieces," the data modeling group argues. "Define the objects that the system must deal with, and the operations that are allowed on each object." Meanwhile, the process modeling group argues, "Use the functions as the basis for deciding how to partition the system. Break each function into smaller, highly cohesive, loosely coupled sub-functions."

To a large extent, the arguments of each camp reflect the kind of systems they build. All systems have some functional, some data-related, and some time-dependent behavior. However, it has often been true that one "dimension" of system

218

complexity dominates the other two. Thus, we can imagine a three-dimensional space, as illustrated by Figure 18.1, in which the X-axis represents increasingly complex functions within a system, the Y-axis represents increasingly complex information (objects and relationships), and the Z-axis represents increasingly complex time-dependent behavior.

From this perspective, it is fair to say that the structured analysis advocates make their arguments with the assumption that all important systems (namely, the ones they worked on) fall into the area marked A in Figure 18.1. Similarly, the database advocates make their arguments on the assumption that all important systems fall into the area marked B, and the real-time fanatics make the assumption that all important systems fall into the area marked C.

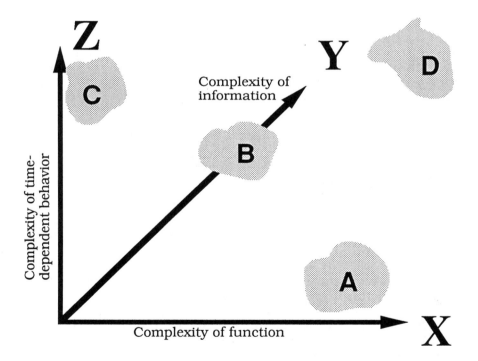

Figure 18.1: **Three dimensions of system complexity**

It is also important to note that the perspective of MIS professionals is strongly influenced by the tools they have available, and by the systems development environment in which they work. As an old proverb says, "If the only tool you have is a hammer, then all the world looks like a nail." System developers working in a classical COBOL environment are naturally going to look at the world from a function-oriented point of view; system developers working in a relational database environment, with powerful query languages and fourth-generation languages, are more likely to take a data-oriented view of the world. And those who work in languages like Smalltalk and Ada have the wherewithal, and therefore the inclination, to also take a data-oriented view.

18.1   THE CURRENT SITUATION

During the past few years, each camp has finally begun to understand the other two; more importantly, we have all begun to realize that there are systems that are complex in all three dimensions shown in Figure 18.1. Thus, we are now finding ourselves dealing increasingly with systems that fall into the area marked D in Figure 18.1. Banking systems now exhibit real-time behavior; real-time process control systems now have complex databases; and on-line database inquiry systems have increasingly complex functions to ensure that the data is entered correctly and retrieved in a meaningful fashion.

The result is a recognition on the part of each camp for the other two. People who build operating systems and process control systems will sometimes acknowledge that a system built with COBOL could have some real-time characteristics, and that not all COBOL programmers are brain-dead. People who are long-time database fanatics grant that data flow diagrams are sometimes useful, and structured analysis fanatics acknowledge that information modeling is an important aspect of most complex systems.

Equally important, most professionals now realize that the function modeling viewpoint, the data modeling viewpoint, and the state-transition models are not mutually exclusive. Rather, they provide three complementary views of a system. A formal relationship among the various views has been sadly lacking until recently. It is now clearly understood, as discussed in Chapter 4, that there are formal one-to-one relationships between the data flow diagram, the entity-relationship diagram, and the state transition diagram; and it is recognized that the data dictionary is the linchpin that holds all three models together.

Naturally, there are still many systems that fall into the category shown as A, B, or C in Figure 18.1. For such systems, one type of model may be the primary one, dominating the other two. But for more and more systems in the 1990s, all three models will be important; to favor one and ignore the others will be an increasingly serious mistake.

18.2   CURRENT ISSUES

Most MIS professionals agree that all three models are important. However, there are still some unresolved questions, particularly two concerning structured analysis and information modeling: Which model should be developed first? At what level in the user organization should the models be developed?

The question of which comes first is best answered by the classic phrase, "It all depends . . . ." Some typical scenarios are the following:

- If there is a strong, centralized database admin-istration group within the organization, then it is likely that the data models will have been developed before your project commences. In that case, the function modeling will presumably take place with an initial data model, though modifications to the data model may be required as a result of the new project.

- If no data analysis has been done, then it is likely that the function model (the data flow diagrams and structure charts) and the data model will be developed concurrently. In practice, it often happens that the data model is derived from some of the questions raised in the function modeling process (for example, "Where does this data come from? What happens to the data? Where does it go after it has been processed?").

- In an organization where there has been no corporate-wide data modeling and where the data itself is not complex, centrally controlled or intrinsically interesting, function modeling may take place without any data modeling.

This last scenario leads us into the second common question: At what level in the organization does all this modeling take place? There are three common levels: the project level, the departmental level, and the enterprise level. When the modeling activities occur strictly within the context of an individual project, function modeling tends to dominate; when done at the level of an entire enterprise, data modeling tends to dominate; and at the departmental level, both types of modeling are equally important. Of course, the third type of modeling, time-dependent behavior modeling, is a third dimension that is extremely important at the project level, less important at the departmental level, and generally unimportant at the enterprise level.

This perspective reflects the political realities that exist at different levels in the organization. If one is working on an individual project to serve the needs of an individual user, then functions are all-important and the global aspects of the data are often irrelevant. Conversely, the systems analyst attempting to model an entire enterprise is uninterested in the functions carried out by any individual group, but is extremely interested in the information common to all groups. At the departmental level, both functions and data are important.

Chapter 19
THE FUTURE OF STRUCTURED TECHNIQUES

When the first edition of this book was written in 1976, the structured techniques were so new and radical that there was no need for a chapter about the future. The theme of the book was that *all* of the structured techniques represented the future of systems development.

Now, more than a decade later, as the fourth edition of this book is being prepared, the concept of structured techniques is well known in many organizations (which has little or nothing to do with the degree of use in those same organizations); the techniques are widely taught in universities; and several hundred thousand copies of textbooks on structured analysis, structured design, and structured programming have been sold. So now, in a sense, the structured techniques are "old stuff," and people are beginning to ask: "What's next?"

The last four chapters have addressed some of the "What's next?" questions that have been debated during the mid- and late-1980s. By the end of the decade, the debate will have ended as current hot topics, such as personal computing, prototyping, fourth-generation languages, and data modeling (a) will have replaced the structured techniques, or (b) been incorporated into the structured techniques, or (c) been rejected as unworkable.

However, several other interesting concepts are appearing that are compatible with the structured techniques and that have not become hotly debated topics yet in most MIS organizations. This last chapter addresses several of these future trends.

19.1 AUTOMATED TOOLS

Throughout this book, we have seen that the structured techniques rely heavily on the concept of modeling. In particular, graphical modeling techniques have been emphasized: Data flow diagrams, entity-relationship diagrams, state transition diagrams, and structure charts have been presented as useful tools for illuminating various aspects of a system. Unfortunately, the graphical models have been hand-drawn in virtually every MIS organization in the world for the past ten years. While this is easy in a textbook where small examples are used and where the author has access to a professional artist, it is not easy in a real-world environment, where (a) large systems involve dozens or even hundreds of diagrams, (b) the diagrams have to be redrawn many times as the user requirements change, and (c) the diagrams are drawn by professional MIS people who don't think of themselves as artists. But there was no practical alternative in the 1970s and early 1980s; although CAD/CAM technology had already been developed in the aerospace and automobile industries, nobody in the MIS world could imagine justifying hardware/software packages that typically cost $100,000 or more.

However, these problems began to diminish in the mid-1980s, when powerful personal workstations began to appear on the market at a cost of less than ten thousand dollars. Indeed, the original version of the IBM PC, in 1981, was substantially below this critical price threshold, but it did not have adequate graphics, storage, or computational power. Similarly, machines like the Apple II were not adequate. But by 1983, the Apple Lisa computer— ill-fated though it may have been— made it obvious that it *was* possible to produce a hardware/software combination of high-resolution graphics and low cost. Also, by then a large number of add-on peripheral products and software packages for the IBM PC made it possible to develop IBM-based hardware/software configurations that would provide appro-priate tools for the programmer and systems analyst.   Others began developing products on the assumption that more powerful and expensive 32-bit machines, such as the Apollo or Sun workstations, would soon fall below the critical threshold of ten thousand dollars.

Since 1985, there has been a veritable explosion of auto-mated tools; these tools have evolved from a "first generation" of sophisticated drawing programs to a "second generation" of true Computer-Assisted Software Engineering (CASE) tools; it is easy to imagine a third- and fourth-generation evolving in the 1990s. In 1987, there were over 50 CASE vendors offering a wide range of products; the activities of such giants as IBM, EDS, and Arthur Andersen indicate that the CASE industry will be a billion-dollar industry in the near future. Because of the volatility of the industry and the technology, I have not listed any of the current CASE vendors in this book; however, you will have no problem finding them if you look at the advertisements in popular computer journals or the vendor exhibits at trade conferences.

All of the CASE products provide some form of the following critical features:

- *Graphic support.* Using a hand-held mouse or some other appropriate device, the CASE tool allows the technician to create a diagram on the screen, revise it, and produce a hard-copy on a standard dot-matrix printer, and/or a laser printer or high-resolution plotting device. Experience has shown us that the technician spends almost as much time on the workstation to compose the initial version of the diagram as he would have done by hand; however, subsequent revisions can be done in minutes instead of hours.

- *Data dictionary support.* In addition to the graphical models, the CASE tool provides some form of data dictionary support so that the data elements, process names, and other items named in the graphical model are properly defined. Many of the CASE tools also allow data dictionaries to be imported and exported from mainframe data dictionary packages.

- *Consistency checking.* This feature is the most important of the CASE tools, and it is an area that will undergo various levels of improvement over the next decade. The CASE tool can ensure, for example, that all items named on the graphical models have been defined in the data dictionary; it can ensure that the items are not defined more than once in the dictionary; and it can verify that net inputs and outputs at one level of a data flow diagram correspond exactly to the net inputs and outputs of the parent bubble in the next higher level diagram.

Since more and more programmers and systems analysts are likely to have personal workstations on their desks in the coming years, the incremental cost of the software and high-resolution graphics monitors for CASE tools should be relatively modest. Nevertheless, making a major change to the MIS "culture" is a slow and difficult process. Although CASE tools have been readily available since 1985, it is estimated that only 10 percent of the programmers and systems analysts in the United States will have such a tool for their use by 1990; it will be the middle of the 1990s before 50 percent of the MIS community is thus equipped.

Early indications from users of CASE tools indicate that an improvement of 20 to 30 percent in productivity is easily achieved, more than enough to justify the cost of the product. The long-term economics should be even more impressive, as we anticipate a factor-of-ten improvement in software reliability and maintainability using such tools.

During the next five to ten years, we can expect to see several more generations of CASE tools that will provide the following capabilities, several of which are discussed in more detail in subsequent sections of this chapter:

- Widespread networking of workstations so that several systems analysts can work together on different components of a large project. Networking could be accomplished with a local area network, or by using a more powerful minicomputer to control and coordinate the activities of the standalone workstations.

- Global error-checking will be performed. If several systems analysts are working on different portions of the same system, there must be a project-wide data dictionary and global consistency checking to ensure that analyst A's work is consistent with analyst B's work.

- Code generation and support of reusable code.

- Complexity models.

- Computer-assisted proofs of correctness.

- Project management and change control.

- Simulation and prototyping.

- "Expert" assistance in the development of the requirements model, and in the transformation of a requirements model into a design model.

19.2   REUSABLE CODE

Observers of the computer field have repeatedly pointed out that programmers have a tendency to write programs that have already been written— maybe dozens of times. At a higher level, systems analysts and project managers build systems that have already been built: How many new payroll systems does the world really need? For at least 20 years, some MIS organizations have tried to remedy this problem by creating libraries of reusable modules, subroutines, programs, and whole systems.

The effort, though well-intentioned, has usually been a failure as programmers continue to write programs that have been written those dozens of times before— indeed, even programs that they themselves have written before. The reasons for the failure of the reusable code library have been threefold:

- The "modules" that were put into the library were often too large and ambitious in scope. A program that tries to do all things for all people often fails, because it doesn't satisfy anyone for any specific application.

- The "modules" were often built in such a way that they could not be used in combination with other modules. Someone writing a logarithm subroutine or a date-conversion subroutine is usually clever enough to realize that the subroutine cannot make any assumption about the environment in which it operates. On the other hand, the person who develops an on-line text editor almost invariably makes the assumption that the environment consists of a human being providing commands through a keyboard. Consequently, the text editor cannot be used in any other environment, even though it contains pattern-matching and string-searching functions that would be useful in many different applications.

- Although it was usually trivial to insert a new module into the library, it was often difficult to retrieve a module from the library, to find out what modules were in the library, what their properties were, and how thoroughly they had been tested.

During the late 1970s and early 1980s, it became apparent that one *could* create an environment conducive to the development of reusable modules. The paradigm of such an environment, in my opinion, is the well-known UNIX® operating system, which I have had the pleasure of using since 1976. Aside from its other advantages and disadvantages, which continue to be debated throughout the industry, the UNIX® operating system environment effectively solves two of the three problems discussed above. By providing a library of some 75 utility routines as a role model, it encourages system developers to create new modules which are small (*very* small— often only 10 lines of code), well-defined, single-minded, and which make no assumptions about the source of their input or the destination of their output. Hence, the UNIX® command language (roughly equivalent to the catalogued procedures on some mainframes, or the batch command files on some personal computers) allows the system developer to create new, unique systems by evoking a unique combination of existing library modules, with perhaps one or two new, unique modules of his own.

Since this system-building process is so easy in the UNIX® environment, it is an attractive option for systems analysts, programmers, and even users. Even in such an environment, there will always be some evidence of the "Not Invented Here" syndrome that encourages MIS personnel to reinvent the wheel for the 3,456th time. Only a vigorous, ongoing management campaign can correct this habit by encouraging, and rewarding the use of, library modules. It is certainly possible to gradually create an MIS culture that looks upon the creation of unique code and custom-built systems as something to be done only in dire emergencies.[1]

The one ingredient that is still lacking in most MIS organizations is the librarian function that will control the introduction of new modules into the library, ensuring that new candidates don't duplicate old ones, ensuring adequate levels of quality, and assisting the MIS technician who wants to know if there is an existing module that fits his needs.

---

[1] Advocates of fourth-generation languages may violently disagree with this approach, since it is apparently so easy to create new, unique, customized code. What is important here, though, is not the duplication of lines of code, but the duplication of intellectual activity. If someone has spent a day developing an elegant implementation of some well-defined task in *any* language, then that effort should not be needlessly repeated simply because another programmer wants to experience the intellectual satisfaction of solving the same problem again.

Some of this innovation requires managerial involvement— for example, the creation of a software tools group if the MIS organization is large enough. Some of it will always involve some human talent— for instance, the concept of a toolsmith that was discussed as a component of the Chief Programmer Team in Chapter 8. But a larger and larger component of the reusable code concept can be accomplished with the assistance of the CASE tools discussed in the previous section. An on-line library of reusable code, designs, and specifications should carry with it an appropriate mechanism for browsing, searching, indexing, and cross-referencing. An appropriate place for this kind of automated support might be the project-level minicomputer discussed above. In the next ten years, we should expect to see some expert system features that will provide automated assistance for the MIS technician who is looking for a module that can't quite be described precisely.

19.3   COMPLEXITY MODELS

Since the mid-1970s, there has been considerable interest in the concept of modeling the complexity of computer programs, and thus, ultimately, the complexity of entire systems. When we use the term *complexity*, we mean complexity as a human observer perceives it. Hence, it may be possible for someone to write a program in BASIC or PASCAL that is easy for another person to comprehend, but difficult for a computer to handle (e.g., expensive in terms of CPU cycles or disk accesses). More importantly, it is easy for a human to write a program that is easy for a computer to handle, but difficult for another human to comprehend. Since the program must be debugged by the original programmer and maintained by as many as ten generations of maintenance programmers before its ultimate demise, this issue of complexity is an important one.

Software complexity is still a controversial subject in the late 1980s; however, some progress has been made. Throughout the 1960s and much of the 1970s, the only metric of complexity was the *length* of a program: It was generally assumed that a longer computer program would be more difficult to understand than a shorter program. While this assumption is often valid as a gross measure of complexity, many times it is not, and it has led to a number of silly programming standards in MIS organizations. History will eventually record the number of programmers who were shot at dawn for writing a 51-statement subroutine when the company's programming standards insisted that no subroutine be longer than 50 statements.

In the late 1970s, Maurice Halstead first introduced the view of program complexity as a function of something more than lines of code. His measure of "volume," documented in [Halstead, 1977], is a landmark; since then, there have been many other models of program complexity, including McCabe's measure of cyclomatic complexity. For further information on this area, see [DeMarco, 1982] or [Grady, 1987].

As mentioned above, considerable debate still exists about many of these metrics, and available statistics can be used to either prove or disprove most of the theoretical complexity models in existence. However, most evidence tends to support the notion of a "Pareto Principle" for components of a system: 80 percent of the complexity of a system (and thus 80 percent of the bugs and 80 percent of the maintenance costs) can be associated with 20 percent of the code; indeed, sometimes the distribution is more like 90:10 or 95:5. The trick is to find out *which* 20 percent (or 10 percent or 5 percent) of the code is critical. The mathematical complexity models are beginning to give us some insights in this area; by the end of this decade, we should be able to pinpoint complex, and thus intrinsically troublesome, modules by the end of the systems analysis phase of a project.

19.4   PROOFS OF CORRECTNESS

It has long been known that testing of conventional computer systems is, at best, a defensive measure. "Testing," as Edsger Dijkstra has said, "demonstrates the presence of errors, not the absence of errors." Exhaustive testing is impractical for almost all MIS projects and is impossible for many; consequently, we must live with the reality that many of today's critical systems may have bugs lurking in them that nobody has yet been able to find.

One solution to this problem has been discussed for nearly two decades: developing a formal, rigorous, mathematical proof of correctness of a computer program. Efforts in this area have been conducted with the academic community, but have been largely ignored within the MIS community because (a) the academic community was attempting to develop correctness proofs for tiny programs (typically less than 100 lines of code) while industry was trying to deal with systems of one million lines of code, and (b) the examples used by academia were of no interest to industry— that is, the mathematical proofs of correctness involved programs that deal with chess problems or other similar game-playing situations.

Academia and industry are still far apart, but the U.S. Department of Defense (DOD) has formed an important bridge between the two. As one can imagine, DOD is currently involved in building a variety of systems for which a proof of correctness has enormous value; the ultimate system of this kind may be the Star Wars system. (See [Bellin, 1987] for more discussion of the problems with this system.) Hence, much of the practical work in this area for the remainder of the 1980s and the 1990s will probably be in the DOD realm, and the economics are interesting: To provide a computer-assisted proof of correctness of a system involving ten thousand lines of code, DOD must be willing to spend approximately half a million dollars. Military systems are an obvious example of the usefulness of proofs of correctness; however, electronic funds transfer systems and other high-volume consumer-oriented systems might also be viable candidates.

In the late 1980s, virtually no commercial, business-oriented MIS organization in the United States has invested money to provide mathematical proofs of correctness for their systems. I predict that this malaise will change drastically as we enter the 1990s, and that the *standard* for large, complex systems will involve such proofs. While most MIS organizations have neither the time nor the talent to pursue this area today, it is an important area to be aware of because most of the practical developments (for instance, software packages that will provide computer-assisted proofs of an application program) will eventually be made available free through the courtesy of the U.S. Defense Department. (It's not usually so blatant, but much of the important R&D work in the computer industry has been done by, or sponsored by, such DOD organizations as DARPA, and the results eventually trickle down to private industry.)

19.5   PROJECT MANAGEMENT

Project management for MIS systems is better than it was twenty years ago; however, it is still commonly true that MIS projects are substantially behind schedule and over budget. As the MIS function becomes increasingly important in both large and small organizations, management will gradually insist on better and more accurate methods of managing MIS projects. In the extreme case, they may abolish MIS projects through the simple expedient of commercial packages and facilities management services if the MIS organization cannot manage itself.

It is widely assumed that software engineering techniques will improve the ability of the project manager to control the events that occur in the development of a large, complex system. By introducing activities and products that show tangible evidence of progress, the project manager is able to avoid the "95 percent done" syndrome that is often evident on the second day of the project. By improving the process of systems analysis, together with the introduction of top-down implementation, the testing phase of the project, which was previously the most time-consuming and unpredictable part of a large MIS project, becomes simple and straightforward.

However, we should not fool ourselves: Software engineering will not eliminate all project management problems. In particular, we are left with the difficult job of estimating the size and cost of a project at a sufficiently early stage so that senior management can make an intelligent decision to approve or cancel the project. Also, we still need better quantitative measurements so that the project manager can evaluate progress during the project. These issues are discussed at length in [Boehm, 1981] and [DeMarco, 1982] and Boehm's COCOMO model has been incorporated into several PC-based estimating programs. However, it is evident that we will have much work to do. When the same data about a new project is fed into five different estimating packages, they produce five different answers— often differing by as much as a factor of three or four.

In addition to the difficulty of making good estimates and deciding what metrics are most appropriate, the project manager has another major problem: Much of the data that he uses is provided by the programmers and systems analysts working on the project. Thus, when he asks Margaret, "How are you doing on the XYZ subroutine?" she is likely to meditate for a moment or two and then respond, "It's 95 percent done, boss!" When he asks Ferdinand, "How many lines of code have you written today?" Ferdinand might open his program listing and scan it for a few seconds before responding, "Oh, about a hundred and ten lines, I guess."

The problem with this information is that (a) it is subject to misinterpretation because the data is being provided by the workers themselves, often in an atmosphere where it appears that the data will be used to evaluate their performance; and (b) it requires additional work and thus will not be done unless the manager insists on it. The long-term salvation for project managers is a mechanism that provides project metrics *automatically* and as a natural by-product of the work itself. The CASE tools discussed earlier in this chapter are a natural tool for capturing this data, and the better-managed MIS organizations will begin taking advantage of such capabilities by the beginning of the 1990s.

An added benefit to the use of such data-gathering tools is that they help create a database of metrics over many projects within the MIS organization. Thus, it will eventually be practical to look at the last ten programs that Ferdinand wrote to see if there are any obvious patterns. It will also be possible to look at the last ten payroll projects within the organization (at which point someone might well ask why it was necessary to write ten different payroll systems!) to see if there are any obvious patterns.

19.6   VISUAL PROGRAMMING

A new form of programming and program design is known as *visual programming*. By using powerful, PC-based work-stations, with high-resolution graphics, programmers can use icon-based facilities similar to the CASE workstations described earlier in order to "diagram" the procedural logic of their programs. One example of such a facility is V.I.P. (which stands for "Visual Interactive Programming") for the Macintosh computer; a typical VIP diagram is shown in Figure 19.1. Other examples of visual programming languages are the command language for the ill-fated Xerox Star computer, FORMAL (see [Shu, 1985]) and Tinkertoy (see [Edel, 1986]).

It remains to be seen whether visual programming will become a major new trend, or whether it will quietly disappear after the initial fascination wears off. There are at least three areas where visual programming may become very important:

- *Teaching programming to children and novices.* Assuming that it is useful to teach programming and algorithm design as part of a general education curriculum (which is a separate area of debate that I do not intend to explore!), then visual programming languages offer a good alternative to the text-oriented programming languages like BASIC and Pascal.

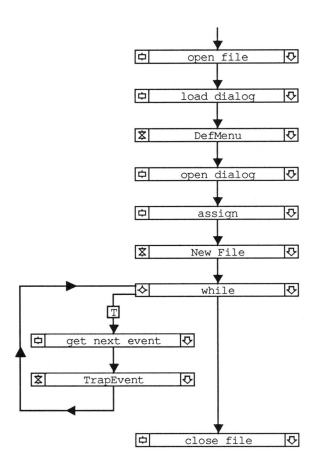

Figure 19.1: **An example of visual programming**

- *Providing a convenient level of abstraction for a professional programmer, in order to hide the difficult aspects of an unfamiliar computer or operating system.* Imagine, for example, a programmer who is familiar with mainframe computers or IBM-compatible PC computers. He is suddenly asked to develop a nontrivial application program for the Macintosh computer that makes use of the Macintosh human interface. One approach, the classic one, is to become familiar with the Macintosh environment by devoting several weeks to studying such bibles as *Inside Macintosh*. But as

Macintosh aficionados like to joke, understanding each of its 70 chapters requires a former understanding, in detail, of the other 69 chapters. An alternative is to use a visual programming language like V.I.P.

- *Providing an environment for nonprofessional programmers—users—to create complex procedures with the word processing packages, telecommunication packages, and spreadsheet packages that they have available.* It is not unusual for a user to want the ability to have his PC automatically dial up several different electronic mail services (e.g., MCI Mail, CompuServe, Telenet, etc.) and check for outstanding messages; he might then want some of the messages downloaded into a file to be formatted by a word processor and printed; others downloaded into a spreadsheet; others perhaps need to be downloaded into a spreadsheet, combined with other spreadsheet files and then uploaded to some other computer. The current approach often requires familiarity with arcane, unintelligible macros, "script languages," and operating system "batch files." It is hard enough for a professional programmer to become familiar with the different syntaxes and structure of these several different languages; for a non-programmer, it is often well-nigh impossible. A common, icon-based, visual programming language would be a welcome alternative.

I personally am very excited about this new approach to program building, and find that it has an enormous intuitive appeal to nonprogrammers. As graphics-oriented, window-based computer environments proliferate and become more sophisticated (e.g., the Macintosh environment, the Microsoft Windows environment on the IBM PS/2, etc.), I believe that we will see a tremendous growth in visual programming languages. For more details, see [Shu, 1988a], [Shu, 1988b], [Raeder, 1985], and [Moriconi and Hare, 1985].

19.7   ARTIFICIAL INTELLIGENCE

Since the early 1980s, artificial intelligence has been an important and exciting topic in the computer industry. Practical applications, ranging from robotics to medical diagnosis, are beginning to appear as commercial products, and we can look forward to a continuing stream of developments in the decade ahead.

Artificial intelligence can be important in developing computer systems and thus, artificial intelligence—or, more specifically, expert systems—will soon be an important adjunct to software engineering.

Consider the analogy of medical diagnosis. A patient describes his symptoms to the doctor—or to an expert system that has been given the rules of judgment that an expert human doctor would use. Based on the symptoms described by the patient, the expert may ask more questions or prescribe certain tests. Eventually, the expert produces a diagnosis, as well as a prescription for medication to cure the problem. In most cases, there is not a 100 percent certainty that the diagnosis is correct; the degree of certainty is both a function of the degree of expertise as well as the nature of the illness.

Now consider the same situation in the field of systems analysis. The patient is the user who has some fuzzy ideas about his needs for automating some portion of his business. He can describe some of his "symptoms," and that initial description usually prompts more questions from the "doctor." At the end of one or more such discussions, the expert (systems analyst) diagnoses the problem and prescribes a cure (inevitably, it's a new computer system!).

The significant point is this: There is a world of difference between expert (human) systems analysts and amateur systems analysts. Over a period of years, the expert has accumulated a number of rules of judgment. He knows what questions to ask and what answers to believe. He has seen enough similar cases (and users) to have a good idea of the problems affecting this user. The amateur, on the other hand, is lost. He doesn't know what questions to ask, nor does he know when to stop asking questions. He doesn't know whether the user is describing a problem, or merely symptoms of a problem, or perhaps symptoms of someone else's problems.

Thus, it would seem highly likely that the expertise of several veteran systems analysts could be captured by an expert system, so that the user-analyst dialogue could eventually occur between a human user and an automated systems analyst. Most probably, this dialogue would be restricted to specific, narrowly defined applications, such as accounting or inventory control. Twenty to twenty-five years from now, though, it is conceivable that we could have general-purpose automated systems analysts.

Finally, we human systems analysts and programmers would be forced out of the systems development profession we have created and would find it necessary to get an honest job. I expect that day to coincide with my 65th birthday, and I look forward to my retirement with great excitement!

Appendix A
SUGGESTED COBOL CODING STANDARDS

Introduction

The objective of this style guide is to produce readable structured code from a structured design of independent, functionally cohesive modules. The standards are not meant for rigid enforcement, but are meant to serve as a springboard for each software development group in deciding what will be acceptable in code reviews.

Topic: **PROCEDURE UNITS**

Standard:
> The basic procedure unit is a paragraph; several paragraphs may be packaged together into a section, especially if their functions are temporally bound (e.g., initialization functions).

Rejected Alternatives:
> 1) Basic unit is a section.
> 2) Basic unit is a separately compilable CALLable entity.

Discussion:
> A module is defined as one or more code statements together fulfilling a single function, with one and only one label by which the function may be invoked.

> The COBOL construct that most nearly satisfies this definition is the paragraph. Using the section as the basic unit with no paragraph names has been recommended because some compilers would then enforce the discipline of an EXIT statement. This is not the case in ANS 74 COBOL. An EXIT statement should be provided only if required as the target of a GOTO within the procedure.

> Having a separately compilable entity as the basic unit, with no labels inside each entity, is possible and gives excellent interface clarity, but the repetition of Data Divisions makes for less readable code and adds overhead.

We envisage micromodules (paragraphs) being packaged into macromodules (compilable entities) by the program designer after completion of the structured design. Where segmentation is important, or in certain forms of CASE structure, paragraphs may be packaged into sections.

Implicit in the definition of a module is that no matter at what level in the hierarchy, it should have only one entrance (the label) and one exit. Control should never be allowed to pass implicitly across any procedure name; that is, control should "fall through" from one procedure to the procedure that happens to be physically next in the code.

Micromodules should be marked off visually from each other by a blank line before and after.

The size of a macromodule or program is not critical for readability. However, it may be desirable to have separately compilable entities for changeability, and there may be constraints on main storage size.

Topic: PROCEDURE NAMES WITHIN A MACROMODULE

Standard:
Each procedure name should express the function of the procedure and should have a prefix, consisting of a letter plus a digit, which gives its relative location within the Procedure Division.

This prefix may be omitted from Procedure Divisions covering less than two pages.

Rejected Alternative:
Use of a suffix.

Discussion:
When micromodules form a hierarchy, they should be numbered A1, A2, etc., for the first level; B1, B2, etc., for the third level, and so on. For example:

```
        PERFORM A1-INITIALIZATION.
        PERFORM A2-PROCESS-RECORDS.
        PERFORM A3-WRAPUP.
A1-INITIALIZATION.
        .
        .
        .
```

A2-PROCESS-RECORDS.

    .

    .

    .

PERFORM B1-READ-RECORD UNTIL ALL-DONE.

Topic: **DATA NAMING AND DEFINITION**

Standard:

1) Data names should be as meaningful as possible while not being overlong, and should be given a suffix if they are used in the macromodule interface: -IN for input and -OUT for output.

2) Working storage (suffix, -WS) will consist of a level 01 for each micromodule. Working storage used by that micromodule will be defined under this 01. Shared working storage will be defined as:

    01   COMMON-WS.

3) No micromodule may modify another micromodule's working storage.

4) The VALUE clause is used to establish only parameters and tables that never change. Variables should be initialized in the Procedure Division, near where they are used. The need for initialization should be kept to a minimum and initialization paragraphs are to be avoided.

5) Hyphenation should be used to add meaning. For example, CD-MF-AC-NO, rather than CDMFACNO.

6) Only counters and binary flags may be coded as literals. All numbers other than 0 and 1 should be coded as initialized variables with meaningful names (*not* TWO, THREE, etc.). Values 0 and 1 should be given names whenever they represent true or false, or similar condition values.

7) The use of level-88 names should be avoided because their use obscures the relationship between the setting and testing of flag values. Instead, make free use of numeric parameters for such values; for example,

    IF RECORDS-LEFT = NO MOVE YES TO DONE.

Topic: **STRUCTURES**

Standard:

Process structures: concatenations of instructions normally involving no transfer of control within the structure, for example, MOVEs, arithmetic statements, input/output statements.

Exception conditions (like AT END, ON SIZE ERROR): If dealing with this condition is part of the module's function, insert the necessary code. If the function should be dealt with by one of the calling modules, set a flag; or better still, use the normal output data parameters to return exceptional information.

A concatenation of structures can normally be treated as a simple process structure, except when it is under the control of a conditional statement (such as IF, READ . . . AT END); and the concatenation of structures must contain an imbedded period. In this case, the process structure is written as a separate paragraph and PERFORMed.

Decision structures: the normal layout is

```
IF condition-1
     imperative-1
ELSE
     imperative-2.
```

Where the logic demands a nested IF (that is, an imperative replaced by another IF), the structure should be rewritten linearly wherever possible:

```
IF condition-1
     imperative-1
ELSE IF condition-2
     imperative-2
ELSE
     imperative-3.
```

NEXT SENTENCE should be revised out of the code wherever possible, even if it means introducing a NOT. Avoid mixing AND and OR in a condition; if you must do so, use parentheses to avoid ambiguity.

Where the code implements a decision table, include the decision table as comments.

Where IFs must be nested, each level of IF should be indented and its corresponding ELSE aligned with it. An obvious exception is the ELSE-IF chain shown above.

As far as possible, the code for a condition should follow the usage of normal speech; if a condition is not comprehensible when read aloud, recast it.

CASE structures: this is a situation in which one variable may take more than two values, with a different procedure performed depending on each value.

For *non-numeric variables*, use the linear chain of ELSE-IFs; for example,

```
IF CODE = A
      PERFORM PROCEDURE-A
ELSE IF CODE = B
      PERFORM PROCEDURE-B
ELSE IF CODE = C
      PERFORM PROCEDURE-C
ELSE
      PERFORM ILLEGAL-CODE-ROUTINE.
```

For *integer variables*, it is permissible to use a GOTO...DEPENDING ON within a section; for example,

```
CASE-STRUCTURE SECTION.
SET-CASE-SWITCH.
      GO TO PROC-1, PROC-2, PROC-3
            DEPENDING ON CODE.
PROC-1.
      .
      .
      .
      GOTO CASE-STRUCTURE-XIT.
PROC-2.
      .
      .
      .
      GOTO CASE-STRUCTURE-XIT.
PROC-3.
      .
      .
      .
```

GOTO CASE-STRUCTURE-XIT.
CASE-STRUCTURE-XIT.

The whole section is PERFORMed from an appropriate place in the program.

Never contrive code just to use a GOTO DEPENDING ON. Unless the code arises naturally in the data representation, use linear ELSE-IFs.

Loop structures: for multiple executions ending on a condition (zero or more times), use:

PERFORM loop-proc UNTIL condition.

For multiple executions ending on a condition (one or more times), use:

PERFORM loop-proc.
PERFORM loop-proc UNTIL condition.

For multiple executions on a counter value (zero or more times), use:

PERFORM loop-proc VARYING counter-name FROM initial-value
        BY increment UNTIL end-condition.

Alternatives Rejected:

PERFORM THRU: This leads to confusion and implies that a functional entity can be addressed to points inside itself. If you need to write PERFORM PROC-A THRU PROC-C, write a "sandwich" procedure, consisting of:

SANDWICH-PROC.
    PERFORM PROC-A.
    PERFORM PROC-B.
    PERFORM PROC-C.

Then PERFORM SANDWICH-PROC as needed.

PERFORM n TIMES: This encourages the use of literals. Use PERFORM VARYING instead, as this will show the exit point more meaningfully.

Discussion:

Note that there are three uses for the PERFORM statement:

1) to invoke a submodule, which performs a complete function and returns (procedure call)

2) to invoke a process block, which cannot be written in-line (a group)

3) to invoke a loop body zero or more times (loop)

Therefore, not all paragraphs may be complete functional modules in the sense of structured design; some may be groups or loop-bodies; that is, sequentially or even procedurally cohesive modules.

Topic: **LOOPS THAT READ SEQUENTIAL FILES**

Standard:

```
MOVE YES TO RECORDS-LEFT.
READ the file
     AT END MOVE NO TO RECORDS-LEFT.
PERFORM the loop
     UNTIL RECORDS-LEFT = NO.
```

At the end of the loop's code, READ again to get the next record.

Rejected Alternatives:

```
MOVE YES TO RECORDS-LEFT.
PERFORM the loop
     UNTIL RECORDS-LEFT = NO.
```

As the first step in the body of the loop

```
READ the file
     AT END MOVE NO TO RECORDS-LEFT.
IF RECORDS-LEFT = YES
     body of loop
     .
     .
     .
```

Discussion:

From the design point of view, it is preferable to carry out an initial read and set a flag, since the executive module can deal with the condition of an empty file straight away. The alternative forces the body of the loop to be a series of clauses within the positive branch of an IF statement.

Topic: **EXPLICITNESS**

Standard:

Arithmetic	Do not write a COMPUTE of more than three variables or constants. Break any more complex formula or equation into intermediate steps.
Notation	Do not use ">" or "<" in the code. People find them confusing, and they may not appear properly on some printers. Use ".GT." and ".LT." instead.
Format	Align all related verbs. Align all PICTUREs (column 32 is suggested). Align all VALUEs (column 44 is suggested).

Topic: **COMMENTS**

Standard:

Use comments ("*" in column 7) to explain code that is not self-evident, or that is not directly related to the function of the module. This usually occurs where the pseudocode of the design cannot be converted directly to COBOL (e.g., swapping the contents of two variables). Rewrite code that needs explaining.

Include any decision tables you develop as comments to be placed immediately before the decision structure that implements them.

If the gross function of the macromodule is not clear from reading the highest-level micromodule, describe the macromodule in terms of pseudocode and include it as comments at the beginning of the Procedure Division.

Include a comment wherever a variable is modified whose values have level-88 condition names, or wherever data is modified by more than one micromodule (unless the data is in COMMON-WS).

Use comments to explain *what* the code is doing and *why* it is being done, not *how* it is doing it.

In general, to determine the need for comments, imagine that someone else is writing this code, and that, in the middle of the night next week, *you* will have to change it under the pressure of time. Moral: Comment unto others as you would have them comment unto you.

Topic: **FORMATTING**

Standard:

1)   Only one statement or procedure name per line.

2)   UNTIL, AT END, ON SIZE ERROR, VARYING, and similar qualifying clauses should be indented from the verbs they qualify (e.g., by two spaces or five spaces). For example,

```
READ CARD-FILE
    AT END MOVE NO TO CARDS-LEFT.
```

3)   Each ELSE should be directly under the IF to which it refers, except in the case of linear ELSE-IF sequences.

4)   In the case of a too-long statement, break it at a word so that it is obvious to the reader that the statement must be continued on the next line.

Appendix B
SUGGESTED PL/I CODING STANDARDS

Introduction

The objective of this style guide is the production of readable structured code from a structured design of functionally cohesive modules. The standards are not intended for mechanical enforcement, but to serve as a point of departure for each software development group in deciding what will and what will not be acceptable in code reviews.

Topic: **BASIC MODULAR UNIT**

Standard:

The basic modular unit is an EXTERNAL PROCEDURE.

Rejected Alternative:

1) Basic module is a PROCEDURE, either INTERNAL or EXTERNAL.

2) Basic module is possibly a portion of a multi-entry PROCEDURE.

Discussion:

The intention of the standard is to create modules that can be compiled, tested, modified, and maintained independently of one another. In PL/I, this is best accomplished by using EXTERNAL PROCEDUREs. Considerations of packaging and efficiency may require moving some modules in-line into others; that is, making them INTERNAL PROCEDUREs. This can be done with great ease late in the project, provided that all identifiers have been explicitly declared (with no exceptions!); in particular, built-in functions should be declared BUILTIN, and ENTRY and RETURNS attributes should be declared in full.

Topic: ENSURING MODULAR INDEPENDENCE

Standard:

Any dependencies, inheritances, side effects, or shared assumptions between modules should be (a) eliminated if possible, or (b) explicitly documented.

Discussion:

1) Declarations of EXTERNAL ENTRYs should specify all parameter and returned-value attributes, such as:

    DECLARE SUBROUT ENTRY (FLOAT, CHAR(*)) RETURNS(FLOAT);

    Parameter attributes can be verified by the compiler if given an ENTRY declaration, and if the programmer reads the attribute and cross reference listing.

2) Shared assumptions, such as the possible range of a parameter, or the meaning of flags, can be described in narrative comments, which form the interface documentation. The most standard place for such documentation is at the beginning of the called module. Defensive programming, or antibugging, should be adhered to wherever such assumptions can be explicitly tested. In production, a section of defensive code can be put into a comment frame if it takes too much execution time.

3) On-units intended to be shared among several modules must be mentioned in a comment in each module. On-units *not* intended to be shared should be established (via the ON statement) and reverted (via the REVERT statement) close to the affected statements so that they aren't inherited by subroutines.

4) EXTERNAL storage must be subject to system-wide controls; a pair of programmers could create tricky maintenance problems by a private agreement to pass information through EXTERNAL storage.

Topic: **STRUCTURED CODING**

Standard:

Programs will be constructed from the basic control structures (SEQUENCE, IF-THEN-ELSE, DO-WHILE) augmented by the multi-way conditional (or "CASE") and the loop termination (or "LEAVE"). Any exceptions to these rules have long-range consequences and require project-wide agreement on the need for and implementation of the exception.

Rejected Alternative:

1)   No restrictions on control structures.

2)   Dogmatic restrictions to SEQUENCE, IF-THEN-ELSE, and DO-WHILE only.

Discussion:

1)   DO-WHILE: Loops should confirm either to the simple iteration form:

      DO J = start TO finish BY step;

      or the general DO-WHILE form:

      DO WHILE (condition);

2)   CASE: The recommended, most general form of the CASE construct is this:

      ```
      /* CASE: alert the reader */
      IF case-1-condition THEN action-1;
      ELSE IF case-2-condition THEN action-2;
      ELSE IF case-3-condition THEN action-3;
                 .
                 .
                 .
      ELSE action-default;
      /* END OF CASE */
      ```

3)   LEAVE: An early loop termination, such as GOTO LEAVE$LOOP, can be allowed, provided that the GOTO goes to the point just past the loop being terminated, *and* that a comment before the loop

alerts the reader to the loop exit, *and* that there is
no simpler way to write the code without the
LEAVE.

Topic: AVOIDING HIDDEN ERRORS

Standard:

A PL/I programmer must adhere to a strict set of rules for
avoiding surprises of PL/I syntax and semantics. The most
important thing is to follow a consistent style, but there is
room for individual selection of the exact style used. The
discussion below lists one set of possible styles.

Rejected Alternative:

Ad hoc approach to each potential hidden error situation.
For example, encountering a nested IF, the programmer
asks, "Hmmm, maybe I should use a DO-END here, or
maybe a null ELSE, or restructure the logic, or . . . ."

Discussion:

1)   Each IF-THEN nesting must have a DO-END around
       its action clause.

2)   All type conversions should be done explicitly,
       preferably by assignment to a variable.

3)   Multiple-closure END statements should not be
       used. Each END should be visually matched with its
       DO.

4)   Use aggregate assignments only for initialization of
       an aggregate.

5)   Perform data editing explicitly with VERIFY rather
       than using the CONVERSION condition.

Topic: PROGRAM READABILITY

Standard:

If a piece of code requires explanation and can be recoded
so as to require none, then recode it.

Rejected Alternative:

Detailed layout rules.

Discussion:

1)   Use a page heading comment before each PROCEDURE.

2)   Adopt a consistent style of spacing and indenting, or use a formatting preprocessor.

3)   Use a consistent system of the following:

keyword abbreviation,
order of attributes and options,
precision,
variable abbreviations,
name-choice conventions,
order of declarations in the listing,
order of identifiers in lists (e.g., always alphabetical)

4)   Good code is capable of being self-documenting at the detail level, but not at the overall concept level. Precede each PROCEDURE's executable code with enough narrative comment to enable reading the code without any further explanation. Examples in programming textbooks can be misleading because the necessary narrative appears in the text, not in the programs. Some especially helpful narrative items are the algorithm used and any creatively chosen data structures.

5)   Design so that the average module's executable code can fit on one page of a program listing. Design and recode a module whose executable code exceeds two pages.

Topic: **MAINTAINABILITY**

Standard:

Write code that can be maintained by someone with less PL/I experience than yourself.

Discussion:

1)   Use the advanced features that are listed below only
      when you have project-wide agreement on their
      necessity and maintainability:

> ENTRY variables,
> GENERIC variables,
> multiple entry points,
> DEFAULT,
> RECURSIVE,
> multitasking,
> compile-time preprocessor statements,
> LOCATE-mode input and output

2)   Eschew magic numbers: Program constants should
      be assigned as INITIAL values to named variables.
      The constants 0 and 1 should be the only hard-
      coded constants in the program, and there should be
      very few of them.   Strive to make it easy to change
      the specific numeric and character values used by
      the program.

Topic: AVOIDING NEEDLESS INEFFICIENCIES

Standard:

When unsure of the efficiency of a PL/I statement, code a
sample and execute it; make use of experimental programs
to avoid depending on out-of-date dogma about inefficient
features.   Devote the most attention to critical areas of
code.

Discussion:

In general, hard-and-fast rules about inefficient features in
PL/I create unnecessary burdens on programmers doing
noncritical code (the major portion of most systems!).
Furthermore, the variability of PL/I implementations and
environments makes many absolute rules somewhat risky.
The following rules are fairly safe:

1)   Wherever possible, declare the same precision for
      arithmetic variables added, subtracted, or assigned
      to each other.

2)   Whenever time is more critical than memory storage, try an experiment with DEFAULT RANGE(*) STATIC.

3)   Require item-by-item scanning of each attribute-and-cross-reference listing to catch the warning messages "data conversion by subroutine call" and "dummy arguments have been created." Both messages reveal time-consuming consequences of attribute mismatches. Try declaring the variables involved with the same attributes.

4)   Don't use a BEGIN block where a DO-group will suffice.

5)   Search each module for inner loops, expanses of repetitive code, and item-by-item (or character-by-character) processing. Experiment with replacing these sections with code using built-in PL/I functions.

Bibliography

[Aron, 1976]   "The Super-Programmer Project," Joel
                      Aron. (*Software Engineering, Concepts and
                      Techniques*, edited by J. M. Buxton, P. Naur
                      and B. Randell, New York: Petrocelli/
                      Charter, 1987)

[Baker, 1972]   "Chief Programmer Team Management of
                      Production Programming," F.T. Baker. (*IBM
                      Systems Journal*, January 1972, pp. 56-73)

[Baker, 1972a]   "System Quality Through Structured
                      Programming," F.T. Baker. (*AFIPS Pro-
                      ceedings of the 1972 Fall Joint Computer
                      Conference*, pp. 339-344)

[Balbine, 1975]   "Better Manpower Utilization Through
                      Automatic Restructuring," Guy de Balbine.
                      (*Proceedings of the 1975 National
                      Computer Conference*)

[Basili, 1984]   "A Methodology for Collecting Valid
                      Software Engineering Data," V. Basili and D.
                      Weiss. (*IEEE Transactions on Software
                      Engineering*, November 1984)

[Bellin, 1987]   *Computers in Battle*, David Bellin and Gary
                      Chapman (editors). (New York: Harcourt,
                      Brace, Jovanovich, 1987)

[Block, 1983]   *The Politics of Projects*, R. Block. (Engle-
                      wood Cliffs, NJ: Yourdon Press/Prentice
                      Hall, 1983)

[Boar, 1984]   *Application Prototyping*, Bernard Boar.
                      (New York: John Wiley & Sons, 1984)

[Boddie, 1987]   *Crunch Mode*, John Boddie. (Englewood
                      Cliffs, NJ: Yourdon Press/Prentice Hall,
                      1987)

[Boehm, 1973]   "Software and Its Impact: A Quantitative
                    Study," Barry Boehm. (*Datamation*, May
                    1973, pp. 48-59)

[Boehm, 1976]   "Software Engineering," Barry Boehm.
                    (*IEEE Transactions on Software Engin-
                    eering*, December 1976)

[Boehm, 1981]   *Software Engineering Economics*, Barry
                    Boehm. (Prentice Hall, 1981)

[Böhm, 1966]   "Flow Diagrams, Turing Machines, and
                    Languages with Only Two Formation Rules,"
                    C. Böhm and G. Jacopini. (*Communications
                    of the ACM*, May 1966, pp. 366-371)

[Brooks, 1975]   *The Mythical Man-Month*, Fred Brooks.
                    (Reading, MA: Addison-Wesley, 1975)

[Brooks, 1987]   "No Silver Bullet," Fred Brooks. (*IEEE
                    Software*, January 1987)

[Bush, 1985]   "The Automatic Restructuring of COBOL,"
                    Eric Bush. (*Proceedings of the Conference
                    on Software Maintenance - 1985*, IEEE
                    Computer Society Press, November 1985,
                    pp. 35-41)

[Buxton, 1976]   *Software Engineering, Concepts and
                    Techniques*, J.M. Buxton, P. Naur, and B.
                    Randell, editors. (New York: Petrocelli/
                    Charter, 1976)

[Canning, 1972]   "That Maintenance Iceberg," Richarg G.
                    Canning, editor. (*EDP Analyzer*, October
                    1972)

[Connell, 1989]   *Rapid Prototyping*, John Connell and Linda
                    Shafer. (Englewood Cliffs, NJ: Yourdon
                    Press/Prentice Hall, 1989)

[Dahl, 1972]   *Structured Programming*, O.J. Dahl, E.W.
                    Dijkstra, and C.A.R. Hoare. (Englewood
                    Cliffs, NJ: Prentice Hall, 1972)

[DeMarco, 1978]   *Structured Analysis and System
                    Specification*, Tom DeMarco. (Englewood

Cliffs, NJ: Yourdon Press/Prentice Hall, 1978)

[DeMarco, 1982] *Controlling Software Projects*, Tom DeMarco. (Englewood Cliffs, NJ: Yourdon Press/Prentice Hall, 1982)

[Dickinson, 1981] *Developing Structured Systems*, Brian Dickinson. (Englewood Cliffs, NJ: Yourdon Press/Prentice Hall, 1981)

[Dijkstra, 1976] "Structured Programming," E. W. Dijkstra. (*Software Engineering, Concepts and Techniques*, edited by J.M. Buxton, P. Naur, and B. Randell. New York: Petrocelli/ Charter, 1976)

[Dijkstra, 1976a] *A Discipline of Programming*, E.W. Dijkstra. (Englewood Cliffs, NJ: Prentice Hall, 1976)

[Edel, 1986] "The Tinkertoy Graphical Programming Environment," M. Edel. (*Proceedings of IEEE 1986 COMPSAC*, October 1986, pp. 466-471)

[Gane, 1977] *Structured Systems Analysis: Tools and Techniques*, Chris Gane and Trish Sarson. (New York: Improved Systems Technologies, 1977)

[Grady, 1987] *Software Metrics: Establishing a Company-Wide Program*, Robert B. Grady and Deborah L. Caswell. (Englewood Cliffs, NJ: Prentice Hall, 1987)

[Halstead, 1977] *Elements of Software Science*, Maurice Halstead. (New York: Elsevier Press, 1977)

[Higgins, 1979] *Program Design and Construction*, David Higgins. (Englewood Cliffs, NJ: Prentice Hall, 1979)

[HIPO, 1974] *HIPO: A Design Aid and Documentation Technique*. (IBM Corp. Form GC20-1851-0)

[Jackson, 1975] *Principles of Program Design*, Michael Jackson. (New York: Academic Press, 1975)

[Jackson, 1983]   *System Development*, Michael Jackson. (Englewood Cliffs, NJ: Prentice Hall, 1983)

[Jones, 1985]   *Programming Productivity*, T. Capers Jones. (New York: McGraw-Hill, 1985)

[Katzan, 1976]   *Systems Analysis and Documentation: An Introduction to the HIPO Method*, Harry Katzan. (New York: Van Nostrand Reinhold, 1976)

[Keller, 1983]   *The Practice of Structured Analysis*, E. Robert Keller. (Englewood Cliffs, NJ: Yourdon Press/Prentice Hall, 1983)

[Kernighan, 1974]   *The Elements of Programming Style*, B.W. Kernighan and P.J. Plauger. (New York: McGraw-Hill, 1974)

[Kernighan, 1976]   *Software Tools*, B. W. Kernighan and P.J. Plauger. (Reading, MA: Addison-Wesley, 1976)

[King, 1984]   *Current Practices in Software Engineering*, David King. (Englewood Cliffs, NJ: Yourdon Press/Prentice Hall, 1984)

[Knuth, 1971]   "An Empirical Study of FORTRAN Programs," Donald E. Knuth. (*Software—Practice and Experience*, April 1971, pp. 105-133)

[Knuth, 1974]   "Structured Programming with GOTO Statements," Donald E. Knuth. (*ACM Computing Surveys*, December 1974, pp. 261-302)

[Kuhn, 1962]   *The Structure of Scientific Revolutions*, Thomas Kuhn. (Chicago, IL: University of Chicago Press, 1962)

[Lientz, 1980]   *Software Maintenance Management*, B.P. Lientz and E.B. Swanson. (Reading, MA: Addison-Wesley, 1980)

[Lister, 1978]   *Learning to Program in Structured COBOL, Part II*, T. Lister and E. Yourdon.

(Englewood Cliffs, NJ: Yourdon Press/ Prentice Hall, 1978)

[McCracken, 1976] *A Simplified Guide to Structured COBOL Programming*, D. McCracken. (New York: John Wiley & Sons, 1976)

[McGowan, 1975] *Top-Down Structured Programming*, C.L. McGowan and J.R. Kelly. (New York: Petrocelli/Charter, 1975)

[McMenamin, 1984] *Essential Systems Analysis*, Steve McMenamin and John Palmer. (Englewood Cliffs, NJ: Yourdon Press/Prentice Hall, 1984)

[Martin, 1984] *An Information Systems Manifesto*, James Martin. (Englewood Cliffs, NJ: Prentice Hall, 1984)

[Martin, 1985] *Structured Techniques for Computing*, James Martin and Carma McClure. (Englewood Cliffs, NJ: Prentice Hall, 1985)

[Metzger, 1983] *Managing a Programming Project*, 2nd edition, Philip Metzger. (Englewood Cliffs, NJ: Prentice Hall, 1983)

[Mills, 1971] "Top-Down Programming in Large Systems," Harlan Mills. (*Debugging Techniques in Large Systems*, Englewood Cliffs, NJ: Prentice Hall, 1971)

[Mills, 1973] "Chief Programmer Teams," Harlan Mills and F. T. Baker. (*Datamation*, December 1973, pp. 58-61)

[Mills, 1986] *Principles of Information Systems Analysis and Design*, Harlan Mills, Richard Linger, and Alan Hevner. (New York: Academic Press, 1986)

[Moriconi and Hare, 1985] "Visualizing Program Design through Pegasys," Mark Moriconi and Dwight Hare. (*IEEE Computer*, August 1985.)

[Myers, 1975] *Reliable Software Through Composite Design*, G.J. Myers. (New York: Petrocelli/ Charter, 1975)

[Neumann, 1985]   "Some Computer-Related Disasters and
                     Other Egregious Horrors," Peter G.
                     Neumann. (*ACM SIGSOFT Software
                     Engineering Notes*, January 1985)

[Noll, 1977]   *Strucutred Programming for the COBOL
                     Programmer*, P. Noll. (San Francisco, CA:
                     Mike Murach & Associates, 1977)

[Orr, 1977]   *Structured Systems Development*, Ken Orr.
                     (Englewood Cliffs, NJ: Yourdon Press/
                     Prentice Hall, 1977)

[Page-Jones,   *The Practical Guide to Structured Systems
1988]   Design*, 2nd edition, Meilir Page-Jones.
                     (Englewood Cliffs, NJ: Yourdon Press/
                     Prentice Hall, 1988)

[Perry, 1987]   DeWayne Perry, "Software Interconnection
                     Models," (*Proceedings of the 9th
                     International Conference on Software
                     Engineering*, April 1987)

[Plauger, 1976]   "New York Times Revisited," P.J. Plauger.
                     (*The Yourdon Report*, April 1976)

[Raeder, 1985]   "A Survey of Current Graphical Program-
                     ming Techniques," Georg Raeder. (*IEEE
                     Computer*, August 1985)

[Ross, 1977]   "Structured Analysis for Requirements
                     Definition," D.T. Ross and K.E. Schoman,
                     Jr. (*IEEE Transactions on Software
                     Engineering*, January 1977)

[Sackman   "Exploratory Experimental Studies Compar-
et al., 1968]   ing Online and Offline Programming
                     Performance," H. Sackman, W.J. Erickson,
                     and E.E. Grant. (*Communications of the
                     ACM*, January 1968, pp. 3-11)

[Scanlan, 1987]   "A Niche for Structured Flowcharts," David
                     Scanlan. (*Proceedings of the ACM Fifteenth
                     Annual Computer Science Conference*,
                     1987)

[Semprevivo, 1980] *Teams in Information Systems Development*, P. Semprevivo. (Englewood Cliffs, NJ: Yourdon Press/Prentice Hall, 1980)

[Shu, 1985] FORMAL: A Forms-Oriented, Visual-Directed Application Development System," Nan C. Shu. (*IEEE Computer*, August 1985)

[Shu, 1988a] "A Visual Programming Language Designed for Automatic Programming," Nan C. Shu. (*Proceedings of HICSS 21*, January 1988)

[Shu, 1988b] *Visual Programming*, Nan C. Shu. (New York: Van Nostrand, Reinhold, 1988)

[Stevens, 1974] "Structured Design," W.G. Stevens, G.J. Myers, and L.L. Constantine. (*IBM Systems Journal*, May 1974, pp. 115-139)

[Strassman, 1985] *Information Payoff*, Paul Strassmann. (New York: Free Press, 1985)

[Thomsett, 1980] *People and Project Management*, R. Thomsett. (Englewood Cliffs, NJ: Yourdon Press/Prentice Hall, 1980)

[Walston, 1977] "A Method of Programming Measurement and Estimation," C.E. Walston and C.P. Felix. (*IBM Systems Journal*, January 1977, pp. 54-73)

[Ward, 1984] *Systems Development Without Pain*, Paul Ward. (Englewood Cliffs, NJ: Yourdon Press/Prentice Hall, 1984)

[Ward, 1985] *Structured Development for Real-Time Systems*, Paul Ward and Steve Mellor. (Englewood Cliffs, NJ: Yourdon Press/ Prentice Hall, 1985)

[Warnier, 1976] *The Logical Construction of Programs*, J.D. Warnier. (New York: Van Nostrand Reinhold, 1976)

[Weaver, 1987] *Using the Structured Techniques: A Case Study*, Audrey M. Weaver. (Englewood Cliffs, NJ: Yourdon Press/Prentice Hall, 1987)

[Weinberg, 1971]   *The Psychology of Computer Programming,*
                    Gerald Weinberg. (New York: Van Nostrand
                    1971)

[Weinberg, 1972]   *Structured Programming in PL/C,* Gerald
                    Weinberg. (New York: John Wiley & Sons,
                    1972)

[Weinberg, 1978]   *Structured Analysis,* Victor Weinberg.
                    (Englewood Cliffs, NJ: Yourdon Press/
                    Prentice Hall, 1978)

[Weinberg, 1982]   *Rethinking Systems Analysis and Design,*
                    Gerald Weinberg. (Boston, MA: Little, Brown
                    and Company, 1982)

[Weinberg and   *Handbook of Walkthroughs and Inspections,*
Freedman, 1982]   Gerald Weinberg and Daniel Freedman
                    (Boston, MA: Little Brown,1982).

[Weinwurm, 1970]   *On the Management of Computer Program-*
                    ming, George Weinwum. (Princeton, NJ:
                    Auerbach Publishers, 1970)

[Weiss, 1985]   "Evaluating Software Development by
                    Analysis of Changes: Some Data from the
                    Software Engineering Laboratory," D. Weiss
                    and V. Basili. (*IEEE Transactions on
                    Software Engineering,* February 1985)

[Wirth, 1968]   "PL/360, A Programming Language for the
                    360 Computers," Niklaus Wirth. (*Journal of
                    the ACM,* January 1968, pp. 37-74)

[Wirth, 1973]   *Systematic Programming,* Niklaus Wirth.
                    (Englewood Cliffs, NJ: Prentice Hall, 1973)

[Wirth, 1976]   *Algorithms + Data = Programs,* Niklaus
                    Wirth. (Englewood Cliffs, NJ: Prentice Hall,
                    1976)

[Yourdon, 1976]   *Techniques of Program Structure and
                    Design,* Edward Yourdon (Englewood Cliffs,
                    NJ: Prentice Hall, 1976)

[Yourdon, 1978]   *Learning to Program in Structured COBOL,
                    Part I,* 2nd edition, Edward Yourdon, Chris

Gane, and Trish Sarson. (Englewood Cliffs, NJ: Yourdon Press/Prentice Hall, 1978)

[Yourdon, 1979]   *Classics in Software Engineering*, edited by Edward Yourdon. (Englewood Cliffs, NJ: Yourdon Press/Prentice Hall, 1979)

[Yourdon, 1982]   *Writings of the Revolution*, edited by Edward Yourdon. (Englewood Cliffs, NJ: Yourdon Press/Prentice Hall, 1982)

[Yourdon, 1985]   *The Perils of Personal Computing*, Edward Yourdon. (Englewood Cliffs, NJ: Yourdon Press/Prentice Hall, 1985)

[Yourdon, 1986]   *Nations At Risk*, Edward Yourdon. (Englewood Cliffs, NJ: Yourdon Press/ Prentice Hall, 1986)

[Yourdon, 1988]   *Managing the System Life Cycle*, 2nd edition, Edward Yourdon. (Englewood Cliffs, NJ: Yourdon Press/Prentice Hall, 1988)

[Yourdon and Constantine, 1989]   *Structured Design: Fundamentals of a Discipline of Computer Program and Systems Design, 2nd edition*, Edward Yourdon and Larry L. Constantine. (Englewood Cliffs, NJ: Yourdon Press/Prentice Hall, 1989)

[Yourdon, 1989a]   *Modern Structured Analysis*, Edward Yourdon. (Englewood Cliffs, NJ: Yourdon Press/Prentice Hall, 1989)

[Yourdon, 1989b]   *Structured Walkthroughs*, 4th edition, Edward Yourdon. (Englewood Cliffs, NJ: Yourdon Press/Prentice Hall, 1989)

[Zloof, 1982]   "Office-by-Example: A Business Language that Unifies Data and Word Processing and Electronic Mail," M.M. Zloof. (*IBM Systems Journal*, Vol. 21, No. 3, 1982, pp. 272-304)

Index

Ada 218
administrator 152
application programmers
    cost of 23
    productivity of 23
    varying abilities of 25
Aron, Joel 150, 151
backup programmer 152
Baker, F.T. 105, 150, 157
Basili, Victor 36
Bellin, David 231
black-box 107
Boar, Bernard 214
Boddie, John 82
Boehm, Barry 18, 25, 33, 36, 59, 232
Brooks, Fred 23, 57, 150, 151
bubble chart 131
bugs
    average number of 31
    critical nature of 32
    interface 29
    lasting forever 30
    likelihood of finding 33
    residual 30
    total number of in a system 31
Böhm,Corrado 106
CASE 5, 62, 138, 143, 223-226
Chapin chart 141
chief programmer 147, 151
chief programmer team
    definition of 3
    history of 149-150, 154
    management problems with 154, 156
    motivation behind 146-149
    nature of 150
Chomsky, Noam 129
COCOMO 232
Code walkthroughs 160
cohesion
    definition of 96

AND TAKE ADVANTAGE OF THESE SPECIAL OFFERS!

a.) When ordering 3 or 4 copies (of the same or different titles), take 10% off the total list price (excluding sales tax, where applicable).

b.) When ordering 5 to 20 copies (of the same or different titles), take 15% off the total list price (excluding sales tax, where applicable).

c.) To receive a greater discount when ordering 20 or more copies, call or write:

Special Sales Department
College Marketing
Prentice Hall
Englewood Cliffs, NJ 07632
201-592-2498

SAVE!

If payment accompanies order, plus your state's sales tax where applicable, Prentice Hall pays postage and handling charges. Same return privilege refund guaranteed. Please do not mail in cash.

☐ **PAYMENT ENCLOSED**—shipping and handling to be paid by publisher (please include your state's tax where applicable).

☐ **SEND BOOKS ON 15-DAY TRIAL BASIS** & bill me (with small charge for shipping and handling).

Name _____

Address _____

City _____ State _____ Zip _____

I prefer to charge my ☐ Visa ☐ MasterCard
Card Number _____ Expiration Date_____

Signature _____
All prices listed are subject to change without notice.

Mail your order to: Prentice Hall, Book Distribution Center, Route 59 at Brook Hill Drive, West Nyack, NY 10995

Dept. 1   D-OFYP-FW(1)

TEAR OUT THIS PAGE TO ORDER THESE OTHER HIGH-QUALITY YOURDON PRESS COMPUTING SERIES TITLES

Quantity	Title/Author	ISBN	Price	Total $
_____	Agents of Change; Bouldin	013-018508-6	$32.00	_____
_____	Building Controls Into Structured Systems; Brill	013-086059-X	$37.00	_____
_____	C Notes: Guide to C Programming; Zahn	013-109778-4	$21.95	_____
_____	Classics in Software Engineering; Yourdon	013-135179-6	$41.00	_____
_____	Concepts of Information Modeling; Flavin	013-335589-6	$29.00	_____
_____	Concise Notes on Software Engineering; DeMarco	013-167073-3	$22.00	_____
_____	Controlling Software Projects; DeMarco	013-171711-1	$41.00	_____
_____	Creating Effective Software; King	013-189242-8	$35.00	_____
_____	Crunch Mode; Boddie	013-194960-8	$31.00	_____
_____	Current Practices in Software Development; King	013-195678-7	$36.00	_____
_____	Data Factory; Roeske	013-196759-2	$26.00	_____
_____	Design of On-Line Computer Systems; Yourdon	013-201301-0	$50.00	_____
_____	Developing Structured Systems; Dickinson	013-205147-8	$36.00	_____
_____	Disaster Recovery Planning; Toigo	013-214941-9	$45.00	_____
_____	Essential Systems Analysis; McMenamin/Palmer	013-287905-0	$37.00	_____
_____	Expert System Technology; Keller	013-295577-6	$31.95	_____
_____	Game Plan for System Development; Frantzen/McEvoy	013-346156-4	$33.00	_____
_____	Intuition to Implementation; MacDonald	013-502196-0	$27.00	_____
_____	Managing Structured Techniques; Yourdon	013-551680-3	$35.00	_____
_____	Modern Structured Analysis; Yourdon	013-598624-9	$34.00	_____
_____	Object Oriented Systems Analysis, Shlaer/Mellor	013-629023-X	$31.00	_____
_____	People & Project Management; Thomsett	013-655747-3	$24.00	_____
_____	Politics of Projects; Block	013-685553-9	$25.00	_____
_____	Practical Guide to Structured System 2/e; Page-Jones	013-690769-5	$37.00	_____
_____	Practice of Structured Analysis; Keller	013-693987-2	$29.00	_____
_____	Program It Right; Benton/Weekes	013-729005-5	$27.00	_____
_____	Software Design: Methods & Techniques; Peters	013-821828-5	$35.00	_____
_____	Structured Analysis; Weinberg	013-854414-X	$46.00	_____
_____	Structured Analysis & System Specifications; DeMarco	013-854380-1	$46.00	_____
_____	Structured Approach to Building Programs: BASIC; Wells	013-854076-4	$29.00	_____
_____	Structured Approach to Building Programs: COBOL; Wells	013-854084-5	$29.00	_____
_____	Structured Approach to Building Programs: Pascal; Wells	013-851536-0	$29.00	_____
_____	Structured Design; Yourdon/Constantine	013-854471-9	$51.00	_____
_____	Structured Development Real-Time Systems, Combined; Ward/Mellor	013-854654-1	$79.00	_____
_____	Structured Development Real-Time Systems, Vol 1; Ward/Mellor	013-854787-4	$35.00	_____
_____	Structured Development Real-Time Systems, Vol. II; Ward/Mellor	013-854795-5	$35.00	_____
_____	Structured Development Real-Time Systems. Vol. III; Ward/Mellor	013-854803-X	$35.00	_____
_____	Structured Systems Development; Orr	013-855149-9	$35.00	_____
_____	Structured Walkthroughs 3/e; Yourdon	013-855248-7	$28.00	_____
_____	System Development Without Pain; Ward	013-881392-2	$35.00	_____
_____	Teams in Information System Development; Semprivivo	013-896721-0	$31.00	_____
_____	Techinques of EDP Project Management; Brill	013-900358-4	$35.00	_____
_____	Techniques of Program Structure & Design; Yourdon	013-901702-X	$46.00	_____
_____	Up and Running; Hanson	013-937558-9	$34.00	_____
_____	Using the Structured Techniques; Weaver	013-940263-2	$28.00	_____
_____	Writing of the Revolution; Yourdon	013-970708-5	$40.00	_____

Total $ _____

Discount (if appropriate) _____

New Total $ _____